LITERATURE AND ETHNICITY
IN THE CULTURAL BORDERLANDS

Intro
2-3 porous borders
3 border v borderland
4 c~ bet 2 ~ nos (Pratt)
5 north v. south as history
7 deconstr. g.b. so "grand narrative"
8 border Nech crossers to cobble they
11 theory v. real border a agrammaticality   Rodriguez
* 12 hunger-strikes   129 gringos
* 13 Pratt's writing in combat zone   130 Rich-heard
14 Arteaga's cross X   131 intimacy a tongue
* 16 effect on traditional lits   132 + silence (mooc.)
→ a writing in English as   133 braceros
    'subversive'
* 18 McCarthy's Spanish

GW00707291

Rodopi Perspectives on Modern Literature

28

Edited by
David Bevan

LITERATURE AND ETHNICITY IN THE CULTURAL BORDERLANDS

Edited by
Jesús Benito
Ana María Manzanas

AMSTERDAM - NEW YORK, NY 2002

The paper on which this book is printed meets the requirements of
"ISO 9706:1994, Information and documentation - Paper for
documents - Requirements for permanence".

ISBN: 90-420-1509-8 (bound)
©Editions Rodopi B.V., Amsterdam - New York, NY 2002
Printed in The Netherlands

CONTENTS

In memory of Moisés Manzanas Sánchez, 1919-1999
En la esfera del reloj
un Hércules soportaba el peso del tiempo-mundo

PREFACE

The impetus for the present volume on literature in the borderlands arose from a conference that the editors organized in Ciudad Real in 1999, as part of the activities of a research project subsidized by the Spanish Ministry of Education (PB96-0531). However, as it is presented here, the volume contains thorough revisions of a selection of the papers delivered there, as well as other articles specifically commissioned and written for this volume, and a substantial introductory essay.

If there was any consensus at the Ciudad Real conference, it was the conviction that the notion of borders and borderlines as clear-cut frontiers separating not only political and geographical areas, but also cultural, linguistic and semiotic spaces, did not fully address the complexity of contemporary cultural encounters. Centering on a whole diversity of literary works from the United States and the Caribbean, the contributors suggested and discussed different theoretical and methodological grounds to address the literary production taking place across the lines. In response to that changing situation and to the diversity of issues touched upon by the different contributors, the editors provide an introductory essay which aims to offer an in-depth exploration of the borderlands as geographical and fictional space from a more general perspective.

The editors are pleased to express their gratitude to a number of individuals and institutions for their support at various stages of the project. We would like to thank the University of Castilla-La Mancha and the staff there for providing us with the opportunity to meet and share our ideas in a pleasant academic environment. Fernando Galván, from the University of Alcalá, has been a generous and wise advisor. Our friends and colleagues in the US also deserve special thanks. Paul Lauter and Anne Fitzgerald, as well as Bernard and Carrie Bell, have given us their support, friendship and hospitality. They have also been inspiration for this volume. Trevor Dawes, librarian at Butler Library (Columbia University, NY), has been a great help and a friend. So have our *compañeros*, Richard and Maria Giacoma-Micelli and their wonderful children, as well as Jerry and Bonnie Whitmire, Anna Tefft and Win Lee. The editors also want to thank all the contributors for their patience and cooperation in coping with queries during the long editing process. We would also like to thank our publisher, Mr. Fred van der Zee of Editions Rodopi, for his belief in our project and his support throughout the final stages of the preparation of this volume. Our colleague Chrissi Harris has always been supportive of the project, and has been generously available for stylistic revisions of the text. For his help with doing the final layout, we are also grateful to Carlos Calzada.

Ana Manzanas would also like to express her gratitude to the Fulbright Commission as well as the Spanish Association for American Studies (SAAS) for her research stay at Cornell University in the spring of 2000. Last but not least, we would like to thank Ciriaco and María Arroyo as well as Lamar and Amparo Herrin for their friendship during our stay in rainy Ithaca.

BORDER(LANDS) AND BORDER WRITING: INTRODUCTORY ESSAY

JESÚS BENITO & ANA MARÍA MANZANAS

The concept of the border(lands) has proved a most fertile one in the current critical debate. But the term 'border' is in itself a 'borderish' concept or hybrid term which implies both a line of division and a line of encounter and dialogue. The border transgresses itself through the borderlands (Anzaldúa 1987; Arteaga 1997), contact zones (Mary Louis Pratt 1992), liminal spaces (Aguirre et al. 2001) or cultural force fields (Porter 1994). This article centers on the blurring of clear-cut cultural, linguistic and racial borderlines, and their substitution by a borderlands which appears as a site of confrontation, appropriation and translation. Frontier spaces, both in America and in Europe, appear as sites which defy previous grand narratives, as well as the traditional tenet that history is a movement from east to west, from north to south. The article further explores the double-voiced discourse of the border: a discourse that renders possible, within the fixed cultural, literary and linguistic bounds of what is permitted, an experience of what is not permitted.

I- Borders

Borders and lines (physical or narrative), like national anthems, give countries and our own selves the limits we live by. They territorialize our thinking, our world vision, and provide the parameters we need to live safely within. And we are all active participants in constantly "mending [the] wall"/border, to paraphrase from Robert Frost's poem. There exists, for example, a fine but clear line which separates the U.S. from Mexico. Like a good and conventional story it has a beginning, middle and end. A similar line, and similarly policed, separates Spain from Africa. It is a fluid line which varies with tides and clear nights; it becomes slightly thinner in the summer and widens in the winter, but like the US-Mexican border, equally separates presumably distinctive nationalities. The border, as Alfred Arteaga has eloquently argued (1997: 92), is an infinitely thin line which truly differentiates the U.S. from Mexico, the haves and havenots, those who are supposedly legitimately rich from those who are (also legitimately) poor of their own accord. The absolute certainty of this discrimination, as Arteaga clarifies, instills confidence in national definition (Arteaga 1997: 92). The thinner the border the clearer and more acute sense of nation it defines and isolates. Thin borders or, should we say, "Good fences make good neighbors." The border is, from this perspective another "grand" narrative, with its own hero (those within), and its antagonist (those without), whose goal is the definition of a national identity and narration.

The concept of the border has proved a most fertile one in current critical works. Together with Gloria Anzaldúa's groundbreaking *Borderlands/La Frontera* (1987), we have to mention Alfred Arteaga's eloquent visions of the border in *Chicano Poetics* (1997), as well as Ramón Saldivar's *Border Matters: Remapping American Cultural Studies* (1997) among many other works. To the seminal writings of Chicano thinkers and writers we have to add the work of Mary Louise Pratt, especially her acclaimed and clarifying *Imperial Eyes: Studies in Travel Writing and Transculturation* (1992), as well as Henry Giroux in his lucid *Border Crossing* (1992), Paul Jay's clear *Contingency Blues* (1997), David E. Johnson & Scott Michaelson, with their cautionary vision of border theory in *Border Theory: The Limits of Cultural Politics* (1997), Elazar Barkan and Marie-Denise Shelton's *Borders, Exiles, Diasporas* (1998) with their selection of essays on comparative literature, as well as the publication of more pedagogically oriented collections such as *Border Texts: Cultural Readings for Contemporary Writers* (1999), edited by Randall Bass, Paul Lauter's *From Walden Pond to Jurassic Park* (2001), and other titles such as *Margins and Thresholds* (2000), edited by M. Aguirre *e.a.*, as well as *A Place That Is Not A Place* (2000), edited by Isabel Soto. All these works have contributed to creating a theoretical and conceptual framework for rethinking U.S. American national and cultural spaces as well as their connections and interactions with other literatures and cultures of the continent. As Paul Jay points out, they have also effectively changed the politics of location of literature and culture "by directing critical attention to the liminal margins and permeable border zones out of which cultures in the Americas have emerged" (1997: 168).

What we can call "border theory," then, is not peculiar to Chicano literature and thinking but has been taken as a paradigm which is present in other cultural and literary manifestations. The decentering of the *locus* of culture has been accompanied by a change in methodological terms. Border theory seems to require a "borderlands approach" to literature and culture, that is, a revisionist position which sees literatures and cultures not as finished and self-contained projects isolated from other influences, but as constructs based on interaction and dialogue, and which evolve and unfold relative to each other. Literary and critical borders, like physical boundaries, are there-fore porous and susceptible to being crossed. Criticizing from the border-lands, as Arlene A. Elder has suggested, implies transgressing the vision of the border as a separating and dividing line to acknowledge the "interrela-tionships of cultures, literatures, hence aesthetic theories and critical prac-tices in the modern and post-modern world" (1996: 9). As Henry Giroux (1992: 26) and Paul Jay (1997: 174-75) have argued, the attempts to theorize that space in between has run parallel to the attempts to challenging, remap-ping and negotiating the boundaries of knowledge which claims the status of master narratives, as well as conventional discursive dichotomies (or bor-ders) such as essentialist/anti-essentialist, centralist/pluralist. As Jay con-cludes in his analysis of Arnold Krupat's *Ethnocriticism*, the space between "is thus a *methodological* as well as a geographic one" (1997: 175).

Although in Chicano literature and culture the theoretical articulation of the concept of the border started with the imposition of an artificial boundary between Mexico and the United States in 1848, the border is not only a geopolitical line, but a site of constant interaction, as Gloria Anzaldúa has remarked: "The psychological borderlands, the sexual borderlands and the spiritual borderlands are not particular to the Southwest. In fact, the Border-lands are physically present whenever two or more cultures edge each other, where people of different races occupy the same territory, where under, lower, middle and upper classes touch" (1987: Preface). As Anzaldúa points out, the image of the border has become fully meaningful not only when we consider it as a physical line, but when we decenter it and liberate it from the notion of space to encompass notions of sex, class, gender, ethnicity, identity and community. In this sense, the crossing of the border is not a stepping of a physical body into a protected "other" national space, as much as a con-stant and potentially creative encounter where differences meet and interact. But some terminological clarification of the concepts of border and border-lands is imperative. The term "border" is in itself a "borderish" concept or hybrid term which implies both a line of division and a line of encounter and dialogue. The very title of Anzaldúa's *Borderlands/La Frontera* seems to identify "borderlands" with the Spanish *frontera* or "border" in English. A few pages into the book, however, Anzaldúa distinguishes between the two terms: "A border is a dividing line, a narrow strip along a steep edge. A borderland is a vague and undetermined place created by the emotional residue of an unnatural boundary" (1987: 3). Alfred Arteaga has taken up this distinction when he clarifies between "the thin and severe borderline," and the notion of a broader zone, a borderlands, "the border zone" (1997: 92-93). Manuel Aguirre, Roberta Quance and Philip Sutton introduce in *Mar-gins and Thresholds* the term "threshold" as one of the ways the border transgresses itself: "If a border is viewed as the line, imaginary or real, which separates these two spaces, then the threshold is the opening which permits passage from one space to the other" (2000: 6). Liminality, for Aguirre *e.a.* "designates the condition ascribed to those things or persons who occupy or find themselves in the vicinity of the threshold, either on a permanent basis or as a temporary phenomenon" (2000: 6-7). Borders, then, engender border-zones, that is, liminal spaces which allow for mestizaje, and racial and cultural hybridization. The two terms, then, imply each other: the existence of the border, however thin and demarcated the line is, requires its own negation, the borderlands. Obviously, different ways of communication evolve and result from these exchanges across the border. Mary Louise Pratt's term ("contact zones" is extremely illuminating to focus on these dialogues: "I use the term to refer to social spaces where cultures meet, clash, and grapple with each other, often in contexts of highly asymmetrical relations of power, such as colonialism, slavery, or their aftermaths as they are lived out in many parts of the world today" (1992: 6). The edging of cultures Anzaldúa refers to bears strong similarities to the meeting, clashing and grappling of cultures. Yet another illuminating formulation of "border zones" and how the term can be applicable to American literatures appears in Carolyn Porter's essay "What We Know That We Don't Know: Remapping American Literary Studies." Porter amplifies the range of the contact zone through the term "cultural force fields," which addresses a wider series of different transcultural axes and exchanges. The term effects a change in the politics of location of American literature by introducing the Latin American vantage point. This vantage point changes the stress of the traditional Anglo-centric critical stance to create a new set of axes: "a quadruple set of relations between (1) Europe and Latin America; (2) Latin America and North America; (3) North America and Europe; and (4) Africa and both Americas" (1994: 510).

But the borderlands, contact zones, liminal spaces or cultural force fields are not the only way the border transgresses itself. There exists not a Border with capital B but unpredictable boundary encounters which show how the border repeats itself in different locations and times. This "repeating border," to use Antonio Benítez Rojo's terminology in *The Repeating Island*, is paradoxically different but also simultaneously the same in its diversity. The limits of this physical border extend beyond the actual U.S.-Mexico Border, as well as the liquid line between Haiti and the U.S., and can reach the outskirts of a big city as in Sandra Cisneros' *House on Mango Street* or a decadent Cafe in Helena Viramontes' "The Cariboo Cafe." As these examples show, literature textualizes the encounters or clashes between cultures, races and classes. Border encounters, however, as well as the interaction implicit in these borderlands, are not peculiar to Chicano literature, but manifest themselves in the rest of the literatures and writings of the U.S. The psychological borderlands, the sexual borderlands and the spiritual border-lands have become textualized in the writings of Native Americans, African Americans and Asian Americans, among others. The line separating pro-slavery from presumably free states, the Mason-Dixon line, is at the center of most slave narratives in African American literature. The permeability of the line, however, tortures the consciousness of the fugitives who have escaped into free territory, as Toni Morrison's characters illustrate in *Beloved*. "124 Bluestone Road," the symbolic location and address in the novel marks a double border, the physical boundary between a plantation ironically called "Sweet Home" and freedom, as well as the time border between the power of the past and the will to live in the present. The encounter with the Europeans and the subsequent removal of Native Americans graphically draw the border which marks their receding territory. The characters in Louise Er-drich's *Tracks* see the encroachment of the border onto their space, the sacred woods, as well as onto their cyclic sense of time. The invisible border between Americans and Asian Americans has come to the fore in the writ-ings of Sui Sin Far, with *Leaves from the Mental Portfolio of an Eurasian*, and continues in the fiction of Maxine Hong Kingston through the separation between Chinese-Americans and "ghosts" in *The Woman Warrior* and *China Men*, to give only a few examples.

Borders, then, link to narrative through literatures which reflect border encounters, as well as the multiple possibilities of crossing and being crossed, silenced and eliminated by the border. But, as Arteaga (1997: 94) has argued, borders also link to narrative through history as another grand narrative. The border expresses the limits, preferably closed and finished, of a nation; history defines time limits in similar terms, for the border is not only concerned with space; it is also a time line which graphically represents and actualizes the flow and the progression of history (Arteaga 1997: 94). History has traditionally established and consolidated borders. Borders not only acted as lines differentiating nations and identities but also established a hierarchy within difference. East has been set up against west; north against south. The very history of the United States was based on a sense of time and space progression; as Roy Harvey claimed more than forty years ago: "The history of American civilization would [...] be conceived of as three-dimensional, progressing from past to present, from east to west, from lower to higher" (qted. in Krupat 1996: 52). Note the way Harvey conflated time and space to express the birth of the United States as the incarnation of north-high ideals, the center of the present as opposed to the lower-south-associated-with-the-past regions of the world. The process of border-making implicit in Harvey's words becomes clearer in this statement by Henry Kissinger, somewhere in 1980s: "You come here speaking of Latin America, but this is not important. Nothing important can come from the South [...] The axis of history starts in Moscow, goes to Bonn, crosses over to Washington, and then goes to Tokyo. What happens in the South is of no importance" (qted. in Krupat 1996: 52). Once more, time and space, south—another word for low/lower—, and past, are conflated to express the insurmountable border between the United States and the rest of the countries which have no say, and to reaffirm the presumably inexorable movement of history. As Krupat reminds us, "In the hegemonic narrative of the dominant culture, the movement of history is always from east to west, and that movement can never be reversed (to go from west to east would be the same as going from higher to lower, from civilized to savage, something unthinkable) nor be adjusted to accommodate the south, where, as Kissinger insists, 'what happens [...] is of no importance'" (1996: 52). The United States is thus presented as the fulfillment of that tri-dimensional movement, another version of the manifest destiny. The movement, as Krupat points out, cannot be reversed.

However, a quick look around us allows us to see Mexicans going into the United States, Haitians traversing a perilous passage to arrive into the promised land of the United States, just like Africans are pressing against European borders in Spain and France. Given the traditional tenet that history is a movement from east to west, it may be worth asking ourselves what kind of history this is. It is a history coming from the South which may be disregarded as "improper" history, but is there, nevertheless, somewhat performing itself through the experiences and stories of hundreds of individuals. They lack any kind of paper or textual form that may identify them. These individuals, to paraphrase from Minh-ha (1989) do not have bodies but "are bodies." Like Beloved in Toni Morrison's novel, all they have is their bodies, bearing the symptoms of a nightmarish Middle Passage. But their experiences have been textualized by journalists and some writers, such as Alí Lmrabet, Michael Finkel, or Mahi Binebine. These contemporary border narratives talk about similar experiences in crossing new versions of the Middle Passage, the space separating Haiti from the richest country in the western hemisphere, and the line which divides Africa from the dream of a prosperous Europe. There are similar preparations for the crossing: like a rite of initiation with no return, the trip starts in Tangier or Tetuán on the African coast, on Port-de Paix or Îsle Tortue in Haiti. The money paid for the passage varies radically depending on the kind of boat or the shade of color—racism in misery, as Alí Lmrabet calls it (*El País* 30 September, 2000)—, but it often requires the passenger's (and his/her family's) life savings; another amount is reserved for braving military positions on the coast. Deception is frequent on both routes. SubSaharan Africans are returned to deserted beaches in Tangier, convinced they are in Spain; Haitians may be dropped off on a deserted Haitian island, thinking they are in the Bahamas (Michael Finkel *TNYTM* June 18th, 2000). A more insidious scheme, Finkel writes, involves taking passengers a mile out to sea and then tossing them overboard. About 75% of Moroccans are ready to leave their country, writes Lmrabet; two-thirds of Haitians, writes Finkel, would leave the country if given the means and opportunity. From Haiti the trip echoes a recurring sense of history: "We came to this country on slave boats," "and we're going to leave on slave boats," clarifies David, one of the passengers on board. The passage recalls the heat, the sickness, and the odor so often described by African slaves such as Olaudah Equiano in his narrative or in the novels of contemporary writers such as Toni Morrison's *Beloved* and Caryl Phillips in *Cambridge*. Finkel describes the heat in the hold which "seemed to transcend temperature," the sickness and the unavoidable humiliation of the bucket. The uncertainties as to the outcome of the voyage itself remain, but the dreams upon arrival have definitely changed; David's dream was to marry an American woman; Steven, another passenger, fantasized with buying a pickup truck, a red one.

This pressing at the borders suggests a different kind, if not a reversal, of history. It also reveals the deconstruction of the border as grand narrative which does not problematize its own legitimacy, and denies the historical and social factors that made it possible. This history talks about a common past in which cultural, linguistic and racial borders are blurred: Mexicans lived in the Southwest of the United States, and claim that territory as part of the mythic Aztlán; Africans lived for eight centuries in southern Spain. As Jose Piedra remarks, "in spite of the early success, persistence, and lingering insidiousness of European colonialism, Africa has been in Europe as much as Europe has been in Africa, and still is" (1993: 822). The same can be said about the impossibility of establishing a border in space and time between the different North Americas, Mexico and The United States. Notwithstanding this common past, history in the United States and in Spain has always revealed a desire for closure and for erasing the migration tracks between countries and continents. From this perspective the border as the outer line of a nation or an identity needs to be closed. The border is thus the *locus* which defines and secures the integrity of a nation. Only a closed border can presumably secure a fixed, stable and finished identity. This image of the closed nation is similar to the concept of the classical body as expressed by Bakhtin in *Rabelais and His World*. The classical body/nation is an image of completeness. On the contrary, the grotesque body/nation is "unfinished, outgrows itself, transgresses its own limits" (1984: 26). The grotesque body "is a body in the act of becoming. It is never finished, never completed; it is continually built, created, and builds and creates another body" (1984: 317). Whereas the classical body/nation is sealed from outer influences, the grotesque is permeable and "stresses elements common to the entire cosmos" (1984: 318). Classical univocality thus contrasts with grotesque duality. Bakhtin's descriptions of the classical/grotesque body have a suggestive applicability to the border in as much as the apertures of the body can be extrapolated to the parts of the body/nation which are open to the outside world. The border can be seen as a sharp line of demarcation which guards and protects an entirely finished and complete political and geographical body, but also as a part of the body/nation "through which the world enters the body or emerges from it, or through which the body itself goes out to meet the world" (1984: 26). As an orifice in the body/nation, the border has to be carefully watched.

The desire for closure or for the finished quality of the classical body/nation is clear in Carlos Fuentes' *La frontera de cristal*, a powerful picture of the border and its inhabitants. Fuentes describes the border as an artificial line of porous contours always in the process of being recreated but also transgressed. Fuentes shows how, as Arteaga expresses, the U.S.-Mexican border instills confidence in national definition and national identity. The U.S. may dislike illegal immigrants but paradoxically needs them to create itself as a nation, and in order to feel good about itself, as a border patroller admits in one of the tales: "detestaba a los indocumentados. Pero los adoraba y los necesitaba. Sin ellos, maldita sea, no habría presupuesto para helicópteros, radar, poderosas luces infrarrojas nocturnas, bazucas, pistolas [...] Que vengan [...] Que sigan viniendo por millones, rogó, para darle sentido a mi vida. Tenemos que seguir siendo víctimas inocentes" (1995: 268). Paradoxically, the border requires border crossers in order to perpetuate itself. The desire for a finished body/nation is however rendered impossible in as much as this image of completion and perfection is contingent and dependent on the arrival of new comers and border-crossers. The southern border may function as a bastion against that history written from the south and the past. The border also signals to what extent so called civilization needs to defend itself from that history, barbaric and regressive, which threatens to engulf it from the south.

At the border, always carnivalesque in its unfinished quality, technology on the cutting-edge represses the transgressors. Democracies loosen up. As Eduardo Galeano suggests, the border is a paradigmatic site to realize the workings of the system: "to the extent that the system finds itself threatened by the relentless growth of unemployment, poverty and the resultant social and political tensions, room for pretense and good manners shrinks: in the outskirts of the world the system reveals its true face" (1988: 113-125). It seems possible to argue that the border is the outskirts of the world, where the systems which fortify the notions of nationality and national identity are truly revealed. In the barbed wire separating The United States from Mexico, the system reveals its true policed nature; likewise, in the border separating the Spanish colonies in north Africa from the rest of the continent, the European dream of a solid and prosperous Europe reveals its true face. "El Estrecho," "The Straight" separating Spain from Africa was described by Paul Bowles as "the center of the universe"; for Mahi Binebine, a contemporary Moroccan writer, it is just "the abyss of the world" (*El País*, 31 October, 1999) which separates the poor from the affluent. But there are not only external borders; in the abandoned *cortijos, mercados* or rundown apartments on the outskirts of wealthy agricultural communities in southern Spain the system reveals who supports a blooming agricultural society, just like that euphemistic Atlas of slavery which supported Southern economy in 19th-century. US, according to Thomas Dew (1963).

But this "regressive" axis of history is already here. Although the U.S. has traditionally contained difference in reservations, internment camps or ghettoes, this act of containment has become increasingly difficult. For Gómez-Peña the demographic facts are revealing: "The Middle East and Black Africa are already in Europe, and Latin America's heart now beats in the U.S. New York and Paris increasingly resemble Mexico City and Sao Paulo. Cities like Tijuana and Los Angeles, once socio-urban aberrations, are becoming models of a new hybrid culture, full of uncertainty and vitality" (1988:130). The effects for Gómez-Peña are clear:

> We witness the borderization of the world, by-product of the 'deterritorialization' of vast human sectors. The borders either expand or are shot full of holes. Cultures and languages mutually invade one another. The South raises and melts, while the North descends dangerously with its economic and military pincers. The east moves west and vice-versa. Europe and North America daily receive uncontainable migrations of human beings. (1988: 130)

This hybrid society is clearly reflected in the words of Kenneth Prewitt, U.S. Census Bureau director: "The 21st century will be the century in which we redefine ourselves as the first country in world history which is literally made up of every part of the world." (The New York Times on the Web, Monday, January 1, 2001). As Rubén Martínez wrote in an article for TNYTM, people from Albania, Ireland, Nigeria, China, El Salvador, Korea and Pakistan are filling the space between America's traditional black and white poles (2000: 12). The border encounters and clashes among so many nationalities are happening everywhere. The importance of this repeating border is assessed by Martínez in the following terms:

> It is not one but many movements at once, whose impact on the course of American history will be as profound as the great migrations of the mid-19th and early-20th centuries and will alter our public life in a way not seen since the

civil rights movement. Unlike that last great lurch forward, however, this revolution is occurring not in the halls of political power but in the work place and
the neighborhood, at class and in church, on John Rocker's fabled No. 7 train. It
is a terrifying experience, this coming together, one for which we have as of yet
only the most awkward vocabulary. One for which new languages are being
written. (2000: 12)

This quiet revolution is written from the south, from the east, in a perpetual
confusion of axes and directions which contrasts sharply with the unidirec-
tionality and simplicity of "nothing important may come from the South."

As a space of confrontation, appropriation and translation, the site of the
border defies all attempts at cultural stasis. It springs, rather, as a subversive
space of transgression, as Gómez-Peña has stated in his bicultural manifesto
"The Border Is" (1993): the Border "means boycott, ilegalidad, clandestini-
dad, contrabando, transgresión, desobediencia binacional [...] But it also
means transcultural friendship and collaboration among races, sexes, and
generations. It also means to practice creative appropriation, expropriation,
and subversion of dominant cultural forms." Like Gloria Anzaldúa, Gómez-
Peña has put forward an optimistic theory of the border and border culture as
a place of cultural and literary negotiation and interaction. Border artists, to
paraphrase from Anzaldúa, "*cambian el punto de referencia*. By disrupting
the neat separations between cultures they create a culture mix, *una mesti-
zada*" (1998: 165). Moreover, the "rich gene pool" of Anzaldúa's "Mestiza
consciousness" (1987: 77) is easily applicable to this hybrid cultural and
literary progeny of the border. Just as the process of hybridity results in a
"new *mestiza* consciousness," the cultural interactions or crossings give rise
to a "*mestiza* literature" or, as Homi Bhabha explains, "to something different, something new and unrecognizable, a new area of negotiation of meaning and representation" (1990: 211) which he calls "the third space." What is
important about this new assemblage, as Homi Bhabha points out, "is not to
be able to trace original moments from which the third emerges [...] This
third space displaces the histories that constitute it, and sets up new structures of authority, new political initiatives, which are inadequately understood through received wisdom" (1990: 211). This hybrid space introduces
difference into the old, and creates new meanings within restrictive literary
and cultural spaces. Hybridity—in identity, community and in literature—is
the offspring of the border. Borders, then, not only separate but also, as
Anzaldúa and Gómez-Peña have suggested, "enlarge the geopolitical space"
(McKenna 1997: 11). But it seems necessary to qualify this enlargement. It
is not only a geopolitical question, but also cultural, linguistic, historic and,
of course, literary. The presence of other cultures, languages, or histories,
does not simply enlarge or amplify the site but radically modifies the mean-

ings of borders, like the meaning of culture and literature, as well as the three axes which articulate progress and the vision of history as we know it.

This optimistic vision of the border or "border theory" is shared by Flores and Yudice, who offer a positive vision of the border as "the locus of re-definition and re-signification" (1994: 202). This process of re-definition is, to some extent, a way of recycling an imposition and transforming it into a feature of self-fashioning. Fearing, however, the theoretical indeterminacy of the border, Flores and Yudice qualify it as "The trope [which] emerges, rather, from the ways in which Latinos *deploy* their language in everyday life. It corresponds to an ethos under formation; it is *practice* rather than *representation* of Latino identity. [...] And it is precisely the projection of this ethos into the culture at large and into the political arena which threatens the dominant 'Anglo' culture with loss of control of its physical and meta-phorical borders" (1994: 203). Rubén Blades somewhat tames the threaten-ing aspects of this vision of the border, as he prefers to call it "a culturally effective crossover," a "convergence," a movement which intends to find a common ground: "Let's meet half way, and then we can walk either way together" (qted. in Flores and Yudice 1994: 216). The crossing of the border, from this perspective, is not an invasion, as many of the voices of the Eng-lish-Only movement see it. Latinos, then, do not aspire to enter an already given America but to participate in the construction of a new hegemony dependent upon their cultural practices and discourse (Cf Flores and Yudice 1994: 216). But this "meeting half way" sounds problematic since it departs from a very asymmetrical relation of power, and requires the dominant Anglo culture to leave aside its hegemony and walk with other groups towards a fairer order.

These and other optimistic visions of the border have raised suspicions and reservations from some critics who caution against the idealistic con-struction of border culture and theory. The border is, together with "race" and "gender," and then "nation" and "sexuality," one of the grand themes of recent, politically liberal-to-left work across the humanities and social sciences, according to David Johnson and Scott Michaelson (1997: 3). In their view the border has become "an imaginary space" which remains unquestioned, and is often "assumed to be a place of politically exciting hybridity, intellectual creativity, and moral possibility. The borderlands, in other words, are the privileged locus of hope for a better world" (Johnson and Michaelson 1997: 2-3). This locus for hope, in Debra Castillo's view, has become "'utopic,' a floating signifier for a displaced self" (1999: 182). The actual border, as Castillo states, remains distant from mainstream centers of theory production in both the U.S. and Mexico (1999: 186). Theory contrasts sharply with reality and actual life. The border, as Castillo reminds us, is a well-known site of refusal—the literal and figural dump for each society's urban, industrial, toxic and sexual wastes (1999: 187). Castillo shares with Galeano a view of the border as the outskirts of the system, the site where the workings of so-called democracies reveal their true face. The border from this perspective is no imaginary utopian signifier but the dividing line between them and us, as Gloria Anzaldúa has stated. However shot full of holes, the border does not always equal transcultural friendship and collaboration among races, sexes, and generations. The border is an imposition which keeps peoples detained and unable to communicate. The language of the border is sometimes the language of hunger strikes and a-grammaticality. For the ones who never make it to the other side, as for those who remain as "illegal aliens" in the Promised Land of the United States or Europe, the language of the border is mere (social) silence. We cannot lose sight of the fact that about 30% of Spanish youngsters, for example, consider immigration as damaging to the race and social mores of the country (*El País digital* 20 October 2000). Along the same lines, the archbishop of Bolonia, Giacomo Biffi, claims that only catholic immigrants may be accepted into Italy to preserve the identity of the country (*El País digital*, 15 September 2000). Somewhat surreptitiously, democracies have established their own internal borders. The Danish minister of interior, Karen Jespersen, suggested secluding the immigrants who commit crimes on an island (*El País digital*, 26 August 2000).

The forms of collaboration, then, are not always creative, as Rus Castronovo explains, "Not only does the border push up against and disturb the nation, but in a strategic turnabout, the nation also employs the border to imagine the limits beyond which it might expand, to scout horizons for future settlement, to prepare the first line of attack" (1997: 196). The porousness of the border may thus signal the dangers of the ever-expanding border of globalization, which only admits one way of communicating, and has very clear notions of how to dominate border language and culture in order to advance its own interests. In return, border-crossing reveals a process of recycling through which old worlds turn into new worlds. But these utopian new worlds present the recurrence of old times. The well-organized humanitarian network which protects Africans in Spain brings echoes of the underground railroad which led African American slaves to freedom. On the other hand, the mafias which control the passage between Africa and Europe recall the profitable business of slave-trade, as well as the new versions of indenture and servitude.

The border configures itself as a most debatable and contested ground. Borders separate but also create borderlands or contact zones which allow for interactions, sometimes abruptly, sometimes creatively, of cultures, languages and world-views. As Homi Bhabha explains, "These 'in-between' spaces provide the terrain for elaborating strategies of self-hood—singular or communal—that initiate new signs of identity, and innovative sites of collaboration, and contestation, in the act of defining the idea of society itself" (1994: 1-2). The border(lands) offer a unique location of culture, literature and language which can be the *locus* of exchange of values, meanings and priorities, but also of antagonism and conflicts (Cf. Bhabha 1994: 2). This is the double edge of the border, as Gómez-Peña has pointed out. This is also the double nature of the contact zone, according to Mary Louise Pratt: "Auto-ethnography, transculturation, critique, collaboration, bilingualism, mediation, parody, denunciation, imaginary dialogue, vernacular expression—these are some of the literate arts of the contact zone. Miscomprehension, incomprehension, dead letters, unread masterpieces, absolute heterogeneity of meaning—these are some of the perils of writing in the contact zone" (1999: 373).

II- Border writing

For the African American slaves who set down their passage into so called "free" territory north of the Mason-Dixon line, the crossing was not only physical but also textual. They created a "fugitive" or illegal discourse which chronicled their appropriation of the white man's language. The discourse of border-crossing can therefore be termed fugitive or illegal. Its practitioners can be called, as Teresa McKenna proposes, "migrants" rather than immigrants (1997: 9). The word seems to suit not only the experience of Chicanos but also that of Native Americans, African Americans and Asian Americans, that is, the cultural groups which have migrated and moved within the inner geography of borders in the United States. It is interesting to see the description of the migrant as "the paradigmatic figure of displacement and oppression and the leading figure of persistence in the vicissitudes of change" (1997: 9). As a double and unassailable figure, the migrant is an expert at recycling experience and carrying over histories, stories and countercultures. The fugitive-migrant is always going to speak with at least a double voice. This is perhaps one of the defining features of border literature: a transgressive discourse whose aim is to render possible, within the fixed cultural, literary or linguistic bounds of what is permitted, an experience of what is not permitted.

An eloquent example of this constant and multiple crossing is Alfred Arteaga's poem "Antecanto" (1991):

These cantos chicanos begin with X and end with X.
They are examples of xicano verse, verse marked with the
cross, the border cross of alambre y río, the cross of Jesus
X in Native America, the nahuatl X in mexico, mexicano,

xicano. It is our mark, our cross, our X, our sign of never
ceasing being born at the point of two arrows colliding, X,
and the gentle laying of one line over another line, X.
It is the sound we make to mark one and other, August
29, familia, raza, as well as to exclude ourselves from the
patterns of death imposed from without. We sign the X
each time we speak we cross at least one border. And
because it is our sign andamos cruzando cruzados,
naciendo siendo xicanos otra vez, cada vez, esta vez. I am
the point of my own X but the arms, los brazos vienen de
lejos, and the arms reach far.

Arteaga's poem turns out into a poem on the cross, the cross that started
with the cross-ing which brought about the cross—*la vera cruz*—but also the
cross of the "atravesados" after the Anglo colonization and artificial imposition of borders; the cross of those who are always traversing or crossing
cultures; the cross of those invisible in the dominant culture who mark their
invisibility and illiteracy with a cross. Also the cross-ing that was the beginning of the cross, the sedimentation of cultures, histories, races and languages that characterizes the historical formation of Latin and Anglo
America. The vision of the X as matrix of constant crossings is not new.
Houston Baker has elaborated on the X as matrix in his superb analysis of
the blues in *Blues, Ideology, and Afro-American Literature* (1984): "A
matrix is a womb, a network, a fossil-bearing rock, a rocky trace of a gem-
stone's removal, a principal metal in an alloy, a mat or plate for reproducing
print or phonograph records. The matrix is a point of ceaseless input and
output, a web of intersecting, crisscrossing impulses always in productive
transit" (1984: 3). We would like to go back to the X as matrix, as the sign of
the multidirectionality and the simultaneity of cultures and languages which
marks the social, cultural and ideological space of the contact zone and the
borderlands. The X signifies and actualizes the meeting, clashing and edging
of cultures, and the heterogeneity of a dialogue which is going to be a
complex mixing of the languages, vocabularies, genres, and strategies of the
different groups. The matrix of the X is present, however, not only in the
blues and in the writings of contemporary Chicano writers such as Arias,
Cisneros or Castillo, and also in the novels of Mexican writer Carlos
Fuentes, but is also one of defining features of the literatures of Chinese
Americans, African Americans or Native Americans and Caribbeans.

Border writing situates itself on the X, the broad area of the borderlands,
the ground which allows space for mestizaje and hybridity. Arnold Krupat
has suggested that "Postcolonial work on Native American history, culture,
and literature cannot help but occur in what Mary Louise Pratt has called
'contact zones', even though we have tended to think of 'contact zones' as

somewhere 'out there' rather than just 'here', close to wherever we think of as home" (1996: 28). These contact zones, however, are not only peculiar to postcolonial work, and to a criticism "on the borderlands," but also to Native American writing, and to the literatures that make up the literatures of the U.S. These contact zones, like the borderlands, are the spaces and sites engendered by the border and the border encounters between cultures and literatures. The concept of the borderlands, like the writing in the contact zones, implies a vision of literature which clashes with the notion of writing as discrete, coherently structured, monolingual edifice. The notion of the classical body, closed and finished in itself, can be carried over to the vision of literature as a classical, perfect body. Writing in the borderlands/contact zones, then, implies opening up the fine line which delimits the body of literature to examine its unfinished quality and the areas of exchange and negotiation it establishes with other languages and writings.

Language is the debatable ground where the borderlands/contact zones are articulated and expressed. As Pratt explains, she takes the term "contact" from its use in Linguistics, where the term "contact languages" refers to improvised languages that develop among speakers of different native languages who need to communicate with each other. Such languages, Pratt clarifies, begin as pidgins, and are called "creoles." This process of language creolization can be easily transposed to refer to hybrid literatures or litera- tures on the border or contact zone. Linguistic exchanges become literary ones. Further, the implications of the impurity of creolized languages travel easily to the field of literatures: "Like the societies of the contact zone, such languages are commonly regarded as chaotic, barbarous, lacking in struc- ture" (1992: 6). There has been something impure about these literatures on the contact zone. This difference has traditionally marked their exclusion from so called canonical or proper literatures, be it American or English literatures. These literatures have inscribed American or English literature with a difference which has been traditionally interpreted and translated as a lack or a sign of imperfection. These literatures were "similar" but not quite "it." Pratt's term "autoethnography" or "autoethnographic expression" is very useful to show a different side of what initially appears as a derivative or mimetic mode: "I use these terms," writes Pratt, "to refer to instances in which colonized subjects undertake to represent themselves in ways that *engage with* the colonizer's own terms: if ethnographic texts are a means by which Europeans represent to themselves their (usually subjugated) others, autoethnographic texts are those the others construct in response to or in dialogue with those metropolitan representations" (1992: 7). Literatures on the contact zone are therefore not only mimetic. This "dialogue" can be further qualified as a very conflicting kind of mimicry. It can be taken as a form of colonial mimicry which seeks to imitate the official language or literary representations (How can we forget Othello in Shakespeare's play and the way he speaks of Africa and Africans as a dark continent populated by cannibals?), but also as a subversive mode of mimicry which plays with and uses official discourse/literature. It is an exchange, as Pratt has further qualified, between dominant and dominated forms which involves "a selective collaboration with and appropriation of idioms of the metropolis or the conqueror. These are merged or infiltrated to varying degrees with indigenous idioms to create self-representations intended to intervene in metropolitan modes of understanding" (1999: 371). In this act of appropriation the writer (and frequently the characters) is aware of the use of a double voice, one that repeats the master's model (in an apparently mimetic mode), and another that plays on it and subverts it. This second move is radically metafictional in essence and carries entirely different messages and world visions. Traditional literatures are thus hybridized and relativized in what initially appears as derivative writing.

Language on the borderlands undergoes a similar process of hybridization which is described by Bakhtin in the following terms: "What is hybridization? It is a mixture of two social languages within the limits of a single utterance, an encounter, within the arena of an utterance, between two different linguistic consciousnesses, separated from one another by an epoch, by social differentiation or by some other factor" (1992: 358). The encounters and the language of cultural crossings can be obvious, like when Chicano, Latino or Anglo writers present a hybrid text which combines at least two languages, but can also be more elusive when the text is apparently written in standard English. For example, Krupat sees the work of some Native American writers who nonetheless write in English as "types of anti-imperial translation" (1992: 35). The same could be said about the literatures of Chinese Americans, African Americans, Chicanos, Latinos, or Arab Americans. This irreducible quality of so called ethnic writing is one of the features of "trickster writing" and the injecting of multiple layers and perspectives under the surface of what apparently is no more than English writing. This English language, however, has been radically transformed to accommodate different cultures and world visions. It is, as Talal Asad has put it, an English "powerfully affected by the foreign tongue" (qted. in Krupat 1996: 36). What on the surface appears as a form of cultural assimilation (writing in English) may be considered as a subversive act, as Frances R. Aparicio has remarked, "that of writing the self using the tools of the Master and, in the process, transforming those signifiers with the cultural meanings, values, and ideologies of the subordinate sector. Subversive also in a literal sense (*sub-verso*, under the verse, under the word)" (1994: 797).

Border writing transcends the idea of an optimistic concept of hybridity to emphasize the instability of the conflation of languages, world-visions and cultures. These new constructions question monolithic visions of identity, culture and reality, as well as purist versions of literature and language. Hybridity then, undoes the logic of the border, the urge to encapsulate and redefine and remake the wall or the barbed wire which separates the different conceptions of literature. Dismantling the wall/border from this perspective equals doing away with the notion of identity, be it personal, national, cultural, or literary as finished entities to rely on inconclusiveness. The grotesque thus replaces the classical to create a new series of relations or assemblages.

The works presented in this volume illustrate different aspects and manifestations of the textual border(lands). As an example of history written from the south, Harriet Wilson's *Our Nig* reveals the darker side of the north and the so-called free slaves. Wilson illustrates throughout her narrative that the line which separated slave from free states was very permeable and the "shadows" of slavery reached liberal and well-meaning abolitionists. In his article "Harriet E. Wilson's *Our Nig*" Aitor Ibarrola shows how Wilson breaks down conventional oppositions between freedom and slavery, male and female, north and south. The South does not finish in the south but like a repeating border threatens the life of supposedly "free" African-Americans like Frado. But Wilson goes a step further to show not only the conventional menacing aspects of the border which materialize through slave catchers, but also the more elusive but equally harmful threat of "professed abolitionists." As Ibarrola reminds us, the "two-story house" which Frado describes appears as a metonym of the larger house of a nation divided into north and south, but Wilson's merit lies also in presenting the divisions and borders within the land of freedom. Wilson, moreover, crosses and subverts generic boundaries to present a work between the slave narrative and the sentimental novel which cannot be reduced to any of these categories. The exploration of generic, literary and linguistic boundaries is further carried out in Justine Tally's "Reality and Discourse in Toni Morrison's Trilogy: Testing the Limits." Tally focuses on *Beloved* and *Paradise* to examine how Morrison undertakes an exploration of borders in her works to disrupt the dichotomies which encapsulate our world and our way of thinking. Morrison upsets the thin line that separates the real and the imaginary, the living from the dead, mind and matter. Her examination of these boundaries reveals, as Tally shows, "fluidity, transgression and instability" on a number of levels, not only in the creation of a character such as Beloved, half way between a ghost and a real person, but also in a vision of time which transcends the division of time into past, present and future. But Morrison's transgressions go even further to question the rigidness of terms such as race through a dislocation of the color line which in *Paradise* ceases to be a line-border. More importantly, as Tally shows, Morrison explores and illustrates these transgressions

through a novelistic (and "novel") language which incorporates the nonliterary, and which, in Bakhtinian terms, creates a *"heteroglossia."* If the transgression of linguistic boundaries or code-switching is one of the most
defining features of Chicano literature, Isabel Soto's "The Border Paradigm
in Cormac McCarthy's *The Crossing*" offers an example of how Anglo
writers are participants of the contact zones between the different languages
and literatures in the United States. Soto explores the border paradigm as the
axis that engenders the novel's strategies at the level of discourse, theme and
plot. Soto bases her analysis on the figure of the *loba*, "the most sustained
signifier of hybridity," a border crosser, a variation of the figure of the
coyote, the trickster in Native American culture, which constitutes patterns
of doubleness throughout the text. This doubleness is achieved on the level
of discourse through a peculiar *mestizo* language which bears McCarthy's
personal imprint. In *The Crossing* McCarthy shows how Anglo writers
participate of the internal contact zones within American literatures.
McCarthy creates a discourse in which both English and Spanish are inflected by each other, thus exemplifying a form of anti-imperial translation
that affects both languages and world visions. As Soto demonstrates, the
border is then realized not only in the creation of a third space in terms of
geography but also through a "third discourse."

Francisco Lomelí undertakes in "An Interpretive Assessment of Chicano
Literature and Criticism" the difficult task of probing into the literary, social
and cultural roots of contemporary Chicano literature. His meticulously
documented literary and critical "archeology" shows that, contrary to the
general opinion, Chicanos, as well as their literature, are no "recent immigrants trying to penetrate the mainstream." Lomelí revises and illustrates the
different stages in the process of self-discovery, as well as the diverse
manifestations of the creative energy from the works prior to 1965 and the
wake of the Chicano movement to the contemporary Chicano Renaissance.
Lomelí couples his literary "digging" for works with the delineation of a
literary history which shows, as he states, that "literary history was no longer
a hegemonic activity pertaining to Anglo American literary circles." Notwithstanding obscurity, silencing and omissions, Chicano literary history
emerges as another manifestation of tricksterism, as another side of "the
clever, survival-obsessed coyote," the character belonging to oral tradition
which, in Lomelí's words, "more accurately reflects the attributes of perseverance and ingenuity to sidestep danger or locate sustenance." The result, as
Lomelí illustrates, is a literature which figures on the map of American
literature, and which participates of a wide variety of models, from Mexican
literature to American science-fiction, from other contemporary Latin
American writers to James Joyce, and has inherent connections with the rest
of the world.

The X of the constant crossings, and the multidirectionality and the simultaneity of cultures and languages which are present in contemporary
Chicano literature is revised and reconfigured in 3-D in Begoña Simal's
"'The Cariboo Cafe' as a Border Text: The Holographic Model." Simal
conflates concepts such as cultural difference and multidimensional text and
truth to analyze a paradigmatic border text. The multiple layers of Viramontes' accomplished story create in Simal's reading a holographic image in
which three gazes are juxtaposed and intersected. Simal defines the model of
holography as the most comprehensive method of representation both of a
multifaceted truth and also of the world of the border and its constant intersection of axes, times, world visions and languages. The holographic model
creates an image of several perspectives, a three-dimensional picture which
captures the complexity of reality. On Viramontes' hands the border metaphor, however, is no optimistic site, as the brutal encounters between the
different gazes in the story illustrate, but a conscious tool to dismantle a
univocal reality and culture. If Viramontes' characters are "crossed" by the
border, Carmen Flys shows in "Shifting Borders and Intersecting Territories:
Rudolfo Anaya," how the writer gives more agency to his characters when it
comes to delineating their own territory and crossing imposed borders. We
move from the border as line or as an imposition which divides those within
as opposed to those without, to the spatial configuration of the circle as
Anaya's characters move through different spaces and thus make borders
shift and fluctuate. After asserting the importance of "a sense of place," Flys
moves on to explore the expanding spatial configurations and mapping of
territories in Anaya's novels. As the characters explore different territories,
"borders continuously shift and the intersections progressively become
larger, creating new territories, spaces of hybridity." A similar process, from
lines of demarcation to contact zones, is illustrated in Markus Heide's
"Transcultural Space in Luis Alberto Urrea's *In Search of Snow*." Markus
Heide shows how Urrea also moves away from the image of the border as
"barbed-wire fence" to articulate both a sense of the border and its different
spaces of intercultural dialogue in the heart of a dessert valley near Tucson,
Arizona. Heide distinguishes three different spaces or territories: "cultural
conflict zones based on static identities," which imply an ahistorical perspective exemplified in the image of the fossil; "utopian spaces in the tradition of
the American 'virgin land,'" based on historical amnesia, and represented in
the image of the snow; to conclude with Mary Louise Pratt's term "contact
zones," and the opening in the novel of a transcultural space which is exemplified in the García home,
    From a linguistic point of view, Eduardo de Gregorio delves into Richard
Rodriguez's exploration of his male identity in "Language and Male Identity
Construction in the Cultural Borderlands: Richard Rodriguez's *Hunger of*

Memory." De Gregorio shows how Richard Rodriguez's construction of gender identity runs parallel to his self-fashioning as an average American. But this standard American male finds that both configurations of the self as male and American are problematic. For one thing the indications of gayness, as de Gregorio illustrates, somehow threaten Rodriguez's heterosexual masculinity. For the other, notwithstanding the fact that he considers himself an average American who endorses conservative cultural and political positions, he is not viewed as average American by the media but as the spokesman for Chicanos. The boundaries of the self which Rodriguez carefully tries to delineate prove, therefore, to be fluid and blurred. This analysis of the linguistic construction of male identity is complementary to S. Suárez's positing of an alternative means of analysis, the m/other tongue. Conversing with postmodern, feminist and deconstructive critical theories, Suárez explores the multiple possibilities opened by the recent loss of credibility of the patriarchal construction of language. The article traces the interstices, the postmodern fissures in patriarchal thought and power, as a borderlands to be occupied by new languages. Suárez poses the mother tongue along with the languages of the other (the immigrant, the native) as the "'new' tongues [that] push against the borders of social definition," claiming their right to be inscribed within a plural "I." At the present moment of transition and instability in this process of cultural uncovering/recovering, Suárez sees the body, whether that of the mother, the native, or the migrant, as "the cornerstone of identity," "the site of social meanings and a political battleground."

The issue of the border and the boundaries of the self in identity construction is further explored in María del Mar Gallego's "The Borders of the Self: Identity and Community in Louise Erdrich's *Love Medicine* and Paule Marshall's *Praisesong for the Widow.*" Gallego draws from a variety of sources, from Van Gennep and Victor Turner and their classic articulations of the rites of passage, as well as from Aguirre *e.a.* and their vision of liminality and threshold, to explore Louise Erdrich's and Paule Marshall's characters. Gallego demonstrates how Erdrich's and Marshall's characters inhabit the area "in between" which is characteristic of the threshold. In Erdrich's *Love Medicine*, Marie and Lulu occupy a liminal position by means of their identification with trickster figures. In Marshall's *Praisesong for the Widow*, Avey undergoes the different stages of the rites of passage and she finally acknowledges her place in the community.

The dismantling of boundaries some spokesmen for border theory like Gómez-Peña argue for, however, is not necessarily a positive process, and the anthology concludes with a different vision of the crossing of borders. In "A Two-Headed Freak and a Bad Wife Search for Home: Border Crossing in *Nisei Daughter* and *The Mixquiahuala Letters*" Janet Cooper cautions against the optimistic vision of border culture and identity as a utopian site. Cooper illustrates the unsuccessful attempts of the main characters in Monica Sone's and Ana Castillo's novels, Kazuko and Teresa, to find a *mestiza* consciousness through physical border crossing. There are more borders to cross in order to be able to articulate a synthesis of the competing values of the different cultures present in the ethnic self.

As David Dabydeen has argued, a sense of the commitment and an understanding of the meaning of boundaries are necessary for creating a sense of belonging or a sense of community. In "Insiders/Outsiders: Finding One's Self in the Cultural Borderlands" Chrissi Harris draws upon such cautionary comments to explore the significance of living in the cultural borderlands of Britain's London and of New Zealand, both areas of a long reaching history of colonization that is perpetuated by degrees in the present day. The works Harris analyses, Andrea Levy's *The Fruit of the Lemon*, Hanif Kureishi's *The Black Album*, and Alan Duff's *Once Were Warriors*, highlight a variety of experiences that are produced by belonging to a cultural minority and the resulting uncertainty of cultural identity that ensues. Harris establishes a series of situations the border condition can give rise to, the creation of insiders, outsiders, or of being caught somewhere in-between, and in this way, provides a suitable ending for the anthology.

The articles presented in the anthology thus question the Anglocentric vision of culture and literature to present, as Carolyn Porter argues for, a more complex set of literary and critical relations. Unlike the commonly sustained opinion that history (read literature) comes from the East to move West, therefore establishing a presumably uninterrupted linear tradition from England to the U.S., there exist other cultures and literatures which link American Literature with the countries within, as well as Europe, the Caribbean, Latin America, and Africa. These creative impulses come, therefore, from multiple directions, and invalidate the dogmatic "What happens in the South is of no importance."

HARRIET E. WILSON'S *OUR NIG*: AN IDIOSYNCRATIC ATTEMPT TO LOCATE THE COLOR LINE IN TERMS OF CLASS, GENDER AND GEOGRAPHY

AITOR IBARROLA-ARMENDARIZ

This article proposes a new reading of Harriet Wilson's *Our Nig* (1859) that would release it from the kind of straitjacketing it has faced in the hands of some highly-programmatic criticism—be it feminist, ethnic, or otherwise. The fundamental argument at the heart of this discussion is that the personal experiences of *Our Nig*'s central character are so singular and often problematical that the text resists any easy, clear-cut categorization as a piece of sentimental, pro-abolitionist or feminist fiction. By looking in some detail into the different aspects of the protagonist's identity, this analysis makes progressively evident that 'the heroine's plight is the total result of interlocking structures of race, class, gender, and religion.' After the discussion of Frado's complex and uncertainty-laden experiences, the article comes to the conclusion that Wilson's autobiographical piece finds its main *forte* in her 'ability to signify from the periphery' or, to put it differently, in her resistance to adopt any inherited discourses/ideologies to portray her sufferings and longings.

> I do not pretend to divulge every transaction in my own life, which the unprejudiced would declare unfavorable in comparison with treatment of legal bondsmen; I have purposely omitted what would most provoke shame in our good anti-slavery friends at home.
>
> Harriet Wilson, Preface to *Our Nig*

> [...] the 'autobiographical' consistencies between the fragments of Harriet Wilson's life and the depiction of the calamities of Frado, the heroine of *Our Nig*, would suggest that Mrs. Wilson was able to gain control over her materials more readily than her fellow black novelists of that decade precisely by adhering closely to the painful details of suffering that were part of her experience.
>
> Henry L. Gates, Introduction to *Our Nig*

One can easily discern the shadow of a contradiction between these two statements by the obscure writer of this 1859 novel and the scholar who rediscovered, authenticated, and reissued it in 1983. While the black woman author of *Our Nig* describes her novel as one full of lacunae and reticences so as not to offend free blacks and white abolitionists in the North, Henry Gates underscores the centrality granted to the protagonist's most gruesome experiences in a literary work whose moving power derives primarily from the poignancy with which her exploitation is depicted. There is, however, a fairly simple explanation to these two antagonistic perceptions of the same text. Wilson's reticent and apologetic attitude throughout her Preface is perfectly understandable if we consider the kind of constituencies to which the novel was being addressed. Contemporary Northern readers were not likely to open a book in which the long-standing oppositions between freedom and slavery, male and female, or North and South, were challenged—or, at least, newly qualified. Thus Wilson's Preface and the three letters appended at the end of the novel serve the purpose of minimizing the effects that her daring exposure of New England's racial, social, and religious double-standards would produce. In spite of the writer's efforts to disguise her strong indictment of Northern racism, and to encourage her "colored brethren [...] to rally around [her] a faithful band of supporters and defenders," (Wilson 1859: 3) the fact that her novel has remained "silent" and ignored for over a hundred and twenty years shows that those efforts were of no avail. As Gates (1987: 137) has argued in his book *Figures in Black*, the "invisibility" of such a seminal contribution to the African-American literary tradition is only explainable if one takes into consideration its heavy criticism of black and white "abolitionists" and the extreme originality in terms of rhetorical strategies and plot of Wilson's fictional autobiography.

I believe, on the other hand, that much more can be learnt from the kind of responses that the work has received this last decade than from the study of the long silence that greeted it after its publication. For one thing, it is quite evident by now that new generations of readers are finding in *Our Nig* a rounder and more complex work of fiction than most of her contemporaries could ever have suspected. Despite the openness of her motives for writing her story: "Deserted by kindred, disabled by failing health, I am forced to some experiment which shall aid me in maintaining myself and child without extinguishing this feeble life" (3), scholars have unearthed several other intentions which turn this text into particularly rich ground in which to debate issues of class, gender, and ethnic identity. If to this fact we add that the ways in which the novel capitalizes on these up-to-date topics are frequently subtle and even ironical, it is no wonder that it should have aroused such a critical flurry from the early 1990s. Elisabeth Fox-Genovese (1990: 192), for one, notes that among nineteenth-century autobiographies by black women, *Our Nig* remains the most "problematical" and "disturbing" as a result of its unconventional structure and fictional cast. It is curious to observe, though, that notwithstanding the strangely idiosyncratic form and the unusual treatment of the themes, most critics have tried to define and classify Wilson's novel as part of, or in opposition to, certain literary trends—be they black or white—which would have determined the shape that her "experiment" ultimately took. Not only this, but according to some specialists *Our Nig* can be re-inscribed in the African-American tradition as a fairly programmatic piece of fiction propagandizing a pursuit of freedom, social equality, or maternal love. In a feminist analysis of the novel, Angelyn Mitchell (1992: 8) explains, for instance, that "in keeping with the tradition of the sentimental novel, Wilson portrays her female characters' quest for freedom through hyperbolic renderings of interpersonal, familial and social conventions." While acknowledging that these contributions may have helped us to gain a deeper understanding of the novel, I do think that more often than not they deface the true nature of a text which gets much of its forcefulness from the singularity of the sufferings and yearnings of the heroine. If it is absurd to deny the impact that some nineteenth-century traditions—most notably the slave narrative and the sentimental novel—had on Wilson's writing, it seems equally nonsensical to pigeonhole *Our Nig* as a representative piece of any of these generic categories.

A close reading of the novel soon reveals that the writer was much more dependent on her personal experiences—ambiguous and disputable as they may be—than on any inherited discourses or ideologies that might have "colored" her narrative. This is by no means atypical among black women's autobiographies, for, as Fox-Genovese (1990: 179) has pointed out, "[they] resist reduction to either political or critical pieties, and resist even more firmly reduction to mindless empiricism." Wilson's text, in particular, proves especially "irreducible" because of its repeated subversions of the distinct paradigms that would permit us to categorize it as a feminist, pro-abolitionist, or domestic piece of fiction. In a recent book under the title of *Psychoanalysis and Black Novels*, Claudia Tate convincingly argues that those narratives by black artists which have focused more closely on the protagonist's personal longings, rather than on public conflict, have been unfairly cast aside by scholars and the common reader in general. According to Tate (1998: 12), "rather than subordinating their expressions of private longing to racial politics, [these novels] exaggerate the distinction between prevalent discourses of racial protest and resonant expressions of personal emotional meaning." Although she does not include *Our Nig* in her analysis, Wilson's novel is one quite obviously concerned with the inner world of her

central character, which does not entirely depend on the material and psychological consequences of a racist social milieu. I will not be offering a
psychoanalytical reading of Frado's story, but my discussion of the novel
should make clear that her self takes the center of the stage here, thus dis-
placing to the periphery all kinds of social and literary rules. On this point,
Beth Doriani (1991: 207) rightly remarks about Wilson's and Harriet Jacobs'
self-narratives that, "in doing so, they bend conventions to their other purpose: the creations of selves consistent with their own experience as black
women."

In the pages that follow, I try to demonstrate that any attempts to read
Our Nig as a representative example of a wider literary tradition are bound to
fail since, above anything else, the achievements of this text derive from the
centrality given to the experiential tensions that the heroine lives through.
Not in vain, the title page of the book already informs us that what we are
being presented with here are simply "*Sketches* from the Life of a Free
Black." Like Harriet Jacobs' *Incidents*, Wilson's fictional autobiography
shows little concern for the genre definitions and constraints that would have
prevented her from exposing the most troubling aspects of her condition as
an indentured servant in New England. In order to develop her black female
identity as far as she could, Wilson needed to defy many of the stereotypes
and cultural boundaries established by black males and white women writers. Of course, such a defiance of the prevalent paradigms brought along
elements of uncertainty and incompletion, as her world grew more and more
in moral complexity. Still, rather than seeing *Our Nig* as a flawed text,
falling short of a radical and unqualified protest against the attitudes of white
women and black males in the North, or of Southern society in general, one
should read it as a representation of the protagonist's personal reactions to
"the betrayal of certain forms of trust, of belief" (Gates 1987: 145). Before I
proceed to discuss the very human ambiguities concerning the boundaries
between class, gender, and geographical affiliations in *Our Nig*, let me
briefly summarize Frado's story to give you a feeling of her circumstances at
each stage of the narrative.

The novel opens with the story of Mag Smith, Alfrado's white mother,
who is an orphan and a victim of an upper-class seducer in her adolescence.
Ostracized by her white society, Mag becomes increasingly isolated and
despondent until she gets married across racial lines to Jim, "a kind-hearted
African" (9). For some time, the couple live comfortably together and their
union bears "two pretty mulattos" (14); but soon afterwards Jim dies of
consumption and Mag is left poor and desolate once more. Having been by
now an outcast for years, she finds it "far easier to descend lower" (16) and
she marries Seth Shipley, a former partner in Jim's business, who talks her
into abandoning Frado, her beautiful six-year-old daughter, at the Bell-

monts'. These are a middle-class white family who take on the protagonist as
an indentured servant and have her variously occupied looking after their
cattle, doing the household chores, and becoming the object of much physical and psychological abuse. Mrs. Bellmont and one of her daughters, Mary,
both of whom are described as "she-devils" (22), scold and beat Frado
regularly. Although the male members of the family and Aunt Abby—Mr.
Bellmont's sister—try to offer Frado some relief, her exploitation at the
hands of the mistress of the house becomes more and more taxing on her
health and her spirit. By the time the heroine turns seventeen and thus nears
the end of her period of servitude, she has become seriously ill: "She had no
relish for food, and was constantly overworked, and then she had such
solicitude about the future" (94).

Before Frado leaves the Bellmonts' home, and encouraged by the patri-
arch of the family, she manages to reverse her plot in a way as she finally
faces Mrs. Bellmont and threatens not to "work a mite more for [her]" (105)
if she is struck once more. This act of resistance and self-assertion has,
however, very short-lived effects on the wicked white lady. After she has
received some severe corporal and mental punishment, Frado is at last
released in the spring of her eighteenth year. "Now she was alone in the
world. The past year had been one of suffering resulting from a fall, which
had left her lame" (117). With a downgraded self-esteem and in possession
of only "one decent dress [...] [and] a Bible" (117), Frado's entry into the
job market is not easy. She works as a servant at several homes but her
health progressively deteriorates until she is unable to support herself and is
forced to depend on public charity on several occasions. However, these few
years as a free individual have allowed her to perfect her needlework and,
helped by two kind white women, Frado is able to enjoy a brief period of joy
and independence. However, already in the last chapter of the novel, the
heroine meets and marries a black sailor and lecturer, Samuel, who claims to
be a fugitive slave. Frado's husband is mostly absent from home and he
reveals that he is a pretender who has in fact never seen the South. Unfortunately, by this stage of the story she is already pregnant and obliged to throw
herself again upon the public for sustenance. "At last Samuel's business
became very engrossing, and after long desertion, news reached his family
that he had become a victim of yellow fever, in New Orleans" (128). Frado's
(and Wilson's) story ends with the protagonist poor and defenseless, fleeing
from slave catchers and "professed abolitionists." She barely manages to
maintain herself by dyeing gray hair back to its original color, and she has to
leave her son in the County House. In a last effort to retrieve her child from
this horrendous institution, and drawing on the limited education she received in the past, she sits to write her own life story. Although she asks for
the sympathy and aid of her "gentle readers" (130), we know now that her

book sold very poorly and her six-year-old son died a few months later.

Very likely, what most strikes the reader in the story of Frado's sufferings and arrested redemption is that not one single trait of her identity could be totally blamed for prefiguring her agonizing existence. No doubt, the color of her skin—as the title of the novel makes plain—stigmatizes her from birth as one whose possibilities in life will be rather limited; but so does the fact that she is born into an impoverished family. In fact, in the late chapters of the book, it is quite evident that Frado is much more concerned with "[her] old resolution to take care of herself, to cast off the unpleasant charities of the public" (124) than with any problems that her dark skin may cause her in the future. Obviously, class and gender do not lend themselves as readily to representation and symbolization as race does, but the novel abounds with hints suggesting that these other components of her identity are also at the very root of her oppression. Still early in the story, Mrs. Bellmont notices that Frado's lively nature and handsome looks are earning her the affection of many of the farmhands. Out of a bizarre type of jealousy, the white mistress decides to keep her servant's hair shorn and to dress her in the rags of her son's worn-out clothes. If anything becomes gradually conspicuous as we advance through the story, it is that the heroine's plight is the total result of interlocking structures of race, class, gender, and religion. A. Robert Lee (1998: 78) has observed on this point that "Wilson's feat [...] is to put in view a heroine caught to her cost within an American confusion of realms." Given these premises, it is not surprising that neither the author nor her fictionalized *alter ego* should find it easy to draw the lines separating friends from enemies in terms of class, gender, or geographical location.

In a profoundly insightful article entitled "Economies of Identity: Harriet E. Wilson's *Our Nig*," John Ernest has discussed the novel as representing a new system of exchange and balanced conflict, or what he calls "a new economy of identities" (425). As he (1994: 430) contends, "it is important to remember that Frado begins as a product not only of racist formulations but also of ethical, gender, and economic formulations." In fact, it is these last factors that seem to restrict much more markedly the protagonist's future horizons as her alienated white mother and professionally enslaved "free" black father cannot provide her with the normal childhood that all children should enjoy. Frado's biological mother is forced to break several important social and moral principles—by self-exclusion, amalgamation, and child abandonment—because, as the narrator explains near the end of Chapter I, "Want is a more powerful philosopher and preacher" (13) than any current ideology. Indeed, one of the first lessons that the heroine has to learn at the Bellmonts' is that regardless of one's skin color, gender, or age, one can become a victim of someone else's will to dominate, which is always more than ready to perpetuate cultural types and class distinctions. This is of course the case of Mrs. Bellmont, Frado's "second mother," whose despotism is most evident in relation to her mulatto servant, but not limited to her. It is interesting to observe, for example, that critics have paid little attention to the remarkable space taken up in the novel by Mrs. Bellmont's rigid marriage arrangements for her daughters or her repeated criticism of Aunt Abby's conduct. Mr. Bellmont's sister tries to tend a helping hand to Frado whenever she can, but each time she has to be extremely cautious not to cause offense to her sister-in-law. In Chapter IV, after the heroine has received a terrible succession of kicks, "Aunt Abby had a glimpse of Nig as she passed out of the yard; but to arrest her, or shew her that *she* would shelter her, in Mrs. Bellmont's presence, would only bring reserved wrath on her defenceless head" (45, italics in the original). No doubt, Harriet Wilson uses the powerlessness of all the other family members to face up the mistress of the house to illustrate metonymically the reduced efficacy of anti-slavery activism in the nation at large. Ernest (1994: 429) argues in this regard that "the sense of a community of silent sympathy among the oppressed becomes another dimension of oppression, another layer of identity defined by others." In *Our Nig* Frado's destiny is mainly determined by the inability of society to implement modes of mutual dependence that would allow the dispossessed (Mag Smith) to regain their humanity and would prevent tyrants (Mrs. Bellmont) from executing their dehumanizing programs.

Although Claudia Tate (1990: 115) and others have claimed that Wilson's novel is primarily concerned with motherly love (or rather, its absence) and maternal responsibility, it is important to underline the fact that Frado's experiences can only be understood in a broader social context. One aspect that speaks quite pointedly of this more variegated and uncertain fictional universe is the fact that the text is populated by blacks and whites belonging to very different strata in the New England society. A major innovation in the novel is that, unlike in most of the sentimental fiction and the slave narratives of the period, character development is very rarely foreseeable. Hence, we meet a high-middle-class woman like Mrs. Bellmont, whose cruelties to Frado seem to have no end but, then, as soon as she is released, she is employed by a Mrs. Moore, another white lady of similar status, who "was a kind friend to her, and attempted to heal her wounded spirit by sympathy and advice, burying the past in the prospects of the future" (117-18). Among the black characters, a clear contrast is established between Frado's father, Jim, who was industrious and caring to his wife, and her husband, Samuel, whose "illiterate harangues were humbugs for hungry abolitionists" (128), and who proved an unreliable spouse. In the heroine's relationships with these figures, race *and* class can be seen to interact in complex and unpredictable ways so that it is impossible to interpret the characters as mere types. Rather than a novel about the horrors of racism or about betrayed love, what *Our Nig* presents is the potential of all human beings to act in a moral and unprejudiced manner, if only they find their niche in a certain society. It is when individuals like Mag Smith or Frado are segregated from their communities that they are driven to unnamable acts— i.e., giving up their offspring—, which do nothing but augment their feelings of rejection and marginality. According to Henry Gates (1983: xlvi), "it is poverty, both the desperation it inflicts as well as the evils it implicitly sanctions, which is *Our Nig*'s focus for social commentary."

If our expectations while reading Wilson's novel remain often unfulfilled due to her challenge to white women's fiction, with its respect for mothers and its veneration of marriage, or to other black narratives, which centered their attacks on the institution of slavery, so are we set off-balance by her handling of gender issues. When, after his wife beats Frado unfairly at one point of the story, Mr. Bellmont admits to his sister his total impotence in governing the matters at home, "How am I to help it? Women rule the earth, and all in it" (44), he is reversing one of the most widespread viewpoints on sexual politics during the nineteenth century. However, his assertion about the power dynamics in his house could not be any truer. The atrocities that Mrs. Bellmont exerts on helpless Frado do not only oppose her to the images of women as angels in the house and merciful beings, but also make evident her incontestable supremacy in the domestic realm. Her husband and sons repeatedly succumb to her evil authority as they are unwilling to cope with any of the rage that would result from keeping a stance against her despotism. Near the end of Chapter X, Jack's (the youngest son's) family are the last to leave the Bellmonts' place: "They followed Jack to the West. Thus vanished all hopes of sympathy or relief from this source to Frado. There seemed no one capable of enduring the oppressions of the house but her" (109). So unforeseen is this inversion of traditional gender roles that some specialists have read it as a satiric note with mysoginistic undertones in the novel. Elisabeth Breau (1993: 462) writes, for example, that having acquired a power never meant for her gender, both Mrs. Bellmont's femininity and her humanity have become completely distorted, and only her feminine flaws remain: she is irrational, tyrannical, manipulative, and given to crocodile tears when thwarted.

It is difficult to admit, however, that Mrs. Bellmont's cruelty and mercilessness are there only to reverse satirically the more conventional portrayal of white women in nineteenth-century fiction as gentle, nurturing, and kind. Once more, Wilson seems to be facing us with a system of complex relations that can hardly be reduced to a dichotomy of black and white.

As interesting as Mrs. Bellmont's characterization as a "devilish" creature is her son's, James', as an "angelic" one. Almost the exact opposite of his mother, he is described as "a fine-looking young man, with a pleasant countenance, placid, and yet decidedly serious, yet not stern" (46-47). A seemingly good Christian, James takes immediate interest in Frado and tries to relieve her of some of his mother's most brutal exploits. He sees some of the most outstanding virtues in her character: her kind heart, inquisitive intellect, and loving nature. Yet, like his father, James also finds excuses not to follow his own judgment:

> But to think how prejudiced the world are towards her people; that she must be reared in such ignorance as to drown all the finer feelings. When I think of what she might be, of what she will be, I feel like grasping time till opinions change, and thousands like her rise into a noble freedom. (74)

There is something weak and unbecomingly overrefined about James that makes his opposition to his mother's rule completely ineffective. Of course he is ill throughout most of the story, but more damaging to the kind of confidence that Frado places in him is the fact that his deep religiosity—a feature which turns him far too compliant—also blinds him to the heroine's most immediate needs. His words to her on his deathbed are very revealing in this sense: "But, Frado, if you will be a good girl, and love and serve God, it will be but a short time before we are in a *heavenly* home together. There will never be any sickness or sorrow there" (95, italics in the original). To the reader these lines cannot but sound rather hypocritical after we have observed the half-infatuated Frado constantly longing to be "saved" from her tormentor's claws by her apostolic friend. It comes as little surprise that after these experiences the protagonist should decide to reject the Christian aspirations that have contributed in several ways to the perpetuation of her "imprisonment":

> Frado pondered; her mistress was a professor of religion; was she going to heaven? then she did not wish to go. If she should be near James, even, she could not be happy with those fiery eyes watching her ascending path. (104)

Unlike most female-male relationships in the literature of the period, which were governed either by economic considerations or by the lustful desires of the white man for the colored woman, Frado's connection with James seems at once purer but more subtly detrimental to her own interests.

Before I bring my contribution to an end, I would like to talk briefly about *Our Nig* as an antebellum piece of fiction that both allegorizes the situation in the divided nation and problematizes any easy judgments on the principles held by both contenders. Evidently, the "two-story white house" where the Bellmonts live overflows with the kind of tensions that the country was going through at this historical point. As Hazel Carby (1987: 44) has noted, the house "increasingly resembles the nation, as the resolve of Mrs. Bellmont's opponents to improve Frado's conditions disintegrates at the slightest possibility of conflict." In fact, Wilson's most drastic critique is not targeted at the mistress of the house who, as she explains in the Preface, "was wholly imbued with *southern* principles" (3, italics in original), but rather at the supporters of the Northern cause who proved unable—or unwilling—to affirm their moral superiority by fighting those unjust principles. In spite of her alleged intention at the outset of the book not to show any of her life transactions that would "provoke shame in [her] good anti-slavery friends at home" (3), it becomes more and more clear that the narrator cannot contain her rage at the unfair treatment she receives in the so-called free states. Her long pent-up emotions explode near the end of her narrative when she is forced to travel across some State lines to find a livelihood for herself and her child:

> Strange were some of her adventures. Watched by kidnappers, maltreated by professed abolitionists, who didn't want slaves at the South, nor niggers in their own houses, North. Faugh! to lodge one; to eat with one; to admit one through the front door; to sit next to one; awful! (129)

It is certainly hard to find a more severe and straightforward indictment of the conditions in the North before the Civil War in American fiction. Too concerned with Dixie slavery, freed slaves and white abolitionist authors very rarely took the time to turn a critical eye to the plight of black domestic workers or single mothers at home. Her own firsthand experiences as an indentured servant for over ten years of her life allowed Harriet Wilson to write movingly and unconventionally about such unspeakable topics in New England as inter-racial marriage, child desertion, domestic abuse of colored servants and a society's inability to provide for those who most needed its assistance.

To conclude, I hope my discussion has brought home a number of points about Harriet E. Wilson seminal autobiography which are essential for the full appreciation of the integrity of the work. On the one hand, it seems both unfair and inadequate to approach *Our Nig* with preconceived ideas about the kind of literary tradition the novel may belong to. Any such attempts are prone to obliterate the true social and literary nature of the text, since the heroine's experiences always prove far too complex and ambivalent to fit into any of those conventional categories. Homi Bhabha (1994: 2) has noted on this point that

> The 'right' to signify from the periphery of authorized power and privilege does not depend on the persistence of tradition; it is resourced by the power of tradition to be reinscribed through the conditions of contingency and contradictori-

ness that attend upon the lives of those who are 'in the minority.'

Evidently, *Our Nig* manages to achieve the type of "reinscription" referred to here, for while it brings together some received conventions of a few contemporary genres, it does so only to generate an utterly new form which successfully resists any easy classification. On the other hand, if it is quite impossible to find *à propos* critical labels to describe the structure and style of Wilson's fictionalized autobiography, little else could be argued about its social and political implications. Despite the increasingly numerous efforts to identify the work as a solely pro-abolitionist, feminist or working-class piece of fiction, my analysis should have made clear that all these facets are unevenly interconnected and that, therefore, neither race nor gender or class can account, separately, for the kind of exploitation that the protagonist is allotted. Like most black women's autobiographies, *Our Nig* reveals a tension in its heroine's relation to the various dominant discourses of her times (Cf. Fox-Genovese 1990: 198). If Frado is eventually forced to reconsider the location of "the color line," it is because her personal experiences teach her to question most of the one-dimensional stereotypes and cultural boundaries present in her society. According to Ralph Ellison (1987: 29), perplexity is very likely to accompany our perception of the complex actualities in the lives of black Americans "because the diverse interacting elements surrounding [or presented to] us, traditional and vernacular, not only elude accepted formulations, but take on a character that is something other than their various parts." In short, Harriet Wilson's *Our Nig* provides us with a moving example of the tremendous possibilities that fiction may grant a writer to give shape to her identity and humanity in a world characterized primarily by the clear-cut divisions it imposes on individuals.

REALITY AND DISCOURSE IN TONI MORRISON'S TRILOGY: TESTING THE LIMITS

JUSTINE TALLY

Although there are many reasons for considering Toni Morrison's three latest novels—*Beloved*, *Jazz*, and *Paradise*—as a trilogy, one of the more interesting is to consider the enigmas respectively underlying each novel: Who is Beloved? Who is the narrator? And who is the white girl? Delving into these questions, which the author purposely leaves unresolved, leads one into Morrison's own exploration of some of the most important questions raised by postmodernism: What is real, and how do we know it is real? How are the texts of reality constructed by language? And, what is history except narrative? Moreover, the relationship of memory/perception, language/story-telling, and history/narrative underlies all three of the novels in such a way that each intellectual discussion of these postmodern questions enriches the reading of the other two.

Although Toni Morrison herself projected her fifth, sixth and seventh novels as a trilogy, the publication of the latest work, *Paradise* (1998), left reviewers and critics in somewhat of a disarray, either ignoring its relationship with *Beloved* and *Jazz* altogether or openly acknowledging that such a relationship was not at all clear. I have argued elsewhere (Tally 1999a) that the trilogy is undergirded by a concern for the relationship of History, Memory and Story, but that in each novel the focus of this concern is altered: *Beloved* foregrounds the problem of memory, *Jazz* of the process of storytelling, while *Paradise* deals with the ambiguities of history. In all, however, their relationship with "Truth," the author's overriding theme in all of her work, is tenuous: memory is fickle, story is unreliable, and history is subject to manipulation.

There are other reasons, however, for considering these three novels as a whole. Perhaps the most obvious is the relationship of their geographical settings and time frames. *Beloved* is set in rural Ohio, just outside of Cincinnati, or in flashback to Sweet Home, a plantation in rural Kentucky, or a chain-gang outside of Alfred, Georgia; Ruby in *Paradise* is a small-town "western" venue in Oklahoma as was Haven, the first settlement of the migrating families; whereas "the City" of *Jazz* is obviously urban New York, even though lyrical regressions in the novel move the characters back to a rural setting in Virginia. Taken together the three represent a wide cross-section of American, or rather, African American social and cultural life. Moreover, while the three novels are historically "grounded" in the 1870s, the focus shifts from the Reconstruction Era of *Beloved* to the Harlem Renaissance of *Jazz* to the Post-Civil Rights Era of the 1970s of *Paradise*, three crucial moments in a hundred years of African American history. Also noteworthy is the fact that these three time-frames all take a major war as their backdrop: The Civil War, World War I, and the Viet Nam War. However, it also seems to me to be just as viable to look at these three works as Morrison's exploration of borders, and in particular of the impossibility of rigidly imposing the limits that human beings set out as norms: physical, geographical, cultural, psychic and linguistic. Her examination of these boundaries reveals fluidity, transgression and instability–a challenge, in effect, to the established (Anglo) social order.

Perhaps more interesting than geographical settings and time frames, however, are the other types of boundaries Morrison explores, highlighted precisely by the unresolved enigmas presented in each book: Who is Beloved? Who is the narrator? *and* Who is the white girl? That the answers are intriguing but unresolved, and ultimately unimportant or even irrelevant, points up the author's impatience with artificially imposed limitations.

Most of the critical work written about *Beloved*—and it is immense!—deals with the importance of memory (both collective and personal) as antidote to a lost cultural history that was never recorded, and in particular with the psychic wounds inflicted on individuals by the institution of slavery. As a *neo*-slave narrative, *Beloved* is freed from the conventions of the nineteenth century, which dictated just how much of the (female) slave experience could be related; Sethe's horror comes alive in the book with chilling precision. Before the arrival of Paul D and then Beloved herself, Sethe spends most of her energy keeping the past at bay, trying intentionally *not* to remember former events. Yet Sethe's memory of things past is fickle: she cannot forgive herself for remembering the beautiful sycamores at Sweet Home instead of the "strange fruit" hanging from them; and the most innocuous stimuli (chamomile sap on her leg, for example) provoke the memories that she struggles so strenuously to avoid.[1]

---

[1] Even as early as *The Bluest Eye* (1970), her first novel, Morrison commented on the absolute unreliability of memory (cf. pp. 187-188). It is also interesting to note

Though Morrison clearly wants her readers to consider the possibility that Beloved is the daughter whose throat Sethe cut, Elizabeth B. House (1990) analyzes the clues in the text that indicate she might actually be a real, seriously troubled human being rather than a *revenant* or a water sprite, or a ghost from the past. More recently, Gurleen Grewal (1998) argues that both Sethe and Beloved are so plagued by traumatic memory (both having been torn from their mothers at too early an age and both having been seriously abused by ruthless masters) that they misread each other as the lost daughter/mother. Cogent as those readings are, they do not invalidate a reading of Beloved as a ghostly re-enactment both of Sethe's violent reaction to the possibility of her children's returning to slavery and of the horrors of the Middle Passage. Indeed, Morrison's dedication of the book to the "Sixty Million and more" clearly indicates her preoccupation with the history of those lost in the black diaspora.[2]

The suspension of disbelief that will allow us to understand the figure of Beloved as Sethe's murdered daughter, returned to her after Paul D has banished the "grief" or "baby ghost" from the house, will help move us beyond the limitations of a Western dichotomy of life and death and onto an African continuum. Let us examine for a moment just what that means. In Western thought we carve up time into "past, present, and future" in which the "present" is so fleeting as to be inconsequential while both the "past" and the "future" spread out almost infinitely. In effect, our concept of time also falls within the binary system so prevalent in our modern-day assumptions: on/off; yes/no; black/white; life/death; human/animal; etc. The past is over;

---

that this author's concern with memory comes to the foreground just as the "recovered memory" movement was gaining in momentum, a movement later debunked as questionable psychology and thrown out of the courts as evidence after certain women falsely accused their fathers of "remembered" sexual abuse when they were children. Cf.. Showalter (1997), Chapter Ten, for an interesting review of this problem.

[2] Her choice of precisely "Sixty Million" reflects, on the one hand, the revised estimates of the number of lives lost in the slave trade (the long standing "10 million" now vehemently disputed by both Afrocentrist and revisionist black historians, but "reaffirmed" as about 12 million in the recent research of historians such as Phillip Morgan [lecture at the conference "Monuments of the Black Atlantic: History, Memory and Politics," Williamsburg, Va., May 2000; forthcoming in the January, 2001, issue of the *William and Mary* Quarterly]); on the other, it alludes to the oft-cited "Six Million" Jewish lives lost in the Holocaust in WWII, an allusion that has irritated more than a few Jewish critics, yet signals the author's concern with substantiating the victimization of Africans over more than two hundred years. In fact, this recent new criticism of *Beloved* focusing on traumatic memory draws heavily on studies of Holocaust survivors; see particularly Felman and Laub (1991).

the future is yet to come. The African world view, however, does not conceptualize reality as strict dichotomy, but rather perceives life and experience on a continuum. The past is very much a part of us, of who we understand ourselves to be.[3] In this view what we know as "life" is only one state or stage of human existence; we lie somewhere on the continuum together with our ancestors and our descendants, and communication from or with them is not only viable, it is an established "fact of life."

Nevertheless, Beloved, as representative of the past, threatens to consume Sethe, who continually tries to explain to her "daughter" just why she killed her. Beloved, however, will not be appeased and literally feeds on Sethe's weakness, so that by the time the community of women has gathered to exorcize what they have come to believe is the devil incarnate, and pregnant no less, Sethe has been reduced to a mere wraith. History is reenacted, and Sethe is given a second opportunity to respond to her traumatic memory by attacking Bodwin, whom she perceives as the hated Schoolteacher. Beloved flees; either this is a ghost of the past which has been redeemed and therefore is banished, or, as Grewal argues, a traumatized young woman frightened away by the appearance of another white man. Even if we argue in favor of Beloved as a "real" human being, both Sethe's and her own confusion of Bodwin as their respective former slave-owners emphasize Morrison's questioning of "reality."

For reality is what we perceive it to be, and the enigma surrounding Beloved's identity—be she a *revenant* in the African American tradition, or a young black slave in the white "rational" view—is left unresolved on purpose. The problem for Sethe is that *she* believes that Beloved was her baby "crawling-already? daughter" whom she has lost once again, and that this daughter was her "own best thing." Without her, Sethe believes that she has no "self," that like Beloved earlier, when Paul D insists that he wants to bathe her, she thinks,

> There's nothing to rub now and no reason to. Nothing left to bathe, assuming he even knows how. Will he do it in sections? First her face, then her hands, her thighs, her feet, her back? Ending with her exhausted breasts? And if he bathes her in sections, will the parts hold? (*Beloved*, 272)[4]

---

[3] For a discussion of time evolving from the predominantly synchronic conception of agrarian culture to the vision of time as diachronic held by industrialized societies, see Bonnie Barthold, *Black Time* (New Haven: Yale UP, 1981).

[4] This image of fragmentation and lack of self is repeated in Denver, who cries "because she has no self" (123), and in Beloved, who examines her lost tooth and

And when she tries to tell him of all her loss—her daughter, her sons, Halle, Baby Suggs, her Mam—, Paul D must help her recenter her belief in herself: "You your best thing, Sethe. You are" (*Beloved*, 273).

There is a warning here: memory may be instrumental in reconstructing the past and in refusing to forget the trauma so as not to allow it to happen again;[5] but to cling to the past even to the annihilation of the present and the suspension of the future can only lead to the obliteration of the self. Sethe must come to terms with a past she tries hard to "disremember," a process instigated by the arrival of Paul D and Beloved, respectively, but she must learn to accept the past without being consumed by it. Just as Morrison gives us no clear answer as to the identity of Beloved, she offers no pat answers as to the boundaries of "reality." The past spills over into the present, just as the dead (memory) keep vigil in the living. And what is "real" is what you *believe* to be so.

The fluidity of the boundaries between past and present, living and the dead, mind and matter is manifest again in the third novel of the trilogy: *Paradise*. As I have argued in *Paradise Reconsidered*, the overwhelming focus of this, her latest, novel is the production of history, or whose version of the "facts" makes it into the written record. Certainly African Americans have every reason to be suspicious of the history that was handed to them by the dominant group, a history that practically obliterated their experience and their agency in the development of the country. Yet Morrison is also clearly suspicious of a re-writing of that history in monolithic terms (*à la* Afrocentrist text) to the exclusion of other groups. The founding of Haven and then Ruby is written as fairly straightforward historical narrative, though the disruptions in chronology defy the pattern of the Western, the *genre* it is based on. Yet there is an(other) undocumented history that is being recovered, again via the use of the psychic.

> The full significance and the extent of the fracture which slavery created for black people can only be appreciated in the light of the African concept of ancestry. In African cosmology ancestors are important because they provide access to the spirits who intrude for the benefit of social cohesiveness into people's lives. Obliterating black slaves' contact with their ancestors thus also destroyed their contact with the spirits. (Peach 1998:102)

The use of the psychic is undoubtedly employed in *Beloved* to reestablish contact with a lost memory, a forgotten ancestry, a silenced history. In

---

ponders the break-up of the rest of her body. Baby Suggs, on the other hand, preaches wholeness and love of the body/self.

[5] "Never again"–and certainly the Jewish community has been adept at keeping the horrors of the Holocaust vividly in view.

Paradise the psychic serves two functions. First, the character of Lone (who has the gift of "stepping in," which she teaches Connie, who is also gifted, to use), links the narrative with the African (American) tradition[6] and draws Connie back toward her own roots in Afro-Brazilian culture. Lone knows

> [...] something more profound than Morgan memory or Pat Best's history book. She knew what neither memory nor history can say or record: the 'trick' of life and its 'reason.' (272)

Though resisting what she sees as "practicing," Connie comes to terms with her special powers by changing the nomenclature to "seeing in." It is notable that while Connie, having been reared by strict Catholic nuns, frets about non-Catholic procedures of helping people, Lone has no trouble using what she considers to be God's gift. Both can "hear" what is unspoken and interpret what is said as well as what remains unstated. Although she is sure that keeping Mary Magna alive with her special gift would be anathema to the Mother Superior (though probably because Consolata does so for selfish reasons, since she has no sense of self without the older woman), it is bringing back Easter from the point of death that initiates (and cements) her friendship with Soane, a source of uneasiness for her husband Deacon.

The second use of the psychic that links Connie with the African tradition is her appearance to Soane as a *revenant*, the spirit of someone who has been violently killed and returns to visit the living. Beloved may be one such case, Consolata another. In this novel, however, no one else ever actually *sees* the apparition; Deacon at first thinks Soane is speaking to him when she says, "You're back," but on realizing that she is talking to someone else, he remains silent. The other women also return as *revenants*: Gigi appears to her father, who has been granted a reprieve from Death Row; Jean spots Seneca as her friend attends to a cut on her hand; Divine sees Pallas carrying a baby as well as a sword but is unable to call to her; and Mavis appears to her daughter Sally for a brief conversation over breakfast.

Unless the reader wants to believe the rather unconvincing possibility that these women were not murdered, that one or all of them survived and escaped in Mavis' "red-as-bruised-blood" Cadillac, Morrison offers the reappearance of these "ghosts" right out of the African belief system. There is, perhaps, an alternative interpretation: that these apparitions are, in fact, the creation of longing and desire, an attempt to fill the emptiness of loss. As in the case of Mavis, who hears the comforting laughter of Merle and Pearl,

---

[6] Lone's and Connie's gift of "sight without seeing" connects them to other Morrison characters such as Pilate of *Song of Solomon* and Thèrése of *Tar* Baby, also guardians of the African American legacy.

the people to whom the Convent women reappear are those who would have an enormous need of comfort, particularly if they felt, as they do, that the loss is intimately connected with their own inadequacies.[7] Morrison herself has stated that she has intentionally left the interpretation of what happens to these women open-ended so that readers can believe what they want.[8] Again, in her writing she does not define the limits of "reality," preferring simply to explore them, and there are numerous occasions in the text in which both interpretations can coexist.

Morrison often reinforces these alternative possibilities in the language she chooses, which allow for a "simultaneous disjunction" in their meaning(s). Trudier Harris states that "the emphasis upon the power of words becomes another way for Morrison to break down the barrier between planes of existence" (Harris 1991:170). Though Harris is specifically referring here to *Beloved*, this observation is equally applicable to the language of *Paradise*. The constant doubling in the text–two brothers, two sisters, two interpretations–is constantly reinforced by language that also encourages double reading:

> She wiped her eyes and lifted the cup from its saucer. Tea leaves clustered in its well. More boiling water, a little steeping, and the black leaves would yield more. Even more. Ever more. Until. Well, now. What do you know? It was clear as water. (217)

The permeability between the psychic and the "real" emphasized in these words, extends to other aspects of the work: on the one hand, the rigid geographical demarcation of Ruby and the exact distancing from the unstructured Convent is continually breached by members of the community who, for different reasons, must secretly defy the sacrosanctness of their town. Deacon for a while maintains a passionate affair with Connie (much to his brother's disapproval), K.D. searches out Gigi for sexual gratification, Arnette goes looking to terminate her pregnancy and then again, after her marriage to K.D., to recover her lost baby, Minus goes there to wrestle with his war memories and the loss of his true love due to the townsmen's insistence on "pure blood," Sweetie sets out for the Convent one chilly morning, half-crazy from caring for chronically ill children, though she never makes it there—Ruby may want to distance itself from all the messiness of life, but such a utopian community is only maintained on the edge of history, not

---

[7] This view, however, glosses over the fact that at the time the *revenants* are "sighted" their hair is short-cropped as they wore it in their later days at the Convent.

[8] Morrison discussed her intentions during a question and answer session after a reading from *Paradise* held at the University of Vienna, October 22nd, 1999.

within it. Gigi's inconclusive search for the rock couple at Wish, Arizona, lends itself to the same speculation: the townspeople of Wish could only be bothered by the "eternally fucking" figures if indeed they bothered to go out of their way to visit them.

On the other hand, the history of the Convent itself, as a school for Native American girls to be instructed in Catholicism, and *out* of their own culture, speaks to the impossibility of eradicating the native culture. Connie's passion for Deacon is not just sexual; she also recognizes in Deacon her own cultural background:

> Consolata virtually crawled back to the little chapel (wishing fervently that He could be there, glowing red in the dim light). [...] No beseeching prayer emerged. No Domine, non sum dignus. She simply bent the knees she had been so happy to open and said 'Dear Lord, I didn't want to eat him. I just wanted to go home.' (240)

Wanting to go "home" is not for Soane the pleasures of sexuality and the traditional hearth; "home" is the African tradition she has recognized in Deacon that connects her with her African American history. Although Connie was snatched from the degradation of life on the streets in Brazil at age nine and reared by devout Catholic nuns, she finds that her assimilation into an Anglo world is not total. The Convent at the (present) time of the story has become a site of inclusiveness, not exclusion, and as such contrasts mightily with the exclusionary politics of Ruby.

The most outstanding challenge to boundaries in *Paradise*, nevertheless, is race, signaled by the very first sentence of the novel: "They shoot the white girl first." Race, then, will be the subject of the book, yet the "race" of the women at the Convent is never mentioned again. Morrison has stated that she "did that on purpose [...] I wanted the readers to wonder about the race of those girls until those readers understood that their race didn't matter. I want to dissuade people from reading literature in that way" (Gray 1998: 67).

Almost all of Morrison's work takes up the question of what it means to be "black." In *Song of Solomon* as in *Tar Baby* emphasis is placed on the legacy of an African tradition as opposed to the adoption of marketplace values of the dominant white culture. Whereas Milkman is judged to have "a heart like the white men who come to pick them up in the trucks when they needed anonymous, faceless laborers" (*Song*: 266), Jadine comes to wonder if her French fiancé loves her for herself or for the exotic color of her skin, while Son returns to his "ancient properties" on the Isle de Chevaliers.

For Pecola of *The Bluest Eye*, just as for the Invisible Man of Ralph Ellison's novel of the same name (1952), blackness renders the protagonist invisible, the totalizing signifier makes it impossible for anyone to see past the colored skin to the real self that inhabits it. In *Beloved* Morrison reverses the trope: the "men without skin" on the slave ship mark the absence of any *human* presence, which renders them invisible as characters or true "selves." And in Ruby of *Paradise* the affirmation of blackness as exclusive and excluding signifier completes the circle, but with little progress in the human condition; the importance of one color has simply been substituted by another. To the contrary, our involvement with the women of the Convent makes their "race" (whatever that may be) irrelevant; the emphasis is on their humanity, their kindness to outcasts, and their inclusiveness. So what, then, does "blackness" mean, and how do we sustain a characterization of individuals based on such an empty category as "race"? The inversion of the infamous "one-drop rule" by the Founding Fathers of Ruby shows up the ludicrousness of such a definition; such boundaries can only be maintained at the expense of full humanity, of those included as well as excluded (cf. the sterility of the women's lives in Ruby and the ossification of the patriarchal order).

In *Beloved*, then, "reality" is enigmatic, and in *Paradise* the limitation of "race" as category is problematic. Who is Beloved? The reader's choice. Who is the white girl? What does it matter? Which brings us to perhaps the thorniest text as far as understanding Morrison's explorations of boundaries are concerned: *Jazz*. In the "middle" novel of the trilogy, some critics have wanted to see Wild as the figure of Beloved—the time frame fits, the fact that she disappears in "water" at the end of the first novel pregnant and reappears in the rain to give birth to Joe in the second, her elusiveness, and her incapacity to relate to other people, most particularly to the man we are led to believe is her son. Yet of the three, *Jazz* has least to do with psychic phenomena, and Wild, though also enigmatic, seems to be a "real" person of flesh and blood.

On the other hand, the unidentified narrator, the style of narration, and the name of the book itself, as well as the time-frame for the central action ("The Jazz Age") have all led critics to center their attention on the author's supposed use of jazz as music both structurally and thematically (Eckard 1994; Gates 1993; Lewis 1997; Rice 1996).[9] As an avid Morrison fan and student, I believe the overt references to music are a distraction from the more serious theme of the book: the ways and means of storytelling.

I have explored elsewhere (Tally 1999b) the clues that Morrison leaves in *Jazz* to indicate why I believe that her emphasis in this novel is on story-telling and its particular importance in the conservation of collective memory

---

[9] For an excellent rebuttal of these critics see Munton 1997.

and consequently of history. One distinct sign is the author's playing with names, a trait characteristic of this writer: Morrison, ever the teaser, plays around with Hunter, Golden Gray's father whose name is alternately Henry "Lestroy" or "LesTroy" (148 & 149) and "Le*story*" (148, 149 & 157), only to wind up definitively as "Lestory" in the following chapter (168 & 172). Bear in mind that Joe has given himself the last name of "Trace" (because his mother had left without a trace) and that "trace" is Stephen Greenblatt's denomination for historical event; also bear in mind that Victory, Joe's best friend and hunting companion, is always associated with memory in the book, and that Hunters Hunter, that is, Lestory, has trained both of them to hunt. Symbolically, then, it is "story" that guides and trains both "history" and "memory," and hence the dominant theme of the book.

There are other indications, not the least of which is Morrison's own ac-ceptance speech for the Nobel Prize in 1993, in which she not only tells a story (of the blind woman and the bird) but emphasizes the fundamental importance of the vehicle for storytelling, that is, language:

> So I choose to read the bird as language and the woman as a practiced writer [...] The systematic looting of language can be recognized by the tendency of its us-ers to forgo its nuanced, complex, midwifery properties, replacing them with menace and subjugation. Oppressive language does more than represent vio-lence; it is violence; does more than represent the limits of knowledge; it limits knowledge. Whether it is obscuring state language or the faux language of mindless media; whether it is the proud but calcified language of the academy or the commodity-driven language of science; whether it is the malign language of law-without-ethics, or language designed for the estrangement of minorities, hiding its racist plunder in its literary cheek—it must be rejected, altered, and exposed. It is the language that drinks blood, laps vulnerabilities, tucks its fas-cist boots under crinolines of respectability and patriotism as it moves relent-lessly toward the bottom line and the bottomed-out mind. Sexist language, racist language, theistic language—all are typical of the policing languages of mas-tery, and cannot, do not, permit new knowledge or encourage the mutual ex-change of ideas. (Morrison 1993: 319)

She goes on to say that perhaps if people had learned to listen to other narratives they would not have been so inclined to build the Tower of Babel in order to reach heaven; perhaps they would have been able to discover paradise in terrestrial rather than celestial space simply through more effec-tive communication, simply by developing the capacity to listen to other texts, stories other than their own.

Another clue that language is very much the subject of *Jazz* can be read in the opening epigraph of the book,

> I am the name of the sound
>> and the sound of the name.
> I am the sign of the letter
>> and the designation of the division,

taken from "Thunder, Perfect Mind," of *The Nag Hammadi*. Several critics have speculated on the relevance of these words, sometimes as justification for their thesis that jazz itself is either the subject or narrator of the text, but more often interpreting them either within the tradition of Gnosticism, since the twelve books of *The Nag Hammadi Library* (1977) deal with gnostic texts, or with the fact that the texts were discovered in the Upper Nile region and that the female voice could be Isis, the African goddess speaking. George MacRae speaks of "a female revealer" (*Nag Hammadi*: 271), while Gurleen Grewal states that

> We can appreciate how Morrison absorbs this figure into the persona of her narrator, who is designated by the sound and name of jazz. Further, the unknown gnostic revelator's stance as a persecuted outsider (an Egyptian's relationship to the dominant Greco-Christian discourse?) allies her with the position of a female African American narrator of the 1920s. Consider these lines from The Thunder, Perfect Mind:

>> Why have you hated me in your counsels?
>> For I shall be silent among those who are silent,
>>> and I shall appear and speak.
>> Why then have you hated me, you Greeks?
>>> Because I am a barbarian among [the] barbarians?
>> For I am the wisdom [of the] Greeks
>>> and the knowledge of the barbarians.

> The ancient one who has been hated everywhere and who declares, I am peace, /and war has come because of me/And I am an alien and a citizen becomes a perfect correlative for the narrator of post-Civil War, post-Reconstruction mayhem (Grewal: 121).

For my part I believe that the epigraph Morrison has chosen (and even the lines with which Grewal has chosen to substantiate her own claims) are best illuminated by the analysis that differentiates "Thunder, Perfect Mind" from the other texts in *The Nag Hammadi* and argues against its inclusion as an Gnostic scripture. Rather, as Bentley Layton (1986) claims, it is much more closely related to the tradition of the Greek riddle in which a paradox is presented that makes little sense until the answer is known. Even when his translation of these same words varies from those Morrison has chosen, the resolution of the "riddle" is important:

It is I who am the meaning of text,
And the manifestation of distinction; [...]
Behold, then, [...] all the texts that have been completed.

("Thunder" VI, 2:20,33-21,12 in Layton: 54)[10]

If we read the answer as "language," both of these texts become powerfully meaningful, and Morrison's focus becomes clear.

To assert that language and the process of storytelling are the underlying theme of *Jazz* is coherent in several ways. In the first place, one of Morrison's stated objectives in writing the novel was to write a post-modern novel, but with a strong narrative line to it. And what is more postmodern than a preoccupation with language, particularly a concern with the way language is used to tell stories? Secondly, we turn to Mikhail Bakhtin, who states categorically that, "As a living, socio-ideological concrete thing, as heteroglot opinion, language, for the individual consciousness, lies on the borderline between oneself and the other" (1981: 294). Bakhtin's sensitivity to language is made absolutely clear throughout the four essays included in *The Dialogic Imagination*. Indeed, and in the third place, his theory of the development of the novel has everything to do with the irruption of the folk (what he calls "laughter") into the "high" literary forms as early as ancient Greek literature. The capacity of language both to represent, and then to parody the representation, in Bakhtin's theory, represents the great innovation of the *genre*; indeed this is exactly what is "novel" about it.

> Cultural and literary traditions (including the most ancient) are preserved and continue to live not in the individual subjective memory of a single individual and not in some kind of collective psyche, but rather in the objective forms that culture itself assumes (including the forms of language and spoken speech), and in this sense they are inter-subjective and inter-individual (and consequently social); from there they enter literary works, sometimes almost completely bypassing the subjective individual memory of their creators. (249, Footnote 17)

It is beyond the scope of the present paper to discuss in detail Bakhtin's theory of the novel, but it is useful to point out some examples of just how Morrison intentionally incorporates the "folk" or non-literary language into

---

[10] Layton's analysis of the whole poem leads him to believe that the answer to the "riddle" posed in the text is actually "Eve." Nonetheless, the part of "Thunder" chosen by Morrison as epigraph to *Jazz* reinforces my thesis that language and storytelling are at the center of this novel.

the weaving of her story in incidences of pseudodiegesis, a kind of doubly-oriented speech, a discourse which simultaneously calls up another discourse:

(*Public signs*)

The City is smart at this: smelling and good and looking raunchy; sending secret messages disguised as public signs: this way, open here, danger to let colored only single men on sale woman wanted private room stop dog on premises absolutely no money down fresh chicken free delivery fast. (*Jazz*: 64)

(*Newspaper headlines*)

Every week since Dorcas' death, during the whole of January and February, a paper laid bare the bones of some broken woman: Man kills wife. Eight accused of rape dismissed. Woman and girl victims of. Woman commits suicide. White attackers indicted Five women caught. Woman says man beat. In jealous rage man. (*Jazz*: 74)

(*Radio serial*)

Taller than most, she gazes at them over the head of her dark friend. The brothers' eyes seem wide and welcoming to her. She moves forward out of the shadow and slips through the group. The brothers turn up the wattage of their smiles. The right record is on the turntable now; she can hear its preparatory hiss as the needle slides toward its first groove. (*Jazz*: 66-67)

(*Folk-sayings*)

They know that a badly dressed body is nobody at all [...] (*Jazz*: 65)

(*Black sermon*)

Who were the unarmed ones? Those who found protection in church and the judging any God whose wrath in their behalf was too terrible to bear contemplation. He was not just on His way, coming, coming to right the wrongs done to the, He was here. Already. See? See? What the world had done to them it was now doing to itself. Did the world mess over them? Yes but look where the mess originated. Were they berated and cursed? Oh yes but look how the world cursed and berated itself. Were the women fondled in kitchens and the back of stores? Un huh. Did police put their fists in women's faces so the husbands' spirits would break along with the women's jaws? Did men (those who knew them as well as strangers sitting in motor cars) call them out of their names every single day of their lives? Un huh. But in God's eyes and theirs, every hateful word and gesture was the Beast's desire for its own filth. The Beast did not do what was done to it, but what it wished done to itself: raped because it wanted to be raped itself. Slaughtered children because it yearned to be slaughtered children. Built jails to dwell on and hold on to its own private decay. God's wrath, so beautiful, so simple. Their enemies got what they wanted, became what they visited on others. (*Jazz*: 77-78)

According to Bakhtin, this parodic rendering of nonliterary languages adds potential to the novel's capacity of exploring the boundaries between the public and the private while adding to the mix of what he calls *heteroglossia*—the necessary voices of different types of speech within the novel.

> Another's speech—whether as storytelling, as mimicking, as the display of a thing in light of a particular point of view, as a speech deployed first in compact masses, then loosely scattered, a speech that is in most cases impersonal (common opinion, professional and generic languages)—is at none of these points clearly separated from authorial speech: the boundaries are deliberately flexible and ambiguous, often passing through a single syntactic whole, often through a simple sentence, and sometimes even dividing up the main parts of a sentence. This *varied play with the boundaries of speech types*, languages and belief systems is one of the most fundamental aspects of comic style. (Bakhtin 1981: 308)

But Morrison's intention is more than comic effect; it is rather the exploration of the limits of language and the ways in which narration is constituted. She echoes Bakhtin's imperative that "the novel must represent all the social and ideological voices of its era, that is, all the era's languages that have any claim to being significant" (Bakhtin: 411), and in doing so she lays claim not only to diversity, but also to the necessity of including narratives other than those of the dominant discourse. And it is this concern that was very obviously on her mind when she began to examine the borders of *Paradise* in her latest novel:

> Whose heaven, she wonders? And what kind? Perhaps the achievement of *Paradise* was premature, a little hasty, if no one could take the time to understand other languages, other views, other narratives. Had they, the heaven they imagined might have been found at their feet. Complicated, demanding, yes, but a view of heaven as life, not heaven as postlife. (1993: 321)

Toni Morrison's trilogy, then, can be understood not as the author's attempt to find answers, but rather to explore the very nature of the postmodern experience; hence the provocative but ultimately unanswered questions. If, as Brian McHale states, postmodernism deals not with the modernist dilemma, "What do we know, and How do we know it?," but with "What is real, and How do we perceive reality?," then *Beloved*'s excursion into alternative realities must be postmodern. If the postmodern concern is with the nature and meaning of language, then *Jazz* is truly a postmodern experiment. And if postmodernism reformulates history as narrative instead of "fact," then *Paradise* warns of the instability of boundaries that can be changed according to whoever is in control of that narrative. Even the boundaries of each of these novels become fluid as their themes and strategies become ever so intertwined.[11] But then, I believe, that is precisely Morrison's point.

---

[11] Cf, for example, Grewal's assertion that "In *Jazz*, history is more like an unfinished plot that must work itself out in the life of the present; as such the novel is in many ways the denouement of *Beloved*" (133).

THE BORDER PARADIGM IN CORMAC
MCCARTHY'S *THE CROSSING*

ISABEL SOTO

In this essay I explore various concepts in Cormac McCarthy's *The Crossing*: the border, space and geography. I argue firstly that the border or frontier is the organizing principle, generating most, if not all, the textual strategies at the levels of discourse, theme and plot. These strategies frequently involve structures of doubleness mediated literally or figuratively by the border paradigm. Obvious examples can be located in such archetypal binaries as male-female, life-death, past-present. Most notably, perhaps, large portions of McCarthy's text alternate English and a form of Spanish defined by, or constitutive of, the United States-Mexican border. I argue secondly, therefore, that the border is closely bound to the concept of space. McCarthy's characters will have to negotiate various sites or spaces: human, natural and otherworldly. Thirdly, I argue that the constructs of the border and space articulate a variation, or perhaps unresolved, version of Heraclitus' notion of geography as fate. Thus, in the mythical contours of the journeys McCarthy's characters undertake, geography does not so much constitute fate as propose experience: always unfinished, always in the making.

Cormac McCarthy's *Border Trilogy* (1992-1998)[1] could be described arguably as a cycle of coming-of-age novels, characterized by such requisite initiation procedures as leaving home, becoming orphaned, confronting death, acquiring sexual knowledge, and so on. Perhaps a more interesting, and productive, focus might be on how those rites of passage are articulated or, indeed, whether they are fully realized. McCarthy's mid-trilogy novel *The Crossing* (1994) is constructed around just such a series of ritualistic maneuvers, each of which acquiesces in the novel's central paradigm. In this essay I propose that the border cannot be disengaged from the concept of territorial space or geography: characters enter alternating or conflicting geographical sites, or acknowledge human spaces alongside those that are

---

[1] *All the Pretty Horses* (1992), *The Crossing* (1994), and *Cities of the Plain* (1998).

not of this world. The novel opens by foregrounding border and geography.

> When they came south out of Grant County Boyd was not much more than a
> baby and the newly formed county they'd named Hidalgo was itself little older
> than the child [...] The new country was rich and wild. You could ride clear to
> Mexico and not strike a crossfence [...] (3)

The border is thus established as the dominant paradigm on the novel's
first page. My overall thesis is that it generates most if not all of the text's
strategies at the level of discourse, theme and plot. Thus, to the extent that
they articulate the border paradigm, discourse, theme, and plot are central to
my discussion. We will see that not the least interesting aspect of the border
paradigm is that it encloses the possibility both of observance and transgression; one can cross it or not. Expressed another way, it denotes a site of
difference between two spaces and, simultaneously, the site, or point, at
which one space may be accessed from the other.[2] Hence I will explore the
border in *The Crossing* both as a static construct or site of demarcation, and
also in its dynamic variant, as a threshold providing access to two spaces,
figurative or real, adjacent to it. Further, if we take the border as the organizing principle in *The Crossing*, we discover that the text frequently yields
representations of doubleness, or equivalences, or variants. Always our
implied mediating structure is the border or threshold. I consider below these
representations of doubleness, whether as figures of difference or figures of
equivalence or duplication. The unfailingly paradoxical nature of the threshold or border is reinforced by these patterns and structures of doubleness, the
effect of which is to stress similitude or magnify difference: in similitude the
border holds fast; in difference it is crossed or transcended.

I will end my discussion by considering McCarthy's contrapuntal—
double—use of Spanish and English and their mutual inflection, in which
respect another, perhaps obvious, point needs to be made: the geographical
context of the *Border Trilogy* is what facilitates the use of Spanish in the first
place, and the alternation, even symbiosis, between English and Spanish in
the second. The narratives do not unfold in Australia or Sweden. To this
extent, then, geography generates experience and the discourse through
which that experience is mediated. Indeed we find geography and discourse
eliding in the service of experience. To repeat the above quotation from the
opening of *The Crossing*, "When they came south out of Grant County Boyd

---

[2] I am indebted here to Manuel Aguirre and Esteban Pujals from the Universidad
Autónoma in Madrid. Our many discussions of the limen or threshold have directly
contributed to my formulation of the border paradigm and to many of the ideas in this
essay.

was not much more than a baby and the newly formed county they'd named Hidalgo was itself little older than a child." Child and land originate and are named together, one in English, the other in Spanish. We read further that his brother Billy "named to him features of the landscape and birds and animals in both spanish and english" (sic). Discourse, human experience and geography conjoin at the border: Mexico is within sight of the family's home, a home which nevertheless is still the United States. The border's ambivalence or doubleness, then, is likewise established in these opening words as a site of demarcation yet also a point of entry or transcendence: "You could ride clear to Mexico and not strike a crossfence" (3).

The novel is organized around three round-trip crossings Billy Parham makes from New Mexico into Mexico. His first trip is driven by a wish to return a she-wolf he has captured on the US-side of the border to Mexico, where he assumes she has originated. The trip ends with the wolf's death and burial at Billy's hands. He makes his second trip accompanied by his younger brother Boyd, the brothers by now orphaned, their parents having been murdered by "indians" while Billy was returning the wolf. This trip too ends in tragedy: Boyd is killed fighting for Mexican rebels. Billy's third and final quest into Mexico is for the purpose of retrieving his brother's body to bury him on his native soil. Having achieved this, the novel ends with an image of Billy watching the sun rise; whether in ecstasy or abject grief is one of the novel's unresolved questions.

As our starting point it is useful to bear in mind just who enforces or po-lices the border, and who contests its presence, thereby drawing punitive reaction from the former. No single being transcends the border, an act equated throughout the novel with transgression, and is punished more formidably on that account than the she-wolf. The reader first encounters the wolf as Billy does, generically, as a constituent member of a group. In his primary boyhood experience in which he leaves his house to venture in the dead of night to within twenty feet of the running pack, the she-wolf is still evoked through the pronominal plural:

> He could see their almond eyes in the moonlight [...] They bunched and nuzzled and licked one another. Then they stopped. They stood with their ears cocked [...] They were looking at him. He did not breathe. They did not breathe. (4)

Note the syntactic—and hence semantic—intertwining of the lupine "they, their" with the human "him, he." At this point Billy is geographically, narratively and discursively occupying the same space as the wolves.

While the quest to recover Billy's father's stolen horses drives much of *The Crossing*'s plot, it is the she-wolf who generates the novel's complex imagery, is the proponent and performer of transgression (she crosses multiple borders) and, ultimately, the repository of doubleness or hybridity. She also inducts Billy into his own desire to transgress or to cross. Billy, then, manages to ensnare the she-wolf, initially in full compliance with the unwritten law of cattle ranching (wolves must be trapped and destroyed) and his father's explicit injunction. Up to this point, Billy acknowledges the border; he literally toes the line. Once, however, Billy decides to abandon familial geography and return the *loba* to Mexico, whence he believes she has come, his mission born of border violation is consistently, even brutally resisted.

Who, then, upholds the border by opposing its crossing? Billy's father in the first instance, who has entrusted his son with the supervision of the wolf-traps. He has also instructed Billy "to come and get him" (59) if Billy catches her, presumably to destroy her afterwards. Billy exceeds however the paternal command: he consults and heeds the advice of Mexican wolf-trapper Don Arnulfo in a scene which also provides the occasion for the first hybrid language sequence. Don Arnulfo seems to supply Billy with the know-how for catching the *loba*, and thus obeying his father or, what comes to the same, observing the border. In order to catch the wolf,

> the boy should find that place where acts of God and those of man […] cannot be distinguished […] Lugares donde el fierro está en la tierra, the old man said. Lugares donde ha quemado el fuego (47).

The doubleness of the discourse, however (English and Spanish), the blasphemous conflation of the divine with the human, and the confession "soy hereje" (I'm a heretic) a few lines down, do not so much foreshadow as confirm a future transgression of major proportions. When, some fifteen pages later, Billy surveys the surrounding geography in an attempt to decide whether to return home with the information his father is awaiting, we know the border has already been breached: Billy has captured the she-wolf and, dragging her behind him, finally chooses to "*cross [...] through the ditch* and [ride] up onto the broad plain that stretched away before him south toward the mountains of Mexico" (63, my italics).

In a series of picaresque adventures, Billy and the *loba* encounter in this first section of the novel persons who express surprise, horror, bureaucratic opposition, and ultimately violence on witnessing the two together. The tragic outcome of this, the first of Billy's quests, is signaled significantly through his abortive attempt to cross the Bavispe river south into the mountain ranges beyond. Unable to help the wolf cross the river's deep waters to the other side, Billy is accosted by two sinister horsemen. The encounter leads to Billy's semi-arrest and the confiscation of the wolf for the purposes of drawing crowds and money at a carnival dog fight. Billy will eventually end her torment by shooting her and trading her body for his rifle.

The bi-cephalous question remains: has the border paradigm held fast or has it been transgressed? That Billy fails to cross the river, a natural border, indeed is lead southwards by the two horsemen by diverging from the river—"they took the path downriver [...] The path diverged from the river [...] The riders rode on [...] and then turned south" (96)—marks the disjunction between desire and plenitude. The novel signifies precisely at these moments of doubleness, problematizing readings that seek to circumscribe it and the other two works in the trilogy, *All the Pretty Horses* and *Cities of the Plain*, within a reductive *Bildungsroman* convention. I suggest that Billy's initiation into adulthood and knowledge is ironic in its clinging to a double discourse that represents a transitional movement even as it subverts it. Billy proceeds in his endeavor to return the wolf to her point of origin: though he initially fails to "cross," he finally does so and closes the novel's first sequence: "At the junction of the rivers he rode across the broad gravel beach" (125) where he first sees the horsemen. This crossing re-writes Billy's original imagining of it (the wolf is now dead, so are her unborn offspring), even as it signals other borders to cross, real and imaginary. As he carries the dead *loba* Billy "sang [...] a soft corrido in spanish from his grandmother that told of the death of a brave soldadera who took up her fallen soldier-man's gun" (125). That Billy's crossing is accompanied by the musical form most closely associated with the border, the *corrido* or border ballad, is hardly coincidental. The *corrido* underwrites Billy's transgression (it is traditionally a form about border conflict) of geographical as well as chronological borders: Billy is here foretelling his brother's death.

There are other moments such as the above where the border is upheld, its crossing checked at the level of desire. Coming-of-age conventions require sexual initiation, a passage from not knowing into knowing. *The Crossing* yields a striking scene of an uncrossed border that inevitably brings to mind Stephen Dedalus's epiphanic commitment to an artist's destiny after watching a girl by the sea-shore who, in his heightened imagination, takes on mythic powers of transformation and seems to adopt the soaring contours of a bird. The scene closes at that frontier moment when day is slipping into evening.[3] Billy's awakening partakes of similar elements: water, here a river; a young woman, naked; a chronological border or threshold, this time sunrise. Billy observes, mesmerized, the morning toilet of a traveling opera diva. The woman's nakedness, beauty and hypnotic movements reveal to Billy "that the world which had always been before him everywhere had been veiled from his sight" (220). A rite of passage? The scene discloses the possibility of true initiation even as it truncates it: "She [...] saw him [...]

---

[3] *A Portrait of the Artist as a Young Man*: 185-187.

and turned her back and walked slowly up out of the river and was lost to his view."[4] In explicit allusion to Heraclitus, for Billy nevertheless "the sun rose and the river ran as before but nothing was the same nor did he think it ever would be" (220). Significantly, perhaps, when sexual initiation does occur, it is displaced: Boyd, Billy's brother, gets the girl, incidentally paying for it with his life.

I have been arguing that the border paradigm is constitutive of doubleness, generating certain textual strategies chiefly through representations of doubleness or alternative maneuvers: the border may or may not be crossed; events appear to offer epistemological certainty, only to yield the paradoxical realization that there is no such thing, just endless variation on or postponement of full knowledge; discourse is bilingual, if not interlingual, as I show below. The most potent representation of that doubleness is the figure of the wolf. For speakers of Spanish generally, in particular Latin American speakers of Spanish and scholars of imperial Spain's *casta* categories, *lobo* is a familiar term. Aside from its standard meaning of "wolf" it also denotes in Mexican usage "hijo de negro e india, o al contrario," according to the *Diccionario de la Real Academia Española*. We are also referred to the term "zambo," meaning the same, and from which the racially offensive English "sambo" derives. The *María Moliner Diccionario de Uso del Español* gives "mestizo" as a synonym for "lobo." Whether or not McCarthy was aware of the semantic range of the word, and it must at least be a possibility, the she-wolf, as I have argued, is the most sustained signifier of hybridity—quite literally of mestizaje—or the border paradigm. Her role as exponent of the border is necessarily fluid: she is a transgressor of real (national) boundaries; she is also an initiator, inducting Billy into his own various transgressions or crossings or attempted crossings; she is, ultimately, a guardian of thresholds, figuratively and rhetorically marking the point of entry into other narrative sequences, other spaces, other worlds.[5]

Billy's early consultation of Don Arnulfo on how he might catch the wolf

---

[4] When in a third and final representation of this moment Billy revisits the spot where he saw the naked diva, he remains unable to cross the river. The most he can muster is to "wade the horse into the [...] shallows" (329).

[5] The wolf is cognate with trickster figures common to all folk cultures. Aguirre, Quance and Sutton identify the trickster as a "liminal" or threshold figure: "the Trickster stands between the wild and the civilized world, sharing in both, committing himself to neither, a figure whose behaviour brings or threatens chaos but, at the same time, offers a promise of liberation or transcendance" (69). Billy's loba is also congruent with the coyote which, in Mexican vernacular, refers to the agent who brokers the passage of illegal immigrants across the Mexican border with the United States. "If you want to work in the US, you get yourself a coyote." (Private conversation with Mexican anthropologist Marta Tello).

yields the answer that he must set his trap in those places "donde ha quemado el fuego" (47). Don Arnulfo's prophetic advice—Billy indeed traps the *loba* among the ashes of a dead fire—generates a series of variants on the initial scene of entrapment, scenarios in which the wolf is physically attached to or guards a space circumscribed by the small circle of a camp fire. The clearest rendering of the mythical role of the wolf as guardian to an otherworldly space occurs early on in her capture. Billy has set up camp for the night on his trek south to Mexico, and secures the wolf by tying her to a piece of wood. While he tends the fire, "her eyes burned out there like gatelamps to another world. A world burning on the shore of an unknowable void" (73). Realization of her threshold status also yields the characteristically Heraclitean and paradoxical insight that extends beyond—*crosses*—the moment: "[...] there would perhaps be other fires and other witnesses to other worlds otherwise beheld. But they would not be this one" (73). The wolf, then, is not only constitutive of doubleness; she also denotes and produces patterns of doubleness, while not necessarily of duplication. Consistent with the border paradigm's duplicitous nature, the *loba* will link up in the text with other, variant canines and who function therefore as dynamic reminders of herself rather than static representational duplicates.

The words of the last quotation typically contain their own realization; they are prophetic. Thus Billy encounters other dogs in the course of the novel: the family dog whose vocal chords are cut by his parents' murderers, a figure of muteness already foreshadowed in the death of the *loba*'s unborn cubs, who "cr[y] out mutely in the dark" (129) at the moment of their burial. More unsettling is the misshapen dog who attends Billy like some grotesque familiar in the closing moments of the novel. The canine figure coheres analeptically with the figure of the wolf, retaining certain elements of equivalence—the color yellow, for instance—just to emphasize the point.[6] More importantly, the deformed dog is *not* the wolf; it is a reminder of difference and the threshold status of something that both is and is not, enacting Billy's earlier realization at the camp fire that "there would be other fires and other witnesses [...] But they would not be this one."

I proposed at the beginning of this essay that the border paradigm is the organizing principle of McCarthy's *The Crossing*, according to which the text's doubleness or equivalences are articulated, commencing with the border's own double signifying practice. While the wolf is perhaps the most obvious figurative representation of the border, it is in the extensive use of

---

[6] "It was an old dog gone gray about the muzzle and it was horribly crippled in its hindquarters and its head was askew someway on its body [...] it was wet and wretched and so scarred and broken that it might have been patched up out of parts of dogs by demented vivisectionists" (423).

58   *Isabel Soto*

Spanish, or rather, the sequences which alternate Spanish and English, where the border paradigm is discursively engaged. The formulation of the interaction between native peoples and colonizing Europeans proposed by Mary Louise Pratt in her influential *Imperial Eyes. Travel Writing and Transculturation* (1992) is particularly suggestive here. Pratt redefines the border or frontier as a "contact zone" ("the frontier is a frontier only with respect to Europe" [7]) which is "the space of colonial encounters" (6). Her use of the term "contact zone" is germane to this section of my discussion not only because of its association with the border, but also because it is a term borrowed from linguistics, "where the term contact language refers to improvised languages that develop among speakers of different native languages who need to communicate with each other consistently" (6). As I noted earlier, in McCarthy's *The Crossing* Spanish and English modulate or permeate each other. The result is a wholly other discourse defined by, or constitutive of, the United States-Mexican border, or "contact zone." Furthermore, that this frontier discourse spreads beyond either side of the border is suggestive perhaps of a growing mestizo hegemony. Geography, as ever, shapes human experience.

The sequences in Spanish and English—sometimes with more of the former than the latter—frequently extend over pages. Consulting McCarthy's voluminous website, one discovers that he learned Spanish as part of his research for *Blood Meridian* (1985), the first of his novels set in the American South West. One also finds that the Spanish passages in *The Border Trilogy* have been translated into English and are available on the website. *All the Pretty Horses*, the first volume, has 12 pages of translation; the most recent, *Cities of the Plain*, has seven; *The Crossing* has 25.[7] That an effort has been made to render the Spanish in English highlights what for bilingual readers such as myself may not be self-evident: McCarthy does not always paraphrase or contextualize his Spanish to render it intelligible for readers of English. Spanish, then, has become an essential part of McCarthy's expressive discourse, and nowhere more so than in *The Crossing*. Puzzlingly, this aspect of McCarthy's output, the same output that has generated most of his commercial success, has attracted relatively little critical or scholarly commentary. William H. Dougherty's very brief article entitled appropriately enough "Crossing" (1995) does little more than identify a handful of instances where the Spanish is seemingly defective. No interpretation is ventured for why ungrammatical Spanish got beyond the editors. In what remains, I will examine instances where Spanish is used, looking at its function in the narrative and suggest why such an unorthodox version of Spanish was allowed to go to print unchallenged.

---

[7] The translator is Lieutenant Jim Campbell.

Few Anglo-American writers of fiction have so self-consciously or so extensively compromised a text's master language through the use of another. Ernest Hemingway is an obvious point of comparative reference and much has been written about his "quaint" or exotic English syntax and lexicon through which the reader is supposed to infer a Spanish-language source. But his direct use of Spanish is not, I believe, comparable to McCarthy's. It is far less widespread in his writings, to begin with. More importantly, the site of Hemingway's "Spanglish" was Spain itself, its otherness to Hemingway or his narrators, certainly his readers, a given. In McCarthy there is no "other" but, following Pratt, a site of encounter or interaction.[8]

This is signaled, as we saw earlier, in the opening lines of *The Crossing*. What also emerges from this passage is McCarthy's use of the lower case— "english" and "spanish"—typical of Spanish usage. This primary instance of one language being modulated by another—the linguistic border transcended—is replicated throughout the text. I noted just now that Hemingway produced texts whose register was inflected by a language other than that articulated at the main narrative level. Spanish is read or sensed or understood *through* English. McCarthy goes further and produces Spanish inflected by English. For example, in one of the many narrative digressions, a Mexican is drawing a map on the dusty earth for Billy and Boyd. One of the Mexican's companions takes a closer look at the map. Here is the ensuing dialogue with Billy:

> Es un fantasma, he said
> Fantasma?
> Sí, sí. Claro.
> Cómo?
> Cómo? Porque el viejo está loco es como (184).[9]

Literally translated, this would read:

> He's a ghost, he said.
> Ghost?

---

[8] Modernist and post-modernist collage and intertextuality perhaps provide closer analogues here. I am thinking of the systematic use not only of varying genres and registers in English, but also of non-English textual fragments or allusions. The destabilizing yet enriching effect is comparable to what McCarthy achieves.

[9] It is not clear to me whether the use of fantasma here is figurative: the old man does not know where he is, he cannot find his way around; or figurative and colloquial: in Castilian Spanish fantasma can denote a person who is full of misplaced self-importance. Either meaning would make sense in the context.

Yes, yes. Of course.
How?
How? Because the old man is crazy is how.

It is not just that American vernacular English has made its way into the
Spanish. American vernacular humor has also. That the reader must be alert
to these cross-linguistic and -cultural nuances is not the least of the demands
McCarthy makes on us. There are further, perhaps less unambiguous, instances but that still produce a palimpsest effect of multi-layered textuality.
Towards the end, for example, a Mexican woman reads Billy's palm, noting
the death in infancy of Boyd's twin as well as that of one of the two remaining brothers—"Uno que vive, uno que ha muerto." "Cuál es cual?" (369)
asks Billy. This is either an inflection of the Spanish by the English construction ("Which is which"?) or, simply, defective Spanish. Note also the missing inverted question mark and missing accent on the second "cual."

Which brings me to the contested issue of the accuracy or otherwise of
McCarthy's Spanish. It would certainly seem to be full of errors. Just one
brief example. In the next passage the doctor tending to a seriously wounded
Boyd holds this dialogue with Billy:

> [...] tráigame una contenidora de agua. Una bota o cualquiera cosa que tenga.
> Sí señor.
> Y traiga un vaso de agua potable.
> Yessir
> Él debe tomar agua. Me entiendes?
> Yessir.
> Y deja abierta la puerta. Necesitamos aire.
> Yessir. I will (307).

Aside from the striking counterpoint between the doctor's commands in
Spanish and Billy's English acquiescence –"Yessir"—what stands out are
the following grammatical errors: un*a* *contenidora*, cualquier*a* cosa que
tenga, or the inconsistent use of verb forms, alternating between the for-
mal—tráigame—and the informal—Me entiendes?—not to mention the non-
normative punctuation.

That my bilingual and bicultural condition make of me perhaps an atypical reader, in other words, that a mono-lingual English reader would be
oblivious to my analysis, is irrelevant to McCarthy's discursive practice. The
fact remains he writes "bad" Spanish. The fact also remains that he chooses
to let it stand thus.[10] His insistence on the status of the Spanish as it is

---

[10] The late Diane Tong, a close friend and proofreader of McCarthy's *Cities of the
Plain* for publishers Alfred A. Knopf, commented to me that wherever a phrase or

rendered in the text draws attention once again, and not coincidentally, to the border paradigm. I propose that McCarthy's Spanish must be accepted on its own terms: as the product of the interaction between two discourses and in line with Myra Jehlen's recommendation that the interaction generated between Europeans and Aztecs be understood as "a concept of commonality [...] a distinct third term" (55).[11] Furthermore, we must understand this mestizo Spanish or "third" discourse as being mediated not through Billy, not through a given speaker of Spanish in the text, but through the rhetorical device of the narrator, who may or may not be a native speaker of Spanish. Once more, it would seem that a site of differentiation—the border— whether between Spanish and English, or narrator and characters, exists only to be transcended.

Thus the unfamiliar or defamiliarized Spanish articulated in *The Crossing* is generated by crossing or transgressing various thresholds, linguistic and/or rhetorical. (Pratt's observation that languages of the "contact zone" are "commonly regarded as chaotic, barbarous, lacking in structure" (6) is instructive here). Its singular quality draws attention to itself, as does the fact that the monolingual Anglophone reader is frequently unable to infer meaning from the surrounding English. For pages at a time, the Spanish in the text contests and displaces English as the primary discourse, even as it absorbs it into itself. Borrowing once more from Pratt's remarkably germane arguments, it would seem that the agency conferred by McCarthy on Spanish, his problematization of hegemonic discourse is grounded in a site which encloses "the spatial and temporal copresence of subjects previously separated by geographic and historical disjunctures, and whose trajectories now intersect" (7).

---

passage in Spanish appeared in the text, the author indicated it should remain unchanged by writing stet in the margin.

[11] Any reference to a "third term," a category generated between two other categories, resonates inevitably with Homi Bhabha's classic formulation of the "Third Space" as occupied by the "translated" or "translational" individual (the post-colonial subject): " [...] we should remember that it is the "inter"—the cutting edge of translation and renegotiation, the in-between space—that carries the burden of meaning in culture [...] And by exploring this Third Space, we may elude the politics of polarity and emerge as the others of ourselves" (38-39). Categories of place, borders, interaction and subject formation are all implied in Bhabha.

AN INTERPRETIVE ASSESSMENT OF CHICANO LITERATURE AND CRITICISM

FRANCISCO A. LOMELÍ

The essay traces the literary, social and cultural roots of contemporary Chicano literature and its relation with American studies in general. Through a literary and critical 'archeology' the article shows that, contrary to the general opinion, Chicanos, as well as their literature, are no recent immigrants trying to penetrate the mainstream. A revision of the different stages in the process of self-discovery, as well as the diverse manifestations of the creative energy from the works prior to 1965 and the wake of the Chicano movement to the contemporary Chicano Renaissance illustrates that American literary history is no longer a hegemonic activity pertaining to Anglo American literary circles. Notwithstanding obscurity, silencing and omissions, Chicano literary history emerges as another manifestation of tricksterism, as another side of the clever, survival-obsessed coyote, the character whose perseverance and ingenuity allow him to sidestep danger or locate sustenance. Chicano culture and literature is finally seen to participate of a wide variety of models, from Mexican literature to American science-fiction, from other contemporary Latin American writers to James Joyce, and to have inherent connections with the rest of the world.

There is little doubt that Chicano literature and the accompanying criticism are currently at productive stages of development. Their expansion and rate of growth have become a phenomena difficult to document, strictly due to the sheer quantitative proliferation. Greatly fueled by the impulsive fervor of the Chicano social movement of the 1960s and 1970s, known as a Renaissance or a "Florecimiento," the literature garnered a messianic bent during that era. At the peak of the social movement, and shortly thereafter, it was common to stress the literary production that addressed the immediacy, and urgency, of a historical situation. Without fully realizing it then, a historical posture was being promoted: we underscored how our people had not emerged out of a vacuum; yet, we seemed to speak from and to that contemporary vacuum. Little was intimately known about our collective background, so we mercilessly clung to our Mexicanness as if it were our last possession. We intimated and even intuited a rich tradition but our knowledge of actual works or artists was at best minimal. Most of us in 1970 were unable to cite a single noteworthy Chicano figure or text—Cesar Chavez being perhaps the lone exception. Our incessant search inevitably resulted in enouncing famous Mexican heroes who ruled the pages of Mexican textbooks or the dynamic realm of oral tradition. Somehow our historical memory had been either scarred or amnesiac in that we had drifted away, or nudged, from our previous cultural matrix. There was a dire need—spiritual as well as physical—to identify a homeland. It is not coincidental, for example, that most of the works during the height of the movement dealt, in one way or another, with providing historical/cultural renditions of Chicanos' search for what they were either in the present or in the past. Two works serve to illustrate this approach: *Yo soy Joaquin* (1967) by Rodolfo "Corky" Gonzales and *Floricanto en Aztlán* (1971) by Alurista. We had become disconnected from our steps to relive that vague ephemeral past. Hence, a Neo-Indigenist trend emerged to try to fill that void. The Chicano Movement, then, represented a concerted effort to regain an ethos, a history and a social context.

But, the general impression of our culture today as well as our literature has been that we are recent immigrants trying to penetrate the mainstream. We have not been altogether convincing, not even to ourselves, that our presence in "el vasto norte," or what in 1848 became known as the American Southwest had deep roots and antecedents. Once landgrant holdings were parceled out, and owners were converted into labor force wage earners, much of our impoverished and powerless people were forced to accept the official Anglo American version of our conquest. What we called Aztlán offered much cognitive evidence as to our background in mythological and historical terms. As an attempt to salvage part of that loss, a quantum leap into a Nahuatl framework was tried, partially minimizing the centuries of Spanish colonial influence and the effects of territorialization under Anglo American rule. These were downplayed to instead highlight the 'brown'/'white' dichotomy that seemed to spell our downfall through the post-industrial chambers of exploitation and second-class citizenry. The two pivotal points of convenient references usually targeted the Aztecs and the Mexican Revolution: the first represented a preferred crib of desired origins while the second marked a niche of redemption. Anything in between resembled a blur or a factor of lesser importance. Our essence rested on the nostalgic consumption of a simplification of ourselves, thus canonizing such important personalities as Pancho Villa and Emiliano Zapata. Somehow, both distance and time had lessened our sense of diverse complexities to the degree that a civil war did not necessarily seem like a civil war, but rather, an extended clash between caudillos. In the meantime, we had been generally reduced to a landless and unskilled mass of people groping for a rightful place in a country that emerged strong as a result of our labor. Likewise, Chicano literature in the 1960s either concentrated, limitedly, on well-known Mexican symbols or identified situational experiences as couched in the barrio or the farm fields. The literary themes revolved around identity and affirmation more than psychological or spatial discovery. This was a necessary and vital stage to undergo, the process of self-discovery, in order to first come to the full realization of how we had been efficaciously compartmentalized, and dehumanized, in American society. In part a purging effect, the politically motivated agenda to establish identity and pride had the function of redefining a new starting point for our people. Most significantly, it altered the focus from serving as work objects for majority society in order to concentrate on our own desires, delights and destiny. At that point we crossed a key juncture: from mechanically living out our external existence to intrinsically exploring our internal makeup. A work that best exemplifies this direction is *"...y no se lo trago la tierra"* (1971) by Tomas Rivera. We began to recognize and tap into our potential as promoters of our creative and imaginative forces.

We did not fully anticipate where this recharged energy adequately fit in the larger scope of our historical gestation. Having regained a sense of awareness and presence, we initially did not know how to contextualize it within our past to measure it as just a one-time event or another symptomatic manifestation of our discontent. Most of our literature at the time centered around more urgent contemporary happenings in barrios, educational institutions, and the farm fields, while some critics opted toward indulging in literary history. The current events sometimes made it a requirement to devote the literary fancy to pressing social matters as they unfolded, but it became equally clear that a literary history was awaiting to be rediscovered. In hindsight, we can now pose the contrast between a sleeping giant about to be awakened (the common metaphor to characterize our people then) and the clever, survival-obsessed coyote (not to be confused with the smuggler of people, although he also depends much on an evasive character) that outfoxed its pursuers. The media promoted the metaphor of the sleeping giant in order to associate it with a social threat, possibly predisposed toward exercising an avenging wrath. However, the coyote, which best suits our oral tradition, more accurately reflects the attributes of perseverance and ingenuity to sidestep danger or locate sustenance. Our people, and consequently our literature, endured famine, turmoil and hardships. Many lows can be pinpointed throughout our development, but, most importantly, numerous significant highs can be highlighted. In other words, we in fact possessed a real past, not one invented out of rhetoric or political idealism, rather, one that had its own pulse and rhythm of existence.

In the area of literature, a massive corpus of uncatalogued Chicano works remained either lost, ignored or simply undisturbed by the watchful eye of a critical readership. These works tended to readily enter the realm of immediate oblivion but the reconstructive approach of the 1970s permitted, perhaps for the first time, to indulge in systematically combing lists or shelves for works from a generally forgotten past. Works prior to 1965 appeared to comprise an amorphous and vague notion of prehistory. Chicano social evolution had been measured according to its association with Mexico and how we related or ceased to relate to our cherished country of origin. This framework is represented novelistically in the polemical work titled *Pocho* (1959) by Jose Antonio Villarreal. Even that latter work serves to illustrate a pre-Renaissance Chicano mindset through its unfolding of conflictive topics, such as assimilation and acculturation, the epic exodus from Mexico, a patriarchal system versus a transitional model concepts of authority, an iconoclastic optic of testing icons and hierarchies, etc. It is also worth noting that *Pocho* was not "rediscovered" until 1971 when an insatiable curiosity set in to systematically identify works by Chicanos prior to the critical year of 1965. Each uncovered text from a dusty shelf—and a foggy past— reinforced a sense of recuperating a part of our cultural expression. That object filled a void and broke new ground for uncovering others. Literary history suddenly assumed the role of an archaeological dig that provided greater and more expansive meaning to our ancestors and, most importantly, to our literary tradition. Each finding marked a coming to face with an empirical artifact from our past by piecing together disjointed fragments that miraculously survived. Together, these fragments provided a larger scope of the unknown by giving depth and breadth as well as concrete samples of writings that spoke of and in preterite modes. Thus, literary history did not have to depend on an in-group intuition of assumptions; clear and substantiating evidence was before us to uncover new ground of critical discourse. Literary history was no longer a hegemonic activity pertaining to Anglo American literary circles. For once, the argument could be supported that Chicano literature had a past, an evolution, stages of development and its own characteristics, oftentimes regionally bound to localized problematics and not totally dependent upon either Mexico or Anglo America. It can be argued that early Chicano literature established a particular discourse with other literatures, although that contact was not necessarily reciprocal. Its predicament was largely due to the stigmatization of being the creation of a conquered people: both American and Mexican literary circles ignored it, perhaps marginalizing it from a stand point of class and social status. In the United States, giving credence to a body of works written in Spanish did not suit well with the homogenizing trends of the nineteenth century. Chicanos basically clung to proven models of literary construct in relatively isolated cases of published works, but oral tradition continued strong despite the onslaught of new foreign influences or the social disintegration caused by the conquest and hardened by the institutionalization of territorial governance.

In other words, a diverse but extensive quantity of literary expression prior to 1965 deserves a rightful place in the annals of what we currently call Chicano literature. Too often, teachers of this literature strictly devote their attention to works after the explosion of the contemporary Chicano Renaissance. Too frequently, professors fail to outline its historical development, thus giving the impression of literary hydroponics as if it does not have a legitimate past. Nothing could be further from the truth. Early works and authors before 1965 merit closer scrutiny and analysis because their situation repeatedly parallel or help explain the backdrop of more modern views. Besides, many of these early works challenge the conventional precepts of traditional genres—a most healthy exercise in order to assess a work's contribution by its intrinsic work and not according to boxed-in categories. Contemporary writers have not come onto the scene out of a vacuum; in other words, there is a history of literary antecedents. There exists a rich but at times modest background in what could be termed a written culture. Chicanos have a tradition of literary creativity and publishing since 1848, and before that the Spanish colony of New Spain evinces numerous samples of writings that are a direct product of what came to be the American Southwest or Aztlán. Therefore, Chicanos have not continued as illiterate or as unpublished as we are made to believe. Many myths set in to perpetuate that very notion because our place in American society oscillated between being low-class, unskilled workers and/or undesirable foreigners. Chicanos have not remained silent; their voice of pure imagination or discontent has generally been ignored or relegated to pockets of localities where the major society did not take notice or repressed acknowledging it. Works abound if we wish to find them: early monographic texts are perhaps scarce but an infinite amount of writings from all genres remain stored in microfilmed newspaper collections that require patience and time to extract. Without trying to sound dramatic, many texts are just waiting to be discovered as significant pieces of a larger puzzle. Only recently since the 1980s has a growing number of scholars proposed regional case studies in order to provide us with the larger picture of Chicano literary history throughout the Southwest and beyond. There is no doubt that the tip of the iceberg is now unveiling a larger mass of creative writings that uncover fascinating and revealing facets of our collective intrahistory.

Although we lack a practical text of literary history, no longer can we find refuge in the argument that no viable samples exist to sufficiently represent early writings. Specific works are readily available—at least in libraries. Chuck M. Tatum's *Chicano Literature* (1982) and *Mexican American Literature* (1990) offer a reasonable starting point with multiple examples and summaries. In two seminal articles titled "Mexican American Literature: A historical Perspective" (1973) and "Cuatro siglos de la prosa aztlanense" (1980), Luis Leal delineates the trajectory of a myriad of texts that, previous to his accomplishing it, had not been incorporated into a single literary historical tradition. Luis Leal, possibly the father of modern approaches to Chicano literary history, has contributed a number of valuable parameters to the field while providing an impetus to recording a legacy dating back to at least 1542. The following list offers some likely selections from before 1900:

1. *Relaciones* (1542) by Alvar Nunez Cabeza de Vaca: the first prose treatment that describes the peoples, flora and fauna of "el vasto norte;"

2. *Historia de la Nueva Mexico* (1610) by Gaspar Perez de Villagra: the first epic poem of the region—which includes the entire U.S.—, comparable to Ercilla's *La araucana*;

3. *Los comanches* (1779?) by an anonymous author: one of the first dramatic pieces to indulge in localized politics in the conflictive frontier involving Hispanics and Comanche Indians;

4. *Writings of Junipero Serra* (1784?) by Junipero Serra: rich anecdotal prose about the early wanderings of the famous priest credited for the founding of many California missions;

5. *Los pobladores nuevomexicanos y su poesia, 1889-1950* (1976) by Anselmo Arellano: consists of the first representative compilation of early poetry from New Mexico that was transcribed from an assortment of newspapers (themes vary; "El idioma español" by J.M. Alarid is highly recommended);

6. "El corrido de Gregorio Cortez" (1895?) in "*With His Pistol in His Hand*," compiled and edited by Americo Paredes: one of the first well-known Chicano ballads from Texas;

7. *Hijo de la tempestad* (1892) by Eusebio Chacon: one of the first political allegories in novel form that closely captures the social turmoil of the 1890s.

8. *The Squatter and the Don*, originally from 1885 by Maria Amparo Ruiz de Burton, recreates an important era of California history;

9.   A variety of individual *corridos*, *decimas*, or *cuentos* can also serve the purpose of highlighting other desired aspects.

To amply characterize the period from 1900 to 1965 with early works prior to the Renaissance period, the following select works offer potential candidates for discussion:

10.   *Cuentos californianos* (1910?) by Adolfo Carrillo: a collection of variegated topics from local color to urban depictions;

11.   *Las primicias* (1916) by Vicente Bernal: a young man's poetic repertoire consisting of nostalgia for his native land, New Mexico, and experimentations with both style and technique;

12.   Again, Anselmo Arellano's *Los pobladores nuevomexicanos y su poesia, 1889-1950* provides evidence of unknown writings from a large segment of writers who originally appeared in newspapers;

13.   *Cronicas diabolicas* (1916-1926) de 'Jorge Ulica' (alias for Julio G. Arce) and edited by Juan Rodriguez in 1982: contains a wide variety of humorous anecdotes, *costumbrista* narrations, plus biting and specious journalistic essays;

14.   *New Mexico Triptych* (1940) by Fray Angelico Chavez: a series of well crafted stories about cultural life;

15.   *Mexican Village* (1945) by Josephina Niggli: provides a scintillating portrayal of a gallery of small town characters;

16.   *We Fed Them Cactus* (1954) by Fabiola Cabeza de Baca: a nostalgic view of pastoral existence in the llanos lamenting the drastic social changes;

17.   Mario Suarez's short stories, beginning in the 1940s, particularly "Señor Garza" and "El Hoyo:" present some of the first excellent depictions of flesh-and-blood characters from the barrios;

18.   *Pocho* (1959) by Jose Antonio Villarreal: represents one of the most comprehensive and detailed views of a Mexican family's adjustments to American life while depicting a first-generation's dilemmas and an individual's awareness of self;

19.   *City of Night* (1963) by John Rechy: offers a disturbing account of a young homosexual's urban picaresque journey through the sameness of alienating urban settings.

As one can see, there exists during the aforementioned periods an abundant quantity of diverse and challenging books to sufficiently engage in animated discussions about content, thematic preference, varied perspectives, relative significance, and uniqueness in characterization. Besides, each work cited is quite distinct from texts that later appear during the Chicano literary movement after the 1960s. There is no longer a justifiable reason why earlier writings are excluded from the core of literary presentations.

The year 1965 witnessed a unique bend of factors that combined to generate a new ethos and reverberated to create a totally distinct concept of Chicano literary imagination. For example, the stage was set through the emergence of two crucial events: as Cesar Chavez's farmworker labor movement solidified, El Teatro Campesino, principally organized by Luis Valdez, revived and developed an artistic form of theater that revolutionized Chicanos' self-portrayal in popular or at times funky, grass-roots skits called actos. These garnished the two necessary sparks to incite the social explosion known as the Chicano Movement. The first provided the concrete framework for political commitment while the second prepared an artistic medium with which to hone *concientización* about our social plight, thus initiating the purging effects of a conquered mind. Commitment and accountability helped unleash a renewed activity among Chicanos in many arenas simultaneously and the poets and other artists joined this communal attempt to act out its self-determination. A cultural and political rebirth emerged by inducing our creative talents, thereby tapping into an integral part of our psyche and heart. Our repressed self emerged to assert our inner makeup with the objective of being active participants in determining modern history. The year 1965 has come to be known as the starting point for contemporary actualization.

Events accelerated to form new avenues of action and artistic experimentation. In 1967 a clear manifestation of a boom was in order: (1) the funding of *El Grito* at Berkeley established an alternative outlet to adequately apply the social sciences to Chicano concerns, plus their inclusion of literary works created what would later be termed the Quinto Sol Generation; (2) Reies Lopez Tijerina, through his Alianza Federal de Mercedes, called attention to the latent landgrant problem of New Mexico when they raided a courthouse; (3) Rodolfo "Corky" Gonzales published his *Yo soy Joaquin*, a nationalistic poetic manifesto that embodied a rallying cry for renewal while rendering a historical outline of the Mexican; (4) the Brown Berets, a militant faction of the Chicano Movement, were formed to support proactive community functions; (5) in the meantime, the movement was crossing over from the farm fields into urban settings and particularly the educational institutions. As a consequence, this movement became one to be reckoned with as a multifaceted social upheaval demanding changes and offering solutions to achieve them.

The years 1968 and 1969 represent the prelude to a full blow-out, that is, the most visible mobilization of Chicanos across the spectrum of socio-economic and political fields of battle. Again, literature played a central role in developing key concepts, such as Aztlán, in modifying symbols, and in legitimizing a Chicano mode of expression called code-switching, Spanglish or bilingual. Alurista was the main promotor of Aztlán. His poetic enterprise became a national Chicano concern at the Youth Conference at Denver in 1969 when *El Plan Espiritual de Aztlán* was adopted into the final platform. That document, along with *El Plan de Santa Barbara,* became the two better-known manifestos of the time: the former to propel a national Chicano social agenda and the latter to address the need for institutions of higher learning to become accountable in creating Chicano Studies departments. By then, Chicanos could allude to their origins, a homeland, a language, and the foundations were being set for greater participation in the political process—which became more defined *in* 1970 through the founding of La Raza Unida Party. Some works reflected this Zeitgeist, namely *Los cuatro* (1969), a collection of militant movement poetry by Abelardo Delgado, Ricardo Sanchez, Raymond "Tigre" Perez and Juan Valdez. The articulation of craft was not of the utmost importance; what mattered, above all, was the emotive, almost visceral plea for identifying and denouncing injustices. Art was definitely at the service of a social movement because Chicano artists recognized that art could only improve concomitantly with the progress of its procreators. So, art was a direct reflection of a group's efforts to break barriers, undermine obstacles, dispel myths, and reconceptualize a fairer social order.

The year 1970 now stands out as a focal epicenter of literary consciousness. It denotes the changing guard from an emerging echo of disenchantment to a bona fide contemporary voice of unbridled imagination. Numerous events coincided that confirm the view: (1) although *Chicano* (1970) by Richard Vasquez fell short of propagating a new thematic agenda, its title became emblematic of referring to a Mexican American story *a secas* as "Chicano;" (2) perhaps more significant was the initiating of the Quinto Sol Literary Award sponsored by the publishing house of the same name from Berkeley which subsequently served as the standard bearer of canon in the novel and short fiction genres—Tomas Rivera being the first recipient of that award for his now classic *"... y no se lo trago la tierra"*; (3) the magazine *La Luz* from Denver Colorado, dedicated a section to the analysis of individual Chicano works; (4) also, the Centro de Estudios Chicanos Publications from San Diego State College embarked on an ambitious project of organizing the first annotated bibliography, which presented a skeletal compilation and whose value rested not so much in the quality of reviews but more in the format used to document such vital inquiries; (5) the founding of the journal *Aztlán* crystallized a sense of homeland through its title at the same time that it advanced 'cientificismo' in all disciplines in order to undergird sophisticated techniques of analyses; (6) the latter two examples further strengthen the area of literary criticism and it received an additional boost from the Ford Foundation when it earmarked funds for graduate studies; (7) a series of Chicano Studies departments were created in that year to address the recent trends of scholarship and cultural studies; and (8) La Raza Unida Party was founded by Jose Angel Gutierrez in Texas in searching for other viable means to represent Chicanos politically. As one can see, a united front of various factors converged to produce a macroscope of collaborative initiatives with direct repercussions in literature and criticism. These two fields not only found themselves in a spiral of productivity but also they were never to be the same again.

The early 1970s constitutes a most dynamic period of development in Chicano literature. The number of works produced exceeded previous projections and, qualitatively, the innovations were dramatic. The openly militant and unobscured expression, although still somewhat prevalent, gave way to more subtle forms of sophisticated techniques and transcendental thematics. Much of the literature had been viewed with smirks and silent assaults by a traditional readership, usually composed of academic departments. Some considered it too contrived with only ulterior motives while others regarded it a mock imitation of 'high-brow' literature which at times it was. The perception persisted to categorize it as being adultered political pamphleteerism and/or folksy popular expression that seemed subpar and unclassifiable. However, landmark works broke new ground: *Floricanto en Aztlán* (1971) by Alurista fuses two languages—while blending Nahuatl aesthetics with a contemporary barrio concerns; *"... y no se lo trago la tierra"* (1971) by Tomas Rivera presents the migrant worker as the collective protagonist in a neo-realist mode by fragmenting time, space and structure; *Bless Me, Ultima* (1972) by Rudolfo A. Anaya establishes a captivating story of apprenticeship, thus signaling a struggle for survival in a changing epoch that ignores spirituality, myth and tradition; *Estampas del Valle y otras cosas* (1973) by Rolando Hinojosa-Smith creates a postmodern novel about a fictionalized Chicano space—much in the tradition of Faulkner and Garcia Marquez, except devoid of magical realism—which is decentered but held together by a gallery of loosely connected characters; *Actos* (1971) by El Teatro Campesino embodies the first modern collection of Chicano skits molded with an unforgettable *rascuachi* flair and wit, creating a stlyle-shattering theatrical form that became internationally known; *The Day of the Swallows* (1971) by Estela Portillo-Trambley offers an ambiguous archetypal play that operates at various allegorical levels while hinting at a burgeoning feminism of either altering the world order or sacrificing oneself for those changes; and *Peregrinos de Aztlán* (1974) by Miguel Mendez contributes a highly poetic *frontera* novel about a people's tragic journeys of suffering, at the same time that variants of language occupy the central focus.

Criticism, however, did not enjoy a popularity parallel to its literary counterpart. Early examples essentially appeared unnoticed. Perhaps the first attempt that remained unacknowledged until 1976 was *Breve reseña de la literatura hispana de Nuevo México y Colorado* (1959) by Jose Timoteo Lopez, Edgardo Nuñez, and Roberto Lara Vialpando, whose modest account traces the literature's longstanding tradition as a natural and well-known phenomenon. They do not indulge in the polemics of definition; they simply discuss its evolution in a matter of fact fashion, citing specific works. They comment on the exclusion of this literature: "tanto en libros históricos como en poesía popular. Nada (se) dice de los tradicionales romances españoles que todavia se cantan en los valles del Rio Grande y de San Luis. Tampoco (se) menciona el teatro popular y tradicional de los campesinos de Nuevo Mexico y Colorado." (8) Already in 1917, Miguel Romera-Navarro, in *El hispanismo en Norte-América: exposición y crítica de su aspecto literario*, prophetically observes: "La historia y exposición del hispanismo literario en Norte-América estan por escribir(se). Ni un solo estudio, comprensivo o superficial, popular o erudito, se le ha dedicado." (1) Critical discourses basically remained undeveloped and rudimentary in nature until the early 1970s. Possibly the best exposé of literary criticism prior to 1970 is Francisco Armando Ríos's "The Mexican in Fact, Fiction and Folklore" (*El Grito*, 1969) in his dealing with three distinct but related areas. Felipe Ortego y Gasca, in his dissertation "Backgrounds to Mexican American Literature" (1971), exemplifies the first comprehensive and encyclopedic treatment of Chicano literature. A non-orthodoxical approach, mixing scholarly analysis with bato loco jargon, is carried out by Jesús "El Flaco" Maldonado in *Poesía chicana: Alurista, el mero chingón* (1971). It was in the early 1970s that the publishing apparatus increased dramatically, including both criticism and creative works, in such journals as *Revista Chicano-Riqueña, De Colores, Caracol, Tejidos, La Palabra, Maize,* and *Mango*. Other journals that later dedicated special issues were: *Latin American Literary Review, Mester, Bilingual Review, Denver Quarterly* and *The New Scholar*. One of the most significant highlights of criticism between 1970 and 1975 was Juan Bruce-Novoa's theoretical precept of "literary space," as modified from Mircea Eliade, George Bataille, Juan Ponce and Octavio Paz. For once, serious theoretical considerations were thought proposed in analyzing and judging this literature, instead of solely depending on thematic approaches.

To best illustrate the meteoric proliferation of Chicano literature and criticism, a quick review of bibliographies is telling. For example, in 1971 *Bibliografía de Aztlán* contains a mere 6 items of Chicano works, the remaining 12 items being of either Mexican origin, Chicanesco works, or other indirectly related summaries. In contrast, by 1976 *Chicano Perspectives in Literature: A Critical and Annotated Bibliography* by Lomelí and Urioste lists a total of 127 annotations, including some early works before 1965. In the same year, Juan Rodriguez began to circulate his *Carta abierta*, an on-and-off-again enterprise, that injected critical dialogue, promoted polemics and satire, and tendered witty and succinct judgements from the editor, plus, most importantly, he inserted didactic materials as well as brief reviews on recent works and trends. Rodriguez served multiple purposes: as a database, he was our Chicano books in print, the first reviewer, the first to provide critical annotations, a general informant about happenings, plus our literary counselor about leads and things to avoid. Ernestina N. Eger, in *A Bibliography of Criticism of Contemporary Literature* (1982), meticulously documents the "explosion of critical activity" in Chicano journals, mainstream sources and international outlets. By 1985 Roberto G. Trujillo and Andres Rodriguez, in *Literatura Chicana: Creative and Critical Writings Through 1984*, compiled a spectacular biography of 783 items, ranging from typical entries to dissertations, video and sound recordings. This incredible rate of growth seems imposing, especially when we consider that less than 20 years ago the anachronistic debate revolved mainly around the existence of such a body of literature.

After 1975, the advantage held by creative writings over criticism waned. Fundamental changes began to occur in both camps. Most of the established Quinto Sol Generation writers (Rivera, Anaya, and Hinojosa as novelists, and Alurista as a poet, with Portillo-Trambley being the exception) grounded their narratives in culturalist terms while receiving sanctions and backing from a Chicano publisher in depicting certain cultural values and social types. Their objectives coincided in destereotyping the Mexican while making concerted efforts to put the Chicano on the literary map of American letters. In essence, their view of the subject conveyed an epic framework that presented a people in a horizontal perspective. The concentration on spatial portrayals (i.e. New Mexico, the migrant worker, Texas) serves to support this contention. Part of their goal was to give a global scope while providing historical depth, sociological heterogeneity and a complexity of characters. They desired to break away from the straightjacket of unidimensionality and stereotypes. Despite becoming classics, they were initially limited to covering much space without grounding their stories on specificity. The next ensuing group of writers, whom I call the Isolated Generation of 1975, answered the call but from totally diverse points of origin. Instead of reporting (in the novel: Alejandro Morales, Ron Arias, Isabella Rios, and Miguel Mendez to a degree; Bernice Zamora in poetry), they advance a vertical conceptualization of marginalized social sectors. The latter group opts toward probing Chicano characters and circumstances with a magnifying glass in order to unearth the internal dynamics of a single place, even if it means exposing the contradictions and the harsh realities beyond an illusory optimism. The Isolated Generation joined the Chicano literary ranks, not through Chicano support, but roundabout by experimenting with other models: from Mexican Literature of the Onda to American science-fiction, from other contemporary Latin American writers to James Joyce. Often-times, they went abroad to publish their works (i.e. Alejandro Morales in *Caras viejas y vino nuevo*, 1975, and Miguel Mendez in *Peregrinos de Aztlán*, 1974, or as in the case of Isabella Rios, she produced her work *Victuum*, 1975, out of her garage). This generation offered works that at first impression did not prescribe to predictable means or ends. At the center of their creativity was the issue of language—not as an Aluristian preoccupation but a linguistically universal one. Thus, their works are wrought with ambiguity: they express more than what we first imagine. Besides, their optic is microcosmic in order to explore the paradox and they resort to the allegory to inject greater meaning and echoes of intertextuality.

Another salient group to emerge with impetus in 1975 was the women writers. They, in a sense, embrace a similar orientation as the Isolated Generation by underscoring female characters and issues. They introduce a focus that had been previously underrepresented as men were usually limited in their perspective of female roles and dimensions. As has become poign-antly clear, these roles and dimensions revealed external male impositions that either bordered on stereotypes or a narrow range of characterizations. Similar to previous Chicano literati, they set out to rectify the situation of a recognizable gap. Unanimity in their approaches should not be sought because their differences are as heterogeneous as any other group. However, certain trends can be traced. For example, the first wave of Chicana writers couched their writings in a cultural setting, obviously influenced by the nationalist vogue. This continues to a degree but changes as they hone their subject matter and explore personalized circumstances. Some of these first authors, that is, Bernice Zamora in *Restless Serpents* (1976), Dorinda Mo-reno in *La mujer es la tierra: La tierra de vida* (1975), Sylvia Gonzales in *La Chicana piensa* (1974), and Angela de Hoyos in *Arise, Chicano and other poems* (1975), engage their writings in a critical dialogue found in the Chicano movement. Their vantage point tried to balance a culturalist with a feminist view. Soon thereafter, the intensity of Chicana feminist became heightened with such works as *Bloodroot* (1977) by Alma Villanueva and *The ivitation* (1979) by Ana Castillo. The double message of culture and gender becomes further fused, but the emphasis now leads towards a femi-nist vein. Consequently, the 1980s, instead of being designated as the decade of the Hispanic should receive the acclaim as the decade of the Chicana writer since they made the greatest strides and that included criticism.

The late 1970s experiences a relative shortage in groundbreaking works in the overall Chicano scene with the exception of Chicanas. Criticism made significant advancements through a series of rhetorical experimentations and paradigms. Joseph Sommers, in "From the Critical Premise to the Product: Critical Modes and the Applications to a Chicano Literary Text" (1977), designs a controversial comparison of three critical approaches (the formalist, culturalist and socio-historical), while dismissing the first two and opting for the last. This spurred defenses and rebuttals, but most of all it generated interest and critical dialogue to deal with Chicano texts. It was no longer safe to hide behind the mechanical process of achieving objective analysis. Thus criticism at this time gains an important ideological element to properly place literature in the context of production vis-à-vis the hierarchical notions of what literature has been for the dominant classes. The new concept of criticism, beyond thematics, style or characterization, was further strengthened by Ramon Saldivar's pivotal article, "The Dialectic of Difference: Toward a Theory of a Chicano Novel," in which he related intrinsic textual dynamics with social and literary history. No longer would Chicano literature be situated as isolated from any other literature, especially American; it became increasingly vivid that it had inherent interconnections with the rest of the world.

The 1980s encompasses a greater acceptance in some mainstreaming. Again, Chicanas appear to spearhead the most noteworthy creative writings. To account for this burgeoning, criticism also has expanded in scope by forming new theoretical foci, ranging from applications of Bakhtin to Walter Ong, or in simply originated theories relevant to minority literatures. One sample of this trend is the upcoming issue of *Discurso Literario* (1990) that offers a diversity of approaches. In addition, other developments have enhanced a wider readership: (1) major conferences zero in on questions related to reconstructing the canon in similar topics to reconceptualize literary sclerosis; (2) internationalization through conferences in Germany, France, Spain and Mexico augment the sphere of acceptability beyond the U.S. borders; (3) ambitious reference books are organized to accommodate the geometric growth of demand such as *Chicano Literature: A Reference Guide* (1985) *and Dictionary of Literary Biography: Chicano Writers* (1989); (4) Chicana authors lead the forefront through a keen feminist mode of innovations and insight, thus leaving an undeniable imprint in both Chicano and feminist letters (i.e. Lorna Dee Cervantes' *Emplumada* (1981); Pat Mora's *Chants* (1984); Lucha Corpi's *Palabras de Mediodia/Noonwords* (1980); Ana Castillo's *The Mixquiahuala Letters* (1986); Sandra Cisneros *The House on Mango Street* (1985); Helena Maria Viramontes's *The Moths and Other Stories* (1985); Cherrie Moraga's *Giving Up the Ghost* (1986); and Denise Chavez's *The Last of the Menu Girls* (1986)); a diverse crop of anthologies appear, such as *A Decade of Hispanic Literature: An Anniversary Anthology* (1982), *Hispanics in the United States: An Anthology of Creative Literature* 1980), *Cuentos: Stories by Latinas* (1983*); Antologia de la literatura chicana* (1986); *Contemporary Chicano Poetry: An Anthology* (1986); the *Palabra Nueva* series of poetry and prose; and Harcourt Brace Jovanovich's *Mexican American Literature* (1989), Sandra Cisneros' American Book Award for *the House on Mango Street,* Nash Candelaria's Before Columbus Foundation American Book Award for *Inheritance of Strangers,* Gary Soto's American Book Award for *Living Up the Street,* and Lionel Garcia's PEN Southwest Discovery Prize for *Leaving Home.*

The 1990s have continued to produce fruitful results in the field of Chicano/a literature for the variety, breadth and range of such expression. If the 1980s served as a strong notice of Chicano/a's presence in literary circles, the 1990s clearly have left an indelible imprint of their impact. Questioning the literature's place in American letters now seems an anachronistic gesture. In other words, it is no longer necessary to state that it has come of age but to reaffirm that it is in fact enriching the general American literary landscape with new voices, groundbreaking thematics and renewed vistas. Experimentation has been taken to new heights while challenging conventions within the literature and outside of it. A proliferation of perspectives has become a stamp of originality in the recent writings, thus exploring every possible social and individualized experience. The variety of trans-generic writings is particularly noteworthy, thereby underscoring hybridities, cross-fertilizations and remapping of literary impulses. It is now more common than not that works transcend a single generic construction, as is well evinced by the proliferation of memoirs, (auto)biographies, cuasi-diaries or journals, *testimonios*, ethnographies, mystery novels, detective narratives and many others. Conventional literary forms have become the central issue of numerous works in which their respective category becomes questioned, defied or altered. Examples of such writings are Norma Cantu's *Canicula: Snapshots of a Girlhood en la Frontera* (1995), Luis J. Rodriguez's *Always Running: La Vida Loca; Gang Days in L.A.* (1993), Ruben Martinez's *The Other Side: Notes from the New L.A., Mexico City and Beyond* (1992), Marisela Norte's poetry recordings, Louie Garcia-Robinson's *The Devil, Delfina Varela, and the Used Chevy* (1993), Luis Urrea's *Across the Wire: Life and Hard Times on the Mexican Border* (1993), Yxta Maya Murray's *Locas* (1997), Michele Serros's *Chicana falsa* (1995), Sandra Cisernos's *Woman Hollering Creek and Other Stories* (1991), Estevan Arellano's *Inocencia ni pica ni escarda pero siempre se come el mejor elote* (1992), and Graciela Limon's *The Memory of Ana Calderon* (1994) and *Song of the Hummingbird* (1996).

Another recent trend is the development of the detective and mystery novels, becoming an important sub-group of Chicano/a writings. Among some of the more outstanding works are Rolando Hinojosa's *Partners in Crime* (1985), Rudolfo Anaya's *Rio Grande Fall* (1996), Michael Nava's *Golden Boy* (1988), Lucha Corpi's *Cactus Blood* (1995), and Manuel Ramos's *The Ballad of Gato Guerrero* (1994).

As can be ascertained, Chicano literature has come a long way from its humble beginnings of epic poems, popular verses of El Viejo Vilmas of the 19th century, *corridos*, hidden writing in a lost newspaper, manifesto, *rasuachi* publications or garage ventures. It is currently gaining much acclaim at an international level and, finally, penetrating the exclusive clubs of American literature circles. Whereas omissions used to be the rule, Chicanos and Chicanas are now highly solicited creative voices and theoretical technicians who can fill the literary shadows of American experience. Chicano literature has garnered a special niche because it has maintained close ties with its sources of inspiration. It continues relatively free of commercialism although this fact is becoming more of a dilemma to avoid. The pressures are mounting to join the mainstream, but it appears that Chicanos and Chicanas are proceeding cautiously to retain authenticity while fine tuning the unpredictable spheres of the imagination. It is precisely for that reason that the literature finds itself in a mushrooming moment of popularity and high regard.

Select Bibliography

Anaya, Rudolfo and Francisco A. Lomelí. *Aztlán: Essays on the Chicano Homeland.* Albuquerque: Academia/El Norte Publications, 1989.

Candelaria, Cordelia. *Chicano Poetry: A Critical Introduction.* Westport, CT: Greenwood Press, 1986.

Corti, Erminio. *Da Aztlan all'Amerindia: Multicuturalismo e difesa dell'identita chicana nella Poesia di Alurista.* Viareggio: Mauro Baroni Editore, 1999.

Gonzales-Berry. *Paso Por Aqui: Critical Essays on the New Mexican Literary Tradition, 1542-1988.* Albuquerque: University of New Mexico Press, 1989.

Herrera-Sobek, Maria and Helena Maria Viramontes, editors. *Reconstructing a Chicano/a Literary Heritage: Hispanic Colonial Literature of the Southwest.* Tucson: University of Arizona Press, 1993.

Horno-Delgado, Asuncion, Eliana Ortega, Nina M. Scott and Nancy Saporta Sternbach. *Breaking Boundaries: Latina Writings and Critical Readings.* Amherst: University of Massachusetts Press, 1989.

Joysmith, Claire, editor. *Las Formas de Nuestras Voces: Chicana y Mexicana Writers in Mexico.* Mexico City: Universidad Nacional Autónoma de Mexico, Centro de Investigaciones sobre América del Norte, 1995.

Kanellos, Nicolas. *Short Fiction by Hispanic Writers of the United States.* Houston: Arte Publico Press, 1993.

Keller, Gary D., Rafael J. Magallan, Alma M. Garcia. *Curriculum Resources in Studies: Graduate and Undergraduate.* Tempe: Bilingual Review/Press, 1989.

Lomelí, Francisco A., editor. *Handbook of Hispanic Cultures in the United States: Literature and Art*. Houston: Arte Publico Press, 1993.

Lomelí, Francisco and Carl S. Shirley, editors. *Dictionary of Literary Biography: Chicano Writers*. Detroit: Gale Research, First Series 1989; Second Series 1993; Third Series 1999.

Melendez, A. Gabriel. *So All is Not Lost: The Poetics of Print in Nuevomexicano Communities, 1834-1958*. Albuquerque: University of New Mexico Press, 1997.

Maffi, Mario. *Voci di Frontiera: Scritture dei Latinos negli Stati Uniti*. Milan: Giangiacomo Feltrinelli Editore, 1997.

Norwood, Vera and Janice Monk. *The Desert Is No Lady: Southwestern Landscapes in Writing and Art*. New Haven: Yale University Press, 1987.

Padilla, Genaro M. *My History, Not Yours: The Formation of Mexican American Autobiography*. Madison: University of Wisconsin Press, 1993.

Rebolledo, Tey Diana, Erlinda Gonzales-Berry and Teresa Marquez. *Las Mujeres Hablan: An Anthology of Nuevo Mexican Writers*. Albuquerque: El Norte Publications/Academia, 1988.

Saldivar, Jose David. *Border Matters: Remapping American Cultural Studies*. Berkeley: University of California Press, 1997.

Saldivar, Ramon. *Chicano Narrative: The Dialectics of Difference*. Madison: University of Wisconsin Press, 1990.

Tatum, Charles, ed. *Mexican American Literature*. Orlando: Harcourt Brace Jovanovich, Publishers, 1989.

Tessarolo Bondolfi. *Dal Mito al Mito: La Cultura Di Espressione Chicana; Dal Mito Originario al Mito Rigeneratore*. Milano, Italia: Ediziono Universitarie Jaca, 1987.

Zimmerman, Marc. *U.S. Latino Literature: The Creative Expression of a People; An Essay And Annotated Bibliography*. Chicago: Chicago Public Library, 1990.

"THE CARIBOO CAFE" AS A BORDER TEXT:
THE HOLOGRAPHIC MODEL

BEGOÑA SIMAL

This article reads Helena María Viramontes's 'The Cariboo Cafe' as a multidimensional re-presentation of border life, specifically of the paradigmatic cross-over character, the immigrant. After exploring several critical attempts to capture the three-dimensionality of border texts, especially the kaleidoscopic and prismatic metaphors, I opt for the more adequate holographic model as put forward by Emily Hicks in her *Border Writing*. Through the holographic model, with its intersection of several referential and cultural threads, Viramontes aims at representing the actual interweaving of multiple realities. In 'The Cariboo Cafe' each of the three sections depicts a different gaze, which in the end overlap as laser beams do in a holographic experiment, with the result of a close-resemblance simulacrum of the multidimensional and hybrid border reality. Viramontes's textual strategy not only enables her to conjure up and denounce the complex tragic reality of border characters, but it also questions monolithic epistemological modes, reinventing border culture and reality as inherently hybrid.

Our world has become a fluid frontier, and yet, there remain some privileged border sites such as the Mexico-US frontier where human nature has become the visible "herida abierta" Anzaldúa explores in *Borderlands/La Frontera: The New Mestiza*. It is difficult to grasp, on both an intellectual and artistic level, the syncretic, contradictory and rich hybrid culture and society that arise in such a space. The closest we can get to an understanding of border life and culture, or rather to a representation of such a reality—which may indeed be the only ultimate knowable object—is by giving ourselves over to the polyphony of cultural difference. One of the leading Chicana writers, Helena María Viramontes has tried to do so by adopting that multidimensional perspective in a paradigmatic border text, "The Cariboo Cafe." In this short story Viramontes explores the tragic reality of illegal immigration and political repression by casting insightful spotlights on three different agents who hover around the same scenario, the cryptic zero/Cariboo cafe. It is out of the conflation of these three converging "light beams" that an image approaching a multidimensional truth arises. It is my aim here to trace this complex and enlightening process of representation through which the projection of "light" from different directions produces a simulacrum suggesting three-dimensionality.

I- The borderlands' Third Space

> It is in this space that we will find those words with which we can speak of Ourselves and Others. And by exploring this hybridity, this 'Third Space,' we may elude the politics of polarity and emerge as the others of our selves.
>
> Homi Bhabha.

As a politically committed Chicana writer, who believes that "fiction has a potential to change the social reality" (Goetz 1996), Helena María Viramontes engages in a disingenuous exploration of the most fierce physical and psychological frontier in the world: that between the affluent life of a "First World" and the poverty-stricken peoples of the "Third World," a threshold epitomized by the borderline between the United States and Mexico. The author's oblique style becomes politically explicit in the third section, where the violence of both army and guerrilla raises its ugly head. However, her narrative focus does not lie in the Central America of the crazy woman's flashbacks, but in the frontier paradigm of immigrants and refugees, a paradigm that is not necessarily found in a physical borderline, but in the imaginary borderland of the displaced person's psyche. Viramontes inhabits the Third Space that Homi Bhabha talks about in "The Commitment to Theory," that "split-space of enunciation [which] may open the way to conceptualizing an inter-national culture, based not on the exoticism or multi-culturalism of the diversity of cultures, but on the inscription and articulation of culture's hybridity" (Bhabha 1988: 209). Throughout "The Cariboo Cafe," Viramontes explores the fundamentally hybrid nature of the characters' culture. She consciously avoids the pitfalls of exoticism and instead articulates the "inter" of "inter-national" and "inter-cultural" communities.

The critic who has most consciously explored the borderlands where Viramontes situates herself and her narrative is Gloria Anzaldúa. In the theory of *mestizaje* she puts forward in the fittingly cross-generic *Borderlands/La frontera: The New Mestiza* (1987), Anzaldúa inscribes a "mestiz@" identity that embraces, in both senses of the word, "the prohibited and forbidden [...]

the squint-eyed, the perverse, the queer, the troublesome, the mongrel, the mulatto, the half-breed [...] in short, those who cross over, pass over, or go through the confines of the 'normal'" (5). In "The Cariboo Cafe" both the children and the crazy mother have crossed over, passed over, and in the case of the woman, she has also crossed the threshold of what we consider "normal," stepping beyond what we term "sanity." As displaced people, these characters haunt the space of in-betweenness, neither "acceptable" America nor their original homeland. At the same time theirs is a critical stance, since their very liminal existence questions the limits of nation and of culture, of "self" and "other": "the problem of the cultural emerges only at the significatory boundaries of cultures, where meanings and values are (mis)read or signs are misappropriated" (Bhabha 1988: 206). Living in cultural borderlands, hiding in their interstices and inhabiting what Mary Louise Pratt calls "contact zones,"[1] all the characters seem to wander without knowing where they have to go. Sonya tries in vain to retrace "her journey home in the labyrinth of her memory" (3084).[2] Even the seemingly static owner of the glowing cafe, where, after her labyrinthine flight, little Sonya apparently finds a safe haven, seems lost in his own loneliness.

When looking for home, however, neither the crazy woman nor the children uphold any sacred, mythic land nor an idealized village. Viramontes has both escaped the easy romanticization of the pre-industrial villages of Mexico and Central America and resisted the enduring appeal of a pre-Colombian, utopian nation, Aztlán, which, according to Juan Bruce-Novoa, constitutes the "axis mundi," the "deep structure" that pervades Chicano culture (Zimmerman 1991). While the Aztlán manifesto still clung to the idealized nation state, "safe in the Utopianism of a mythic memory of a unique collective identity" (Bhabha 1988: 206), the new feminist and/or postmodernist Chican@ writers shook the ethnic culturalists out of that fallacious security. Therefore, in a postnationalist strategy, Viramontes locates her characters not in an imaginary, utopian Aztlán, but in the atopian/distopian cafe of the double zero. There all characters seem to drift, slide, float. Their feet can't take root in a non-existent soil. There, with no other props, the author indulges in long forays into the depths of the charac-

---

[1] They "refer to the space of colonial encounters, the space in which peoples geographically and historically separated come into contact with each other and establish ongoing relations, usually involving conditions of coercion, radical inequality, and intractable conflict [...] By using the term 'contact,' I aim to foreground the interactive, improvisational dimensions of colonial encounters [which] emphasizes how subjects are constituted in and by their relations to each other" (Pratt 6-7).

[2] Page references correspond to the reprinted version of the "The Cariboo Cafe" included in the 1998 (3rd) edition of *The Heath Anthology of American Literature*.

ter's psyches. The resulting interior monologues succeed in both "de-composing" reality and in "re-composing" or "re-membering" it.

II- The multidimensional perspective: searching for a model

The multiple perspectivism of "The Cariboo Cafe" makes it a con-sciously multidimensional text, the epitome of border literature. Viramontes presents us with three main interior monologues in three different sections, and only at the very end of the story do these coalesce, intermingle and even shift from third to first person narrative mode. The same event is perceived from diverging personal standpoints. At the same time, different hermeneutic paradigms can be read into the narrative. This intersection of points of view and referential codes pervades many self-conscious narratives and is present in different guises in several critical approaches: the kaleidoscope, the prism and holography are some of the tropes used in order to encapsulate this multi-perspectivism.

Victoria Carchidi describes Bharati Mukherjee's narrative in *Braided Lives* as kaleidoscopic: "an image of the interweaving of diverse points of view to create a new perspective that is neither wholly like nor wholly different from the elements that make it up, an image well-suited to Bharati Mukherjee's vision of America" (1995: 91). Also in "The Cariboo Cafe," the three narratives function as three small color beads that, upon being shuffled, combine into different patterns, magnified and given depth by superimposed lenses/mirrors. The double zero would stand for the two circles that confine the kaleidoscopic tube. Still, however colorful, the trope does not succeed in conveying the sheer three-dimensional realism of the resulting representa-tion.

Carchidi's article fails to probe deeper in the dissection of the kaleido-scopic vision in terms of representational significance, though it may well fit the amalgamation of cultural traits of different characters, "the intermingling of cultures that makes up what has been called the United States's melting pot" (1995: 95). However, it is not the amalgam of the melting pot nor the variety of the Canadian mosaic that Viramontes addresses. Hers is a border text, dealing with the frontier in both its literal and figurative senses. But, as we have seen, far from indulging in utopian culturalist dreaming, Viramontes and her work advocate cultural difference rather than cultural diversity, alternative notions which Bhabha explains as follows:

> Cultural diversity is an epistemological object—culture as an object of empirical knowledge—whereas cultural difference is the process of the enunciation of cul-

ture as 'knowledgeable,' authoritative, adequate to the construction of systems of cultural identification. If cultural diversity is a category of comparative eth-ics, aesthetics, or ethnology, cultural difference is a process of signification through which statements of culture or on culture differentiate, discriminate, and authorize the production of fields of force, reference, applicability and capacity. Cultural diversity is the recognition of pre-given cultural 'contents' and cus-toms, held in a time-frame of relativism; it gives rise to anodyne liberal notions of multiculturalism, cultural exchange, or the culture of humanity. Cultural di-versity is also the representation of a radical rhetoric of the separation of total-ized cultures that live unsullied by the intertextuality of their historical locations. (1988: 206)

Viramontes upholds the constructivist concept of cultural difference and does not endorse of the implicit tenets of cultural diversity, especially the contention that there is (or even, that there must be) such a thing as an undefiled, unalloyed culture, never tainted by its geographical and historical "intertextuality." Therefore, rather than accepting and adopting the domesti-cated motto and label of multiculturalism, foisted upon much of the so-called "ethnic writing," Viramontes delves into the underlying, radical question of cultural difference and its unsettling consequences.

Another contribution to the study of multidimensional textuality is Paula Gallant Eckard's "The Prismatic Past in *Oral History* and *Mama Day*," where she utilizes the trope of prismatic refraction in order to account for the multiple perspectives encountered in Lee Smith's and Gloria Naylor's novels. In those works it is the past that seems to act as prism: "like light passing through a prism, the past enters human lives and produces assorted perceptions, illusions, and distortions. However, even with such refraction, its power is not diffused. The past is still a singular force that shapes human life with a fierce intensity" (1995: 133). However, the critic uses the motif in a slightly superficial way and does not integrate the trope in the main body of criticism, just mentioning it at the beginning and the end: "In the hands of Lee Smith and Gloria Naylor, the past becomes a multi-dimensional, pris-matic entity that shapes familial, community, and cultural history [...] Taken together their novels yield a portrait of the past that is prismatic and yet, at the same time, strangely unified" (1995: 121).

The only point of intersection in Viramontes' short story that could be said to possess prismatic qualities is the double zero in the Cariboo Cafe. There, all three conflicting and complementary lights (child, man, mother/ghost)[3] coincide and converge, to produce a more complete white

---

[3] The trinitarian analogy does not escape an informed reader. The triad in the story embodies not only the basic traditional family unit, but also, in a figurative sense, the Catholic Trinity (child, father, spirit).

light, a light made out of all three original colors, which, combined, throw out a realistic representational simulacrum in all the colors of the rainbow. However, the prismatic model does not seem to suffice, since it does not exhaust the possibilities of the story.

The multidimensional aspect of the texts under study becomes more coherently articulated in the unorthodox critical model put forward by Emily Hicks' *Border Writing: The Multidimensional Text*. There the tropes of the frontier and the critical analogy of the holographic image acquire central relevance, and, despite their being intermittently used, confer the necessary critical unity to the book. It is Hicks' image that I intend to use, notwithstanding the rich modulations with which the other two tropes furnish the critic.

III- Composing and de-composing: the holographic model

> Structural man takes the real, decomposes it, then recomposes it.
>
> Roland Barthes

In the introduction to *Border Writing*, "Border Writing as Deterritorialization," Emily Hicks explains the mechanics of holography:

> A holographic image is created when light from a laser beam is split into two beams and reflected off an object. The interaction between the two resulting patterns of light is called an 'interference pattern,' which can be recorded on a holographic plate. The holographic plate can be reilluminated by a laser positioned at the same angle as one of the two beams, the object beam. This will produce a holographic image of the original object. (1991: xxix)

Hicks then goes on to draw the parallel between the holographic method and the kind of conflation, overlapping and intersection of perspectives, cultures and critical paradigms found in border texts:

> A border person records the interference patterns produced by two (rather than one) referential codes, and therefore experiences a double vision thanks to perceiving reality through two different interference patterns. A border writer juxtaposes the two patterns as border metaphors in the border text. The border metaphor reconstructs the relationship to the object rather than the object itself: as a metaphor, it does not merely represent an object but rather reproduces an interaction between the connotative matrices of an object in more than one culture. The holographic 'real' is less solid, and as a result it cannot be dominated as easily as the monocultural or nonholographic real. (1991: xxix)

As a border writer, Viramontes not only perceives and grasps those inter-ference patterns resulting from juxtaposing two different cultural codes, she also manages to transpose that holographic image on to the narrative mode. Viramontes attempts to dissect or, in Barthes's words, de-compose "reality" as seen from different perspectives. It is the intersection of the three gazes (child's, man's, woman's) that the narrative tries to capture in an attempt to re-construct the most credible simulacrum[4] of what is happening at the Cariboo Cafe, and, by extension, in the borderlands of experience. However, this re-presentation is not—cannot be—unbiased, because, as a simulacrum of an object, as Barthes points out in "The Structural Activity," it is indeed an *"interested* simulacrum, since the imitated object makes something appear which remained invisible, or if one prefers, unintelligible in the natural object" (quoted in Rowe 1990: 35). The author carefully chooses the three points of view so as to cast light on each other and illuminate the plight of the marginal population teeming in dilapidated border cafes such as the "double zero" one. Not even the signpost of the Cariboo Cafe remains intact in this intraculture of survival, inhabited by prostitutes, transvestites, drug-dealers, exploited illegal immigrants, lost children and crazy women.

For the increasingly complex world of the border, both in the Southwest frontier, and in other urban borderlands inhabited by the immigrant, the mestiz@, and the marginal "underclass" (Steinberg 1989), the model of holography is the most comprehensive method of representation, "because it creates an image from more than one perspective" (Hicks 1991: xix). The all-encompassing nature of the holographic model registers the multiple interactions between different referential and interpretative codes.[5] It also permits a new, multi-perspectivist understanding on the part of the readers who become aware of the different codes and begin to see their clashes, complementary aspects and reciprocal questioning: "Only readers who are able to negate their assumptions about all of these codes until they can hold both strands of the double code simultaneously will be able to 'see' the text in its full dimensionality" (Hicks 1991: 68).

In his preface to Emily Hicks' *Border Writing: The Multidimensional Text*, Neil Larsen poses the question of whether the reader can appreciate this multidimensional interplay of codes and whether it can be politically

---

[4] See the notion of "simulation" coined by French hyperrealist Jean Baudrillard (in *Simulations*, "Pataphysics of Year 2000," "Radical Thought," etc.).

[5] Indeed, at one point Hicks, in her analysis of Latin American writer Luisa Valenzuela, lists the following critical paradigms that can be found in her work: "(1) the traditional tale [Propp]; (2) the hermeneutic code; (3) the Freudian-Lacanian psychoanalytic code; (4) the code of Marxism and politics in Latin America; (5) the code of feminism and (6) the code of the real" (Hicks 1991: 68).

effective. He believes we run the risk of undoing the discourse of resistance inherent in all border texts, since "there is nothing in the logic of [any theory of the text] to explain why the interpreting subject for whom the effect itself is devised might not, in practice, undo the effect by resolving the multiplicity of perspectives in her or his unifying gaze" (Larsen, in Hicks 1991: xvii). Furthermore, the reader can choose to remain aware that the narrative holography is just "an illusion of three-dimensionality produced by the mixing of interference patterns" (ibid.), that is, to keep on seeing it as mere representation.[6] The fact remains that the strategy of border resistance through the holographic model can always be ignored or viewed as mere simulacra. However, for the reflexive reader the holographic real comes close to providing a thorough (holographic) picture of the represented object, in this case the liminal reality of displacement, political oppression and illegal immigration.

IV- The double-zero holographic image

In "The Cariboo Cafe" the author goes into the mind of three characters narrating the same event, the confrontation of a woman and two lost children (whom she "adopts") with the *polie/Migra*, from different perspectives, giving at times contradictory information,[7] but in the end providing the reader with a rich narrative version of a holographic image. Another of Hicks' metaphors helps us convey the realistic nature of the representation that the readers can perceive: "This can be imagined by remembering the experience of wearing 3-D glasses. The image is printed twice, in two color

---

[6] Larsen soon realises that the theory of simulations could easily be invoked here, but both he and Hicks dismiss it: "Of course the claim might be lodged, a la Baudrillard, that *all* objects of perception have now been reduced to the virtual status of holograms. But Hicks seems, wisely, to aver this sort of reasoning" (xvii). We must note that Emily Hicks and Neil Larsen employ the term "hologram" as a synonym of "holographic image." However, although for her purposes of critical assessment of literary works Hicks conflates the two concepts into one, scientifically speaking, "hologram" and "holography" are not exactly the same. See pp. 233-238 in K. Thyagarajan and A.K. Ghatak's *Lasers: Theory and Applications.*

[7] Thus, the woman/Llorona believes she is protecting her son from violent men, whereas the cafe owner, who in a sense stands for the Establishment, tells us she is kidnapping the child. And we get little Sonya's meaningful looks (the text gives us no direct first person narrative from the child, and at this point not even a third-person stream-of-consciousness technique is used) that give us yet another connotative interference pattern. The truth is thus shown to be multifaceted and complex.

of ink. The glasses make it possible to see both at once, to perceive depth" (1991: 68-9). Although the first section only takes us to the meeting point, the cafe, the information it provides is crucial for us to understand who these two lost children are and the reasons why they are easily coveted by both the man and the Llorona woman.

The first beam of light shines from the mind and experience of a little immigrant girl, probably from Mexico ("Mi'ijo," p. 3085). Hers is a vision dominated by fear of the *Migra*, the *polie*, as the immigration agents are variously known, who "get kids and send them to Tijuana" (3085). The fear is as real for illegal immigrants as the threat of deportation. However, choosing an innocent child's eyes as the projector of the first flat image is no coincidence. It purports to give us a naïve and simplistic vision which is not "sullied" by adult interests and prejudices. Sonya only needs to get home, that is, to reach a site of safety and, we assume, love. She is, in a way, the embodiment of the guileless immigrant lost in a culturally and linguistically strange world, in the threatening, hostile world of an "illegal existence," as if just being alive were a crime.

In her desperate flight from the feared *polie*, Sonya finally reaches the "beacon light at the end of a dark sea" (3085), an ironic reference to the Cariboo Cafe. Sonya's beam will then coalesce with the one shining from the glowing cafe. However, a further threat lurks under the double zero on the signpost. To begin with, Sonya and Macky are two zero individuals, they do not even exist—legally—as far as American society is concerned. Furthermore, no one seems to notice them either in the streets or in the cafe: "Funny thing, but I didn't see the two kids 'til I got to the booth. All of a sudden I see these big eyes looking over the table's edge at me. It shook me up, the way they kinda appeared. Aw, maybe they were there all the time" (3086). The children's big eyes again conjure up the Carib-o-o double zero, the mark of the status of non-entity that they acquire as immigrants. Eventually, the children take refuge in the apparent safety of this anonymity.

The second beam is projected from a person on the opposite end of the spectrum of experience and innocence. Far from naïve, the cafe proprietor is skeptical about everything and has betrayed those who make up the bulk of his customers, the vulnerable illegal Mexican immigrants. His personal disappointments, especially his regret for having lost his wife and son, tinge his skepticism and render him more human, even though his betrayal of the immigrants qualifies and ultimately determines his psychological makeup.

As in the case of the other adult beam, the cafe owner speaks to the reader directly, using a first person narrative and addressing us as "you." His linguistic code, his nuanced slang gives us some insight into his social standing. The double zero cafe is for him the "story of [his] life" (3085), the story of a working-class existence (even though he does not want to identify with the illegal workers) and of a double disappointment, JoJo (the son who dies in Vietnam) and Nell (his Spanish-speaking ex-wife). He himself tells again and again that he is trustworthy, although his deeds prove otherwise. He also complains of the futility of this honesty: "That's the trouble. It never pays to be honest" (3085). And of course we learn that he has informed on the illegal immigrants that had hidden in the restrooms. This first betrayal anticipates that of the woman and children, when they next come to his cafe, a sequence described in the third section.

The last section takes us again to the cafe, where the lost children and the "crazy" Llorona woman have come a second time. The second account has "englightened" us and we know already which frame of mind leads the bar owner and cook to be ruthless in telling on all the immigrants. The looks he gets from Sonya (3087) and one of the illegal immigrants caught at his cafe (3088) tell us of his betrayal, they tell us that he is not to be trusted, or at least not when you have no documents.

This third pencil of light comes from a real mother, who is at the same time that more encompassing mother, La Llorona, "screaming enough for all the women of murdered children, screaming" (3092). The real mother has lost his five-year-old son, Geraldo, to the volatile political situation of Nicaragua in the eighties. The child has been taken and accused of being a contra spy. The first-person flashback explains the terrible consequences of war, but it also hints at the transformation of the real mother into the mythical Llorona. This figure supersedes all other inconsolable mothers who wail for their lost children:

> The darkness becomes a serpent's tongue, swallowing us whole. It is the night of La Llorona. The women come up from the depths of sorrow to search for their children. I join them, frantic, desperate, and our eyes become scrutinizers, our bodies opiated with the scent of their smiles. Descending from door to door, the wind whips our faces. I hear the wailing of the women and know it to be my own. Geraldo is nowhere to be found. (3088)

Just as Sandra Cisneros in *Woman Hollering Creek* or Gloria Anzaldúa in *Borderlands*, where she connects the myths of Guadalupe, La Malinche and La Llorona, Helena María Viramontes chooses to rewrite one of the "Chicano male-centered macro-mythologies" (Zimmerman 1991). In the version of the legend of La Llorona Viramontes gives us, the mother does not kill her children out of spite or as a revenge, as happens in most of the stories. Rather she loses one of her children, blames herself for it, although we know it is external agents who have taken him away. This corresponds to one telling of the story that Marta Weigle includes in her *Spiders and Spin-*

sters (1982): "In another [version], she is a mother driven mad by the loss of her son in a village drainage ditch; thereafter she seeks to kidnap any small children she encounters" (qtd. in *Heath I* 1329). This apparently coincides with what happens with little Macky: he is kidnapped by the crazy weeping mother, or, as she would perceive it, he is "adopted." The woman herself seems aware of the potential danger which lies in her identifying with La Llorona: "When the baby comes I know Tavo's wife will not let me hold it, for she thinks I am a bad omen. I know it" (3090). She finally becomes the archetypal weeping mother found in many Western and non-Western cultures. The real, historically grounded Nicaraguan mother becomes the wandering, insane and inconsolable mother spirit. And, it is no coincidence that "I" should become "she" (3091) when the woman becomes delirious and raves about little Macky being her lost Geraldo.

In the third section we see at least two conspicuous references to light. This time, however, it is not a shining beam from a metaphorical lighthouse, as it was the case in the first vignette. Here they take the form of both the searchlights from the police and another misleading beacon that burns stupid moths, both a description of what the inquiring mother sees and a metaphor of the political situation of her country: "I think about moths and their stupidity. Always attracted by light, they fly into fires, or singe their wings with the beat of the single bulb and fall on his desk, writhing in pain. I don't understand why nature has been so cruel as to prevent them from feeling warmth" (3089).

The three gazes, little Sonya's, the cook's and the woman's, finally converge. All three lights focus on the little child. Everybody wants to appropriate him as a hope for the future: the bartender soon calls the boy "Short Order" and comes to regard him as his lost son; the Llorona woman actually takes him to be her little Geraldo; whereas his sister, Sonya, just wants to keep him, and in so doing, to keep their innocence.

Now the police flashing lights remind us of the holographic image we are witnessing, not just a flat picture described or imagined by one of the characters involved therein, but the convergence of three stories with their width and depth to render the scene a three-dimensional simulacrum of the real: "by multiplying the levels of representation, or, if one prefers the Barthesian schema, by pluralizing the various reference codes, one achieves a non- or trans-representational access to the 'real'" (Larsen 1991: xvii). It is finally the restored I/eye of La Llorona that sees it all and tells it all as she finally dies and resurrects as the eternal weeping mother (3092-3093). Hers is also a life of death and disappointment, which intersects with the first beam of fear and innocence, and the second one, full of skepticism and betrayal, to bring about the tragic dénouement.

CODA

Viramontes has chosen "a portion of the matrix" of border life to signify on the liminal condition as a whole: "In the same way that one part of a hologram can produce an entire image, the border metaphor is able to reproduce the whole culture to which it refers" (Hicks 1991: xix). The three perspectives collide, overlap, intertwine, and ultimately expose the disorientation, alienation and chaos encountered by the children, here the embodiment of those trapped in between cultures and "nations." The very fragmentation of the text reflects how these holographic images, in their "re-creat[ion of] the whole social order," are faithful to that same fragmentation of postmodern life (Hicks 1991: xix) at a metaphysical and social level: all three characters belong to broken families, where violent death,[8] deterritorialization and separation have wrought havoc.

The author not only denounces the social and political evils that bring about the final death in the story. She also consciously uses her border metaphor as a dismantling tool in the deconstruction of univocal reality and culture, since "it is the 'inter'—the cutting edge of translation and negotiation, the in-between, the space of the *entre* that Derrida has opened up in writing itself [l'ècriture as the site of the difference]—that carries the burden of the meaning of culture" (Bhabha 1988: 209). Thus, Viramontes textual strategy, while not eluding political and social issues, questions fundamental modes of epistemology and cultural understanding. Rather than staying in the postmodern impasse of indeterminacy, the author depicts the American scenario "as a cultural map with endless living borders," borrowing Zimmerman's metaphor. At the same time as the holographic picture questions monolithic interpretations of culture and the "real," it reinvents culture as inherently hybrid. Zimmerman provides us with an example of a typical crosscultural product: salsa, "a crossover combination of many musical forms" (1991). Just as this type of music and the popular culture associated with it constitute a typically cross-cultural phenomenon which draws from different sources and includes "heterogeneous elements rather than going back to some place of origin," the border text seeks to destabilize safe positioning in a totalized culture.

The double zero holographic image both points at the postmodern indeterminacy and fragmentation, and, in a second beam of light, draws the picture of a hybrid non-culture and a three-dimensional simulacrum, which

---

[8] Significantly enough, the death of the two "lost children" is directly or indirectly caused by war, be it the army/guerrilla confrontation in Nicaragua, or Vietnam.

is actually the interweaving of many referential and cultural threads. In this sense, this strategy opens up an optimistic panorama for future developments, where "[c]ultural richness is not defined by past myths but the generation of new possibilities, and new, if sometimes chaotic, energies," and we do not aim at finding "some original axis mundi or fixed essence, but distinct sets of identity possibilities from within the givens of an expanding multicultural universe" (Zimmerman 1991). In de-composing reality and re-composing it as a multidimensional holographic image, "The Cariboo Cafe" not only manages to create a sophisticated rendering of the multiple threads that conform the "real," but it also dismantles the false security of a monolithic culture and reality.

SHIFTING BORDERS AND INTERSECTING TERRITORIES: RUDOLFO ANAYA

CARMEN FLYS JUNQUERA

This paper analyzes Rudolfo Anaya's transgressions of borders, particularly in the creation of hybrid cultural, expressive and literary borderlands through his use of imaginative spatial configurations. The article traces Anaya's constructions of primary, secondary and tertiary territories, throughout his novels and how the borders between these territories are erected, crossed or changed during the journey to self knowledge of each one of the protagonists. The learning process of each character, for Anaya, is always one of valuing the diverse and hybrid Chicano culture as the only way to attain inner harmony. Anaya's portrayal of cultural borderlands present a true *mestizaje* of cultural expressions, beliefs and customs, literary genres and techniques such as the subversion of the popular hard-boiled detective genre, the use of magical realism, and linguistic code-switching. Through these aesthetic strategies, not only do the characters attain self-knowledge, but Anaya, who also subtly challenges the expectations of the reader, seems to follow his self-proclaimed role of the shaman-storyteller, trying to bring knowledge, alternatives and harmony to his audience and community.

A sense of place is one of the most primal human needs—the need to feel roots, a sense of belonging. The sense of rootedness, according to Simone Weil, lies in a full participation in the life of the community, which is formed, among other things, by the place of birth and the environment. Place is inhabited space, a space which is enclosed and humanized and the center of established values. Place, whether natural, constructed or imaginative, affects people's inner states of being[1] and therefore is an essential given in our sense of identity. Rudolfo Anaya, one of the major Chicano writers, often considered "a founder of the canon of the contemporary Chicano literary movement" (González-T. 1990: xv) clearly acknowledges the importance of place. In an essay "The Writer's Landscape" he states: "My earliest memories were molded by the forces in my landscape: sun, wind,

---

[1] For definitions of place and space, see humanist geographers Tuan and Steele.

rain, the llano, the river. And all of these forces were working to create the people that walked across my plane of vision" (1977: 99). The purpose of this paper, therefore, is to analyze Anaya's use of place and spatial configurations and see in what manner his construction of imaginative space affects the characters, and by extension, how it can affect his readers.

The latter claim needs some clarification. Anaya is a writer clearly committed to a mission, that of the empowerment of his readers. In a comment he wrote on his stories, he equates the storyteller to a shaman, a curandero, and he considers that "the story goes to the people to heal and reestablish balance and harmony" (1984: 57). One of Anaya's strategies for "healing" and empowerment is his portrayal of place and space. The spatial configuration that will be discussed in this paper is that of his continuous shifting borders and the mapping of intersecting territories.

In order to understand Anaya's use of space, one must first analyze his sense of the basic territories which inform the life of every individual. I am speaking of how each person perceives private and public space, or more specifically, the differences between primary, secondary and tertiary space. Technically, privacy can be defined as "a changing process whereby people attempt to regulate their openness/closedness to others" or as a "selective control of access to the self" (Altman and Chemers 1984: 75, 77). The implication of this concept to that of a sense of identity is evident: psychological well-being centers on the successful management of privacy; self-identity implies an understanding of the self as a being and knowing where one begins and ends (Altman 1975: 49), of being able to control one's boundaries. Privacy mechanisms "define the limits and boundaries of the self" and when these mechanisms are under control, in other words that one can regulate contact when desired, then "a sense of individuality develops" (Altman 1975: 50). In this manner, privacy mechanisms contribute to self-definition.

A primary territory is one in which the individual can exercise control and regulate its accessibility, usually the room or home. A secondary territory is one where the individual has a lesser degree of control, such as the neighborhood or social clubs and usually these territories, again following Altman and Chemers, present a great potential for misunderstanding and conflict. Thirdly, a tertiary territory, or public space, is the place which "almost anyone has the right to use on a temporary, short-term basis as long as he or she observes certain minimal rules" (1984: 134). Altman and Chemers continue to note, however, that the term "almost anyone" is particularly crucial as cases of segregation, apartheid or caste poignantly illustrate.

But the moment we establish a territory, the border between different territories appears. The concept of border, a dividing line, which is apparently so clear, has been expanded and re-conceptualized, generating a whole area of critical debate. That deceivingly simple boundary, from an essentialist point of view, becomes a constructed one, physically, historically, politically, culturally, linguistically, and so forth. Edward Said views the marking of boundaries as arbitrary, "only a fictional reality" (1979: 54). He comments on the age-old custom of marking territories as "ours" or "theirs," thus constructing a sense of identity negatively, by opposition. If these boundaries are fixed arbitrarily in the mind by "social, ethnic and cultural" expectations as Said claims (1979: 54), these borders can fluctuate and shift, according to the degree of control exercised over the access to the enclosed territory or according to changing mental or social attitudes. If the border is constructed and can shift arbitrarily, the establishment of a territory is not only arbitrary but also subject to continuous changes.

Evernden, in his essay "Beyond Ecology," provides a useful paradigm for the concept of territoriality which relies on natural science yet gives us another insight into the meaning of what it feels like to have a territory. In this illustration (Fig. 1) he speaks of the cichlid, a small fish, that during breeding season, seems to forget any rationality of size. He establishes himself in a territory and will attack anything, despite its size, that comes into his circle. It is "as if his boundary of what he considers to be himself has expanded to the dimensions of the territory itself. The fish is no longer an organism bounded by skin, it is an organism-plus-environment bounded by an imaginary integument" (1996: 97). Within the territory, the further from the center the intruder lies, the fish is less likely to attack, the boundary being a kind of gradient. "It's as if there is a kind of *field* in the territory, with the 'self' present throughout but more concentrated toward the center" (1996: 98).

Following these descriptions of the concepts of territory, we can map the territories of each of Anaya's protagonists. These territories can be viewed as different circles, each representing primary, secondary and tertiary territories. As the characters develop, the circles end up intersecting each other more and more and thus establishing in the intersection a larger territory whose boundary becomes a gradient and in which the protagonist, as the cichlid fish, moves effortlessly and at ease, assured by his sense of place.

Thus, a border or boundary can be seen in constant flux and continuously being negotiated. Gloria Anzaldúa defines this territory where the border lies, part of that gradient, as a "place of contradictions" (1987: preface) where, much like the cichlid, there are moments when "dormant areas of consciousness are being activated, awakened" in that need to shift identities. She, like Said, views the purpose of setting up these arbitrary borders "to define the places that are safe and unsafe, to distinguish *us* from *them*. A border is a dividing line, a narrow strip along a steep edge" (1987: 3). Her definition of the borderlands remind us of that temporary "emotional" state of the cichlid. She writes that "a borderland is a vague and undetermined place created by the emotional residue of an unnatural boundary. It is in a constant state of transition" (1987: 3). But precisely the existence of that undetermined place allows for racial and cultural hybridization. It allows the cultures in contact, as Mary Louise Pratt would say, to "meet, clash and grapple with each other" (1992: 6), and therefore, possibly, negotiate new terms of belonging. This meeting of cultures, of crossing from one to the other and back again, interacting, changing, and adapting allow for a new territory, a larger space where the mixing and re-defining of both the territory and the individuals who inhabit it takes place. As in the case of the cichlid, the primary territory of the individual expands, encompassing a larger hybrid territory which becomes part of his sense of place and a site for enacting his identity.

From this rather distant and theoretical exposé, let us now review the three territories as they are presented by Anaya. In general, throughout Anaya's novels, the home, usually represented by the kitchen or garden, constitutes the basic primary territory. However, the home is only fully described in the case of his first novel, *Bless Me, Ultima* where the protagonist, Antonio Marez is a child. In the rest of his novels, homes are not described physically, but rather in terms of the aromas of the kitchen or the flowers of the garden. For the adult male protagonists—all protagonists are male—home is a warm, comforting place that nourishes both body and soul. The home is clearly a woman's domain and the heart of it is the kitchen. The fact that most have some kind of garden is also significant, given Anaya's belief in the need for harmony with the land and nature. In the city of Albuquerque, all characters who have a balanced and harmonious sense of identity have a garden.

The home is an obvious primary territory although not necessarily so in other writers.[2] But it is not the only primary territory. Anaya includes another site as primary territory: Nature. In most of his novels, reaching a sense of intimacy and harmony with nature is a key factor in achieving a balanced sense of identity. Anaya believes that communion with nature is part of the Chicano world view, as is the sense of community just mentioned. All his characters achieve privacy and moments of illumination while in close contact with the land. Identifying with nature and with the spirit of the earth constitute crucial epiphanies. Characters are free to retreat into themselves and meditate while at harmony with nature; the forces of landscape are key

---

[2] For example, in most of James Baldwin's novels, the only primary territory lies within the mind of the protagonist. The home is clearly a secondary territory. For a detailed study of the case of Baldwin, see Flys 1998.

factors on their road to self-actualization. Therefore, I see nature as another primary territory for Anaya's characters.

Particularly interesting is, however, yet another site viewed as a primary territory. In many parts of Anaya's novels, the barrio can also be considered a primary territory and it is often described as being an extended part of the home, similar to the enlarged field of the cichlid fish. While the barrio can be at times a clear secondary territory where children and adolescents are socialized and confront their peers in gang fights, more often than not, it is perceived as primary territory. This shifting perception of the barrio as a primary and/or secondary territory is of particular significance. The arbitrariness of this border becomes very apparent: at times there is no border and the barrio is lived as a primary territory, an extension of the home where the characters move freely and have no trouble regulating boundaries. The boundary is clearly distant, at the end of the barrio where the Anglo world begins. Within the barrio it seems as if there is one big family where the kitchen aromas of different houses mix, where neighbors are perceived as part of a large extended family, as the traditional welcome states: "mi casa es tu casa." Yet paradoxically, the same space, the barrio, can become a secondary territory for a few characters. Psychological and cultural boundaries are continuously erected. For example, when adolescents band together, forming gangs, each claims its own territory and fights for primacy and control over it. This is evident in the gang rumbles of *Heart of Aztlán*. Likewise, in *Alburquerque* we find cultural-psychological borders being set up. Abrán is not accepted as one of the barrio boys because his skin is too fair. He is forced to transgress violently, engaging in fights to prove his "mexicanness." Only when he "conquers" can he destroy that border and feel the barrio as his own. But upon learning of his true parents, again the boundaries shift making him perceive the barrio as a different cultural site and the city as another. His insecurity builds borders where there had been none and until he resolves his own mental borders and accepts his mestizaje, he cannot destroy the borders and inhabit his space freely. Thus the barrio presents itself, in Anaya's fiction, as a clear hybrid site with dividing lines that are continuously transgressed, crossed over in both directions, a contact zone where the terms of belonging are under constant negotiation.

The barrio, however, from a legal and jurisdictional point of view, is clearly a public space, a tertiary territory, where the dominant authority has control and the power to access that space. Given that the barrio is, socioeconomically speaking, a ghetto, and is usually not a secure, comfortable, middle-class place of leisure, should merely underscore the power of the dominant culture. For instance, in most novels written by or about minority groups, the hostile presence/invasion of the police in the barrio/ghetto serves as a constant threat to the local people and thus construes that territory as a tertiary one. The fact that Anaya rarely mentions the menacing presence of the police in the barrio—except in *Heart of Aztlán*—illustrates his perception of the Chicano view of community. In *Heart of Aztlán*, Anaya's most politically committed novel, the police does appear to break up the gang rumbles and the strike. In these two cases the clash is between us and them, a cultural, class and racial clash. This clash is between boys of different barrios who choose a "neutral" public territory—the Anglo territory near the school which in itself is tertiary territory from the start. The other case is that of the strike where there is a clear confrontation of the railroad workers, who live in the barrio and threaten to enter, to transgress, the railroad yard—again a clearly hostile tertiary territory dominated by Anglo bosses. Thus in both these cases, the threat is based on the "barrio" invasion of Anglo territory, so the law enforcers must defend their territory. The Chicano community values remain intact and the barrio remains predominantly a primary/secondary territory for its residents.

Often parts of the *Alburquerque* city of Albuquerque, particularly for the modern young men, protagonists of the Quartet[3] can be also viewed as a secondary territory. Abrán or Sonny move easily between the barrio and the city and, at the onset of the novels are quite assimilated, belonging more in the Anglo world than in the Chicano world. Therefore, it is an extremely permeable border, in sharp contrast to the novels of the initial trilogy. Nevertheless, often enough, the city scenes constitute part of the public, tertiary territory which can often be intimidating for the characters, as they exercise no control over the boundaries, rather, they are often made to feel as intruders. This is particularly true of the Anglo residential areas. Abrán reflects on "the line between Barelas and the Country Club" (*Alburquerque* 37)[4] as a border which was not to be crossed and Sonny sees the same line as "the Great Wall of China" meant to "keep out the hordes" (*Zia* 174). Ben Chavez comments on "class lines, ethnic lines, [...] Borders in our own backyard" (*Alburquerque* 67).

The dividing line, the border, is portrayed in many ways. There are many types of borders, physical or metaphorical and in Anaya we find multiple images, from shut doors of the hospital wards, to rivers and walls or cultural

---

    [3] Although the name of the city in New Mexico is spelt Albuquerque, Anaya, both in his fiction, the title of the novel and in press articles, is calling for a return to the original Spanish spelling of Alburquerque. Therefore, I have respected the two spellings, as they apply.
    [4] Given that I will be quoting often from all of Anaya's novels, I feel it is clearer to include the title of the novel, often abbreviated, in the parenthetical notation and the page, rather than the year. Years are indicated in critical articles, including those of Anaya himself. All page numbers refer to the editions cited in the bibliography.

mores. Crossing the border is also reflected in many ways, from physical walking to one of Anaya's most recurrent image, the popular Chicano image of the coyote which is, by nature, a border image with multiple meanings. Coyotes are those who help others cross the border, or the mestizos, and also a legendary trickster figure or the animal guardian, nagual, for character Sonny Baca. In crossing the border, we evidently find images of bridges and paths. Anaya's novels are also full of physical and metaphorical bridges which seem to lengthen or shorten, according to the character's ability to cross—with fear or with confidence—as we shall see. All characters are forced to cross these lines, to transgress. Only by doing so, can they integrate their multiple identities and territories into a larger, hybrid one, that of their intersection. This intersection of different territories is clearly a hybrid space, a space where several languages, cultures, customs, races and social classes meet, clash and negotiate. This space is also the space of the hyphen in ethnic America, a kind of no-man's land, until claimed as a space of hybridity or cultural syncretism. It is clearly a subversive space where norms are challenged and re-defined. Cultural mores interact, being rejected, appropriated, changed or subverted, syncretically creating a new "more malleable species with a rich gene pool," (Anzaldúa 1987: 77), a new cultural mix. By appropriating this hybrid space, characters re-define their identity, becoming more "malleable," tolerating ambiguities and contradictions, but also being enriched by multiple bloodlines and legacies. This intersection becomes a large borderland, full of new meanings, creativity and possibilities.

These spatial configurations, constructed by the author, can take on different aspects. Iain Chambers reflects that in the West, there is an inherited fear of cultural fragmentation and mobility (1994:71) and Gayatri Spivak confirms the same when she says that "there is a longing for a center, an authorizing pressure, that spawns hierarchized oppositions" (qtd. in Chambers, 1994: 71). This fear drives us, then, towards stark polarities, a space which seems to be perceived, in reality and in many novels, clearly in a dialectical manner, full of dichotomies and polarities of ours and theirs and with characters hovering or floating in between, feeling forced to chose one and reject the other, or to remain in a kind of limbo. The current cross-cultural framework, with its increased awareness of diverse histories, cultures and memories, however, leads us, according to Wilson Harris, "to a deeper and stranger unity of sensibility through and beyond polarized structures" (1983: xviii). Rudolfo Anaya can be a point in case. I see Anaya's spatial configurations in more of a dialogical manner, full of interdependent circles—each representing different histories, cultures, territories—which can or cannot intersect. The geometric figure of the circle is important to Anaya and to his spiritual vision. We can see this in his frequently used symbol of the Zia sun of New Mexico; the circular sun with rays extending in each of the cardinal directions. In most significant moments, those filled with a sense of the supernatural and mystical, a circle is clearly present and central. Don Eliseo, Sonny's mentor and guide to the spirit world, while talking about the particular meaning of the region of New Mexico and the Rio Grande valley, considered sacred by many, claims that the region is "a circle that holds together, provides harmony. Self is also a circle, so is family, community, earth, universe. Raven [the representative of evil] seeks to destroy the sacred circle" (*Shaman* 56).

Therefore, I posit that Anaya's predominant spatial configuration is that of a circle, each territory being a circle which intersects more or less with others, depending on the character's ability to regulate his own crossing of the boundaries. The intersection of these territories, thus, will become the space in which each character can move freely and regulate access to himself and to the other territories. As we will now see, in each novel, the borders continuously shift and the intersections progressively become larger, creating new territories, spaces of hybridity, where the protagonist, who has learned to bridge the gaps and integrate his heritages, can move, making that new space his own. In this study I have mapped both physical and mental/cultural spaces, as both can be perceived as territories in which a character moves.[5]

In the first novel, *Bless Me, Ultima*, we can see that at the beginning (fig. 2), the child Antonio Marez is torn between two heritages, that of his father, Marez and of his mother, Luna. As a child, he is more at ease with his mother, at home or in her garden. He has nightmares over the father and his family fighting over his afterbirth and future. Since Antonio's dreams are an essential part of the novel, I have also mapped them as a kind of mental territory. At first they are uncontrollable and unintelligible. Thus the Luna sphere represents his primary territory, his mother's "castle on the hill" (26). The father's world, the llano, although familiar, is a secondary territory which Antonio can enter, but is not fully at ease. The home is clearly separated, both physically and mentally from the town by the river and the bridge. He is afraid to cross, fearing the "awful *presence* of the river" (15). Yet, since the novel is written by an adult Antonio with hindsight, he comments that "the innocence which our isolation sheltered, could not last forever, and the affairs of the town began to reach across our bridge and

---

[5] In the figures an arbitrary coding has been used and is indicated in the key. Physical territories are designated in shades of gray and with a continuous line/border while cultural and metaphorical territories are designated by stripes and their boundary has a broken line.

enter my life" (15). This intrusion is violent, beginning with Antonio's witnessing a death at the river.

During the progress of the novel (fig. 3), Antonio begins crossing the bridge, the border, to go to school. After his first year of school his confidence increases and he dares to face the river: "it was the first time I ever remember talking to it [...] I cross you and leave town, I cross towards the llano!" (77). As we see from the first terrifying image of the town "hidden in the mist" and the school where "a million kids were shoutinggruntingpushingcrying [sic]" (57) and where he feels "an outcast" (59) things progressively change. He becomes able to go alone with confidence and use the knowledge acquired in school. On the other hand, through Ultima, he learns the secrets of the llano and increasingly appreciates his father's heritage, admitting that he "love[s] them both yet [he is] of neither" (38). The llano no longer intimidates him and he realizes that he "was no longer lost in the enormous landscape of hills and sky. [He] was a very important part of the teeming life of the llano and the river" (37). Also, through Ultima, his mentor, he learns the value of dreams and progressively accepts them as informing his spiritual life.

By the end of the novel (fig. 4), Antonio accepts his heritage: "I am neither Marez nor Luna. Perhaps I can be both" (247). He has integrated the town and school, learned English and participates actively in school. He now understands Ultima's world of the llano as well as accepts her spiritual powers—shamanism and dreams. Antonio has learned to bridge the gap—he can now race across the bridge—of his various territories, creating a large intersection and expanded boundary of his self, where he has developed his own individual identity but in communion with his environment, both natural and cultural.

In Anaya's second novel, *Heart of Aztlán*, the Chavez family is forced to move from the small town of Guadalupe to Albuquerque. Clemente is torn by the move knowing that by selling his land he "will be cast adrift" (3) because "every adobe, every nail contains a memory" (3). The llano has been his environment and his home, a place where he felt elated and, in his dreams, he felt he could fly (fig. 5). As the family enters the city, they feel the hostile environment; they are "lost in the melee" and in "the snarl of confusion" and Clemente "cursed the city" (9). Once in Albuquerque, they arrive to the barrio of Barelas, where their older son lived. Here they find a new home, "a welcome place to drive into" (10) and where the people say "every barrio is my barrio" (62). The wife, Adelita, had brought a can of earth from their land in Guadalupe, which they plant to initiate their garden and their new roots. The barrio feels like home, a primary territory which adolescent Jason identifies with home. As he walks, "In the tree-dappled light of the afternoon he felt a flow of energy in the barrio street, like the force of the river in Guadalupe" (68). Clemente and Jason meet Crispín, the barrio poet whose house has a lush green garden. As he sings his inspiring poems, "each man traveled where he would on the chords of the blue guitar" (14).

This atmosphere contrasts sharply with the railroad yards where "the black tower of steel loomed over" and the "trains thrashed like giant serpents" (22), a clearly hostile territory. As Clemente enters the railroad yards for the first time, he finds a job as a result of Sanchez' death. The ominous sign couldn't be clearer: the yards are a kind of hell on earth, where the workers are exploited and manipulated by both the bosses and the labor unions. The border separating the railroad yards from the barrio, a few blocks away, is evident as the "houses near the yards were dark with soot and the elm trees withered and bare" (22). The city itself is separated from the barrio and yards by the zoo and a park. Anaya's description, here too, reveals a tertiary territory. As Jason crosses the boundary from the lyrical, welcoming "tree-dappled light" of the barrio, he hears the "shrill cries of birds" (56) from the man-made, controlled and locked-in nature.

Jason, although not the protagonist, reflects the development of the adolescents, Clemente's children, in their new environment (fig. 6). He learns to cross the park into the Anglo sector of the city, he crosses into the railroad yards and lives in the barrio. Although the first two are public territories, as the novel progresses he does learn to integrate these spaces to a degree, as his brother Benjie and his sisters will also. Each one of the young people represents a different degree of assimilation and the ease with which they move in the different spaces reflects their adjustment.

As the strike in the railroad yard progresses and the situation becomes more desperate, Clemente is more able to negotiate his terms of belonging to that hostile territory—even if only to protest (fig. 7). Crispin's words, spoken in dreams and legends, increasingly influence him more, and he becomes obsessed with finding the Aztlán of the legends. Thus the mythic or imaginative territory progressively becomes more his.

By the end of the novel (fig. 8), Clemente, in a dream-vision, has realized that "[he is] Aztlán!" (131) and therefore is capable of making the dream/legend come alive. He realizes that "the space between us can be bridged, a bond can unite us all!" (147). This enables him to lead the protest strike march, uniting all Chicanos and workers against the bosses. He is now capable of transgressing the border and entering the steel yards to destroy their evil, physically and politically with the march. The space of dream-visions has enabled him to integrate other territories, controlling the terms of belonging as he wishes.

The third novel of Anaya's initial trilogy, *Tortuga*, picks up where *Heart of Aztlán* left off. Benjie, who had fallen from the "evil" steel tower, is paralyzed and is traveling South, crossing both a physical and spiritual desert on his way to the town of Agua Bendita, known for its "magical springs." The religious and magical connotations of the novel are made clear from the beginning. Benjie, as we have seen previously, moved freely in the barrio, his primary territory, and naively considered Albuquerque as a comfortable secondary territory (fig. 9). He now arrives to the unknown and intimidating space of the hospital at Agua Bendita, where his cultural/spiritual block is underscored by his physical paralysis. The town is unknown, as he can't even see it from his supine position. He is not even aware of crossing a bridge. All is foreign. In the hospital, which is described as "a dumping station between life and death" (61), the hostility is clear by the fact that he cannot move nor control access to himself. This is exemplified when he is accidentally abandoned in an isolation room for a long period of time, despite the initial friendly doctor and nurses aide.

Locked within his shell/body-cast (fig. 10), for which he is nicknamed Tortuga (turtle), he slowly begins to interact with his roommates, but he still cannot regulate access to himself, as illustrated by the unwelcome visits of Danny, or the time he is punished and taken to Salomon's ward, the so-called "vegetable patch," (36) where all the children are totally paralyzed and connected to respirators. Progressively, he begins to integrate with the people of the hospital and this greater control is signified by being moved into a wheel chair, where he can control some of his movements. The ward, now, becomes a secondary territory. There are still limitations and threats, as the possibility of being taken to Salomon's ward of the "living dead." The doors of the ward, which he cannot manage, constitute terrifying borders.

As Tortuga begins to move freely both in his room, the ward and occasionally through the hospital, Solomon's stories begin to filter through his mind as dreams, bringing hope. As he grows stronger (fig. 11), he dares to visit Solomon, who despite being in the ward of the "living dead," has some "small potted plants and vines" (39). Solomon wants him to learn about suffering, but the shock is too great and he cannot accept the message of suffering. Another test of strength is the visit of all the hospital children to the public territory of Agua Bendita to the movies. The hostile townspeople insult the children, calling them freaks, but these, who have acquired the will to "walk the street" and to "be proud and walk tall" (91) fight back with snow balls. In Tortuga's dreams and through Solomon's dream-stories, he sees himself going up the bridge to the magic Tortuga mountain, where there is love and healing for all. Increasingly, the dream space becomes his source of strength.

At the end of the novel (fig. 12), Tortuga has accepted the dreams and the responsibility of taking the torch from Crispín, the barrio poet who has died, and sent him the blue guitar. Solomon dream-transmits to Tortuga that *"Now it's* [his] *turn to sing"* (171) because Tortuga has *"felt the roots of sadness ...* [Their] *pain and suffering had meaning in* [his] *heart!"* and he is *"the one hope that the darkness will never cover* [them] *completely!"* (172).[6] Solomon, as all in his ward, dies due to an accident caused by Danny, but Solomon's dreams of hope and love survive in Tortuga. Tortuga has accepted all the children of the hospital as his family and primary territory. He walks about the hospital "looking clearly into every part so [he] could take it with [him]" (185) as he leaves. He is now able to walk, with the help of crutches, but he walks "tall" around the town, still public but not hostile and able to interact and negotiate his belonging. He is able to undertake the return journey to Albuquerque, and to cross the bridge separating/joining the town and the hospital; and he is able to integrate the people, suffering and emotions of all his spaces into a more comprehensive and richer identity.

Alburquerque marks the beginning of Anaya's *Alburquerque* Quartet, a series of novels revolving around the four seasons in the city, dealing with contemporary issues and having young men as protagonists. The Quartet, as its name indicates, takes place in the city of Albuquerque, New Mexico, which constitutes the over-riding territory. Nevertheless, within the city, there are clearly separated territories, both physical and cultural, which will inform our map. Although *Alburquerque* begins when Abrán is a student in medical school, we learn much of his childhood and therefore the mapping of his earlier life is relevant (fig. 13). Like most children, home constituted his primary territory, a warm and sheltered haven. The barrio was a clear secondary territory. Although he played on the streets, we learn that he had a difficult relationship with the other barrio boys because he was so fair-skinned. He was insulted as a "güero" (21) and often had to fight to prove his "mexicanness." Therefore, he did not always control the situation in this territory. The greater city, and the dominant Anglo culture, however, were clearly hostile and public. The borders between these worlds were not easily bridged.

At the beginning of the novel (fig. 14), Abrán is totally integrated in the barrio. He had been a barrio hero, a junior boxing league champion; the cantina is perceived as a "friendly watering hole" (2) and he calls the barrio "Barelas barrio and home" (16). Therefore, both home and barrio are primary territories and given the ease with which he has learned to move

---

[6] In all of Anaya's novels, when dreams are narrated, italics are used.

through the city, as a student, integrated with the dominant institutions, the city itself has become a secondary territory in which he knows the rules.

Abrán enters a severe crisis when he learns on Cynthia's deathbed that she, a well-known Anglo painter, daughter to a wealthy Anglo boss of the town, is his mother, not Sara and Ramiro. His father is an unidentified barrio boy. Abrán's memories of childhood fights come back as he realizes that he, in fact, is a mestizo, a coyote and the accusations of being güerito were all too true. This revelation leads him to question his terms of belonging to the barrio, to his family and to the Chicano tradition. Although his home remains a primary territory with Sara perpetually watching over him, he finds himself floating in the air, hovering over two worlds, both accepting and rejecting and incapable of integrating them (fig. 15). He runs into an old "bruja" who gives him a cryptic message, "Tu eres tu" (23) which throws him into a confusing morass. The barrio which had become a primary territory now again becomes a secondary space, where his terms of belonging are no longer clear. Moreover, Albuquerque, in this new light, becomes suddenly a new place, one in which he no longer feels confident, very public. Because of Cynthia's fame, Abrán becomes a pawn in the hands of wealthy politicians who are enmeshed in an electoral battle for mayor. Thus the Anglo part of town seems to become his territory, yet he is manipulated and his mestizaje is exploited for political purposes. The city he thought he knew, is now "awash in blood and beer" (213). Initially, it seems that the borders between Hispano and Anglo cultures/neighborhoods so prominent in the past, as his biological parents learned, have almost disappeared but as he quickly learns, "one didn't cross to date Anglo girls. Not now, not then" (37). He is the result of that transgression, but he is still not allowed to cross—only when it is convenient. Finally, he begins to question and challenge his Chicano traditions. Those elements which had been givens, taken for granted, but neither carefully learned nor cherished, suddenly take on new meanings and become a new spiritual space which intersects with his other spaces.

The novel unfolds as Abrán searches for the identity of his father. At the hospital he meets a young nurse who becomes his girlfriend. Lucinda, steeped in Chicano lore, helps him and brings back significance to his mixed cultural heritage. At the end of the novel (fig. 16), Abrán discovers who his father is, the barrio writer, Ben Chavez, sworn to secrecy by Cynthia and her father who refused to acknowledge a mestizo grandson. Abrán learns to accept himself and his mestizo heritage, thus understanding Doña Tules' words. He realizes that he is a "child of this border, a child of the line that separated white and brown" (38). Abrán reaches victory, as the barrio champion, by winning the match in the boxing ring and defying the political bosses who had plotted his downfall. Thus, Abrán finally integrates the different territories and finds his own hybrid space in their intersection.

The following three novels, *Zia Summer*, *Rio Grande Fall* and *Shaman Winter* form one continuous story with a progressive evolution of the same main character. Therefore, they will be dealt with as one process. Initially, in *Zia Summer*, we meet Sonny Baca, a handsome well-integrated young man, considerably assimilated to the Anglo world (fig. 17). He has attended college, worked as a high school teacher, but has now achieved his license as a private investigator so "he came and went as he pleased" (3). He "did weights at the gym," "loved women," "had taken up rodeoing" and ate "too much junk food" (6-7). He lives at the margin of the barrio—not Barelas, but Los Ranchitos, in the North Valley. However, he rarely partakes of any of the traditional Chicano customs, often neglects visiting his family and community, despite his repeated intentions "to see his mother more often. They had to stay together as familia" (181). The territories in this series are both physical but even more cultural and their borders are marked: "the rift between the cultural groups seemed to grow" (182).

The novel begins with the cult murder of Sonny's cousin Gloria which affects him seriously; he is contracted by his aunt to investigate the murder. The novels repeat the formula of the hard-boiled school but with some subversions.[7] In the investigation he is helped by his old neighbor, Don Eliseo and his friends, and he also has the support of his girlfriend Rita. Both Eliseo and Rita try to bring him closer to his Chicano traditions, particularly as the murder case brings him into the occult. He begins having dreams and Don Eliseo teaches him that dreams speak of the spiritual world. He meets the typical formulaic and enigmatic temptress, Tamara, who not only speaks of dreams and cults to the sun god, but who has the Zia sun represented all over her house. Sonny is skeptical although respectful of Don Eliseo and intrigued by Tamara. By the end of the novel, he manages to solve the murder and appears to have defeated the enemy, Raven. But much of this comes from accepting Eliseo's help, listening to the traditions and accepting some, such as praying to the sun every morning or accepting the interconnectedness of everything: nature and human beings. His recurring dreams of coyotes seem to mean something but he is still hesitant and very surprised when Tamara hails him as the new Raven, a brujo.

If one doubts about the importance of place and spatial configurations, we find that Anaya himself has mapped the novel, including a map at the beginning with all the places where Sonny goes to. From a physical point of view, Sonny moves very freely, with his pickup truck. Both Albuquerque

---

[7] For different aspects on the subversive elements within the detective genre in Anaya, see Flys 2000.

and the surrounding mountains are a comfortable tertiary territory, while Los Ranchitos and Barelas are secondary territories. But maps can be misleading. As Jeanette Winterson states, "maps growing ever more real, are much less true" because they cannot reflect the places of the imagination (qtd. in Chambers, 1994: 16). Despite so many maps, what we really don't find, due to his physical, psychological and spiritual restlessness, is a space of his own, a real primary territory (fig. 18). If we plot these mental and cultural territories, we find that the world of dreams, heavily involved with Chicano lore, never intersects with the Anglo world. Sonny definitely feels more comfortable in the latter which he combines occasionally with his Chicano customs.

The next novel, *Rio Grande Fall* also begins with a murder, this time of the prime witness. Sonny is still suffering from "susto"—a belief in the invasion of the soul by a dead person looking for revenge—as a result of Gloria's death. Finally, at Rita's insistence, he accepts undergoing a "limpieza" to get rid of the susto. In doing so, Lorenza, the curandera, teaches him about his nagual—his animal guardian spirit—the coyote and he learns to harness "their energy [which] flowed to him" (129). He finally begins to remember his "grandfather's farm, the adobe house" (128) and accept his traditions, as the belief that "the world of nature is our world [...] Our nature is linked to that of our ancestors, to their beliefs" (121). He increasingly dreams more and learns to remember his dreams, which are interpreted by Eliseo. He also begins to read up on Chicano history, ancient Aztec beliefs and the syncretic Chicano belief system which combines elements from Christianity, several Indian tribes and Aztecs. Through this process he discovers that by trusting his intuition or his dreams, he can solve the crimes. He now begins to accept the relationship between the dream life and reality. By the end of the novel we find that Sonny's position in the web of territories has shifted (fig. 19). He now accepts the dreams and his Chicano heritage and finds himself increasingly more at ease in those territories than in the Anglo one. Again Anaya provides a physical map of the places Sonny visits, yet the spiritual map presents a shift, as Sonny integrates his territories more closely, straddling both sides of the border and particularly incorporating nature and the spiritual world of dreams. As Eliseo points out, the land "was the meeting ground of spiritual ways" (124).

As we reach *Shaman Winter* Eliseo teaches Sonny to harness his dreams and to create them in order to act in them. He learns that dreams and the past affect the present and reality. Anaya presents time as circular, much as the sacred hoop of the Plains Indians where "all movement is related to all other movement—that is, harmonious and balanced or unified" (Allen 1996: 243). The novel is devoted to his learning process and a review of the crucial moments in Chicano history, a history of mestizaje and cultural syncretism.

He learns that the Anglo world and harsh reality live alongside the world of dreams and he partakes of both. Eliseo insists on the "interrelatedness of everything" including the "minds of men and women communicating across space and time. Space and time became their thoughts, their ideas" (105-6). Anaya uses the novel to develop a complex philosophy of dreams and spiritual world and the eternal fight between the forces of good and evil. In the end, the different territories (fig. 20), the Anglo territory together with the official legislated reality, Chicano traditions and lore, and the spiritual world combine as Sonny learns to move in all, becoming a new brujo or shaman, taking up where Eliseo left off. In this novel Anaya provides three maps, two geographical and historical and one genealogical. One is that of Oñate's route in 1598 (2), the second portrays the invasion of Col. Kearny's army in 1846 (124) and thirdly, Sonny's family tree (234). Thus Anaya maps place and time and identity, highlighting their inter-dependence and relevance to actions in the present. In my mapping of mental and cultural territories, Sonny's increasing awareness of his mixed cultural heritage is clearly portrayed. By integrating his territories, he has been enriched and has learned to use his powers. The Anglo becomes less relevant, although he moves freely in it, whereas the spiritual world of Chicano heritage become much more significant. His own personal territory is far larger and his identity far richer.

The circle, therefore, is the dominant spatial configuration in Anaya. He seems to reject the polarity of a line, of the either/or. Anaya presents his characters with their multiple legacies represented in circles, destined to intersect. The degree of intersection, the size of that new space is the measure of a character's integrated, harmonious identity. Anaya's circles/legacies are basically cultural ones. We have seen both physical spaces defined culturally such as the barrio and the city and we have also seen metaphorical spaces representing the cultural traditions. These cultural traditions are made up of beliefs, language, history and customs. All aspects interact, all influence each other, as the sacred hoop of the Plains Indians. Christianity and indigenous beliefs mix; the rational, empirical approach to knowledge blends with the intuitive and spiritual; English mixes with Spanish; different versions of history, United States, Spanish, Mexican, Aztec, Pueblo, all meet; rituals, foods and celebrations from all these cultures come together. Anaya truly creates a hybrid cultural space where all traditions are integrated. But, as always, the question of dominance is present. The different legacies are not equal as their power relations are asymmetrical. Although Anaya portrays the Anglo culture as dominant, in the hybrid space he creates, the Chicano world view has greater significance. His re-definition of this culturally syncretic space places emphasis on the Chicano legacy, suggesting its superiority for his characters. Indeed, Anaya's purpose is clear: only by wholeheartedly embracing the Chicano heritage, one of mestizaje of Spanish, Native American and Anglo, can his characters/readers effectively cope in this world. In his first two novels, the quest is that of learning to cope with the Anglo culture. In the last four, the quest is recovering the Chicano heritage. Assimilation to the dominant culture is not the answer.

Nevertheless, there are other areas of hybridity that Anaya is less clear about. Most theoretical articulations of the borderlands discuss racial, class and gender issues, as well as cultural and literary. If Anaya's portrayal of cultural borderlands is very articulate, this is not the case with race, class or gender. Although in his novels he presents Chicanos as clearly a race of mestizaje, the predominant racial/cultural strains discussed are Spanish and Indian—clearly viewed in his first novel, *Bless Me, Ultima*. There is virtually no expression of the mestizaje with the so-called "white" race or the Northern European/Anglo-Saxon extraction.[8] Nor does he seem to encourage it in his fiction. Abrán, is of course, the exception. And his racial mix, Mexican-Anglo/white, is precisely the central problem, not the Spanish-Indian. Ironically, Anaya, as most other writers and critics, is immersed in the American racial dichotomization of "white" vs. "non-white," forgetting the paradox that the Spaniards, in origin are of the same racial and genetic extraction as Northern Europeans and therefore, equally "white" as the latest genetic study led by Semino and Underhill at the University of Stanford has just proven.[9] Scientifically speaking, then, the mix Spanish-Indian-Anglo is predominantly "white," unless the one-drop rule reigns here, too. But this is beside the point, except for the obvious implications of cultural impositions and dominance. Of all of Anaya's characters, only Abrán is portrayed as mestizo (Mexican-Anglo/white), just because he has one grandparent who is Anglo. Yet, he is viewed as a "child of the border," the only one apparently.

This ambiguity as far as racial mestizaje, also appears in terms of class. Only in two novels, *Heart of Aztlán* and *Alburquerque* does Anaya address class issues. In the former, there is a clear confrontation between Chicano workers and Anglo bosses. The spatial configuration of this clash is that of radical polarities and the borders are not transgressed. Although Clemente does try to establish a dialogue with some apparent intermediaries such as

---

[8] In this article I have presented the central dichotomy as one of Anglo vs Chicano. I resist accepting the American dichotomization of racial issues, white vs non-white, when this dichotomy is clearly a constructed one of power relations; all races are mixed, lines are not clear and often cultural extractions are used as racial categories.

[9] See *El País*, Nov. 10, 2000 and the November issue of *Science*.

union leaders and the priest, he discovers that they, too, side with power and wealth. In the latter, Abrán is the biological son of wealthy painter Cynthia and a poor barrio boy—now the also well-established writer, Ben Chavez. Her rich father was the cause of hiding Abrán's birth and existence, mostly for racial reasons rather than class. Even at the end, Abrán is not accepted by his grandfather. Likewise, wealthy Frank Dominic and mayor Marisa Martinez try to manipulate the barrio boy; here the issue is one of class, since both Dominic and Martinez claim Hispanic ancestry, if only for political reasons. But these borders are not crossed. In the rest of the novels the class dichotomy is radical. Class transgressions are not allowed, but they are not central to Anaya's themes. He does not explore nor problematize these borders.

And finally, neither are gender borders transgressed in Anaya's fiction. All his protagonists are men. Although his portrayal of women is almost always positive and he does present several very strong women, anywhere from the powerful Ultima to modern, entrepreneur Rita, they all continue in the traditional role of supportive and loving mothers, wives and girlfriends. The mothers strive to keep the family together and always stand by their husbands, despite their possible inadequacies, such as alcohol, violence, infidelities, illness or depression. The girlfriends look towards marriage and children. Only Ultima, Tules and Lorenza have no male couple, but they are curanderas and/or brujas, women who have traditionally remained alone because of their powers.

Therefore, Anaya's creation of new territories is basically limited to spaces of cultural interaction and hybridity. These expanded cultural borderlands are portrayed in a very positive, almost idyllic manner with little hint of negative or conflictive relations between groups. This representation clearly attests to his view of the shaman-storyteller and the purpose of empowering his community. These cultural borderlands are not only presented through the spatial configurations of the novels, the subject of this paper. Anaya also hybridizes literary genres and expressions in constructing his cultural borderlands. The novels present expressive crossings of language. Words and phrases in Spanish dot the pages, lending both ambiance and emotional verisimilitude and truth to the characters. Yet, the use of Spanish is limited in such a way as to not alienate a non-Spanish speaking readership. Anaya also, consistently draws on his Latin American legacy of magical realism. The use of magical-realistic techniques is particularly surprising and they constitute clear transgressions when used in his detective novels. One could suggest that his use of magical realism is a manner of "speaking from the margin," a way of writing "ex-centrically" as Theo D'haen posits in his article "Magic Realism and Postmodernism: Decentering Privileged Centers." Magical realism can constitute a de-centered and subversive discourse which reflects, in the words of Rawdon Wilson, "a conflicted consciousness, the cognitive map that discloses the antagonism between two views of culture" (1997: 222). In this manner, Anaya plots the Chicano culture, represented by the extraordinary, the intuitive, the spiritual, and the magical, clashing with the routinely, the ordinary and empirical of Anglo culture. Perhaps Anaya's greatest cultural/literary crossing is precisely his subversive disruptions of the hard-boiled detective genre. Incorporating magical realism into the centered discourse of the hard-boiled genre, one in which the dominant values are confirmed and where the detective solves the mystery precisely due to empirical evidence, is a manner of appropriating the centered discourse only to dis-place it in order to create an alternative world. Thus, Anaya's transgression of borders are particularly rich in creating hybrid cultural, expressive and literary borderlands. He does so, among other techniques, with the construction of his fictional spaces, subject of this article.

Therefore, we find that consistent with his use of aesthetic strategies for empowerment, Rudolfo Anaya uses his spatial configurations to illustrate and propose solutions to the real conflicts of his ethnic community. The imaginative space Anaya creates and the way he plays with it, allows his characters to selectively integrate their diverse territories, their diverse heritages, creating new harmonious primary territories where they can regulate access, where they can determine their terms of belonging and thereby define their identity. Through the model proposed, I feel that Anaya is suggesting that his readers attempt to follow suit: that they create or dream their own space, and transgress the borders that separate their territories, integrating them to the degree they wish, creating their own imaginative space where each reader can negotiate the terms of belonging.

Key to textures

Primary territory
(house, home)

Secondary territory
(barrio, school, semi-public)

Tertiary territory
(public, semi-hostile)

Chicano tradition

Anglo tradition

Dreams, spiritual world

Tertiary territory

Secondary territory

Figures

Fig. 1

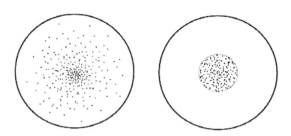

Fig. 2

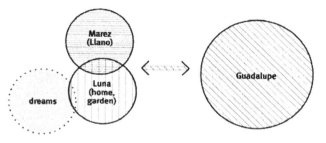

Fig. 3

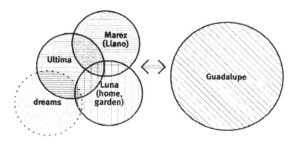

Fig. 4

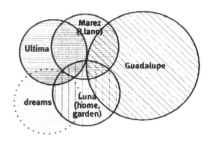

Fig. 5

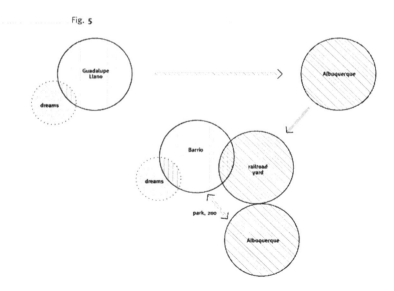

Figures

Fig. 6

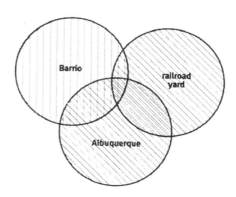

Fig. 7

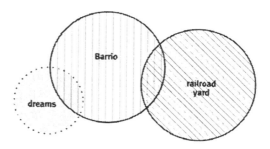

Fig. 8

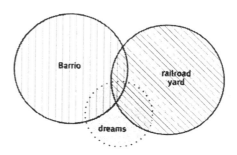

Figures

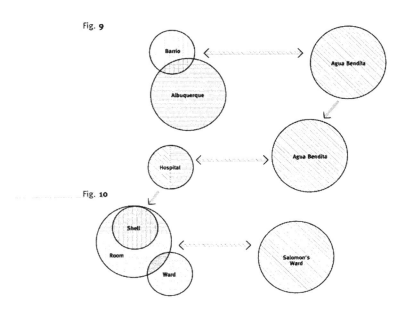

Fig. **9**

Fig. **10**

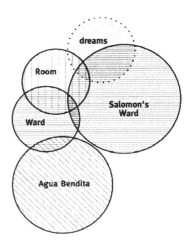

Fig. **11**

Fig. **12**

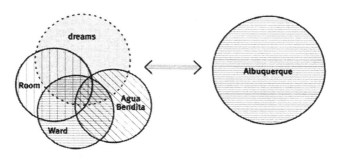

Fig. **13**

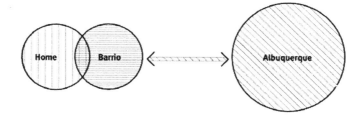

Fig. **14**

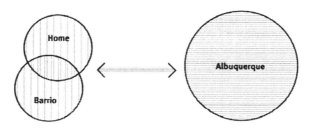

Fig. **15**

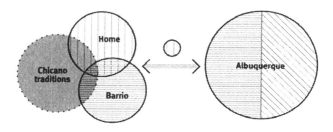

Fig. **16**

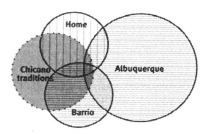

Fig. **17**

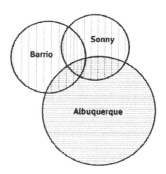

Fig. **18**

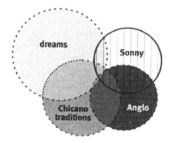

Fig. **19**

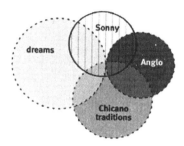

Fig. **20**

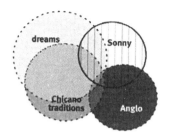

LEARNING FROM FOSSILS: TRANSCULTURAL SPACE IN LUIS ALBERTO URREA'S *IN SEARCH OF SNOW*

MARKUS HEIDE

This article analyses the staging of cultural contact in Luis Alberto Urrea's 1994 novel. While the novel at first sight does not seem to be composed as a fictional exploration of the U.S.-Mexican borderlands, a close reading shows that the narrative structure and the imagery are sketching different spaces of intercultural exchange; these spaces do in fact 'speak' to the history of Chicano identity formation. Reading the text through the theory of transculturation (Fernando Ortiz), Mexican-American history and the traumas of the Southwest surface as 'concealed contact histories' that have affected and are affecting the different cultures interacting in the Southwest.

In his non-fiction books *Across the Wire* (1993) and *By the Lake of Sleeping Children* (1996) Luis Alberto Urrea gives a first person account of his experiences among the poor on the Mexican side of the USA-Mexico border. In the autobiographical introduction to *By the Lake of Sleeping Children* Urrea writes: "If, as some have suggested lately, I am some sort of 'voice of the border,' it is because the border runs down the middle of me. I have a barbed-wire fence neatly bisecting my heart" (1996: 4). Himself the child of a Mexican father and a US-American mother, in this passage Urrea writes himself into characteristic Chicano enunciations of border subjectivity and border-space. He uses the border as a metaphor for being divided, for having two parts, for his hybrid identity. The self, community, territory and the body are inseparably intertwined in this imagination of border space. The figurations for expressing his border subjectivity seem to place Urrea in the imagery of Chicano literary articulation: "I have a barbed-wire fence neatly bisecting my heart," intertextually connects with Gloria Anzaldúa's *Borderlands/La Frontera* that refers to the border as a "1,950 mile-long open wound / [...] / running down the length of my body" (1987: 3). The kinship of imagery illustrates the author's self-positioning in Chicano/a discourse on space and identity.

In view of this positioning the detachment from matters of Mexican and Mexican-American community life in Urrea's 1994 novel *In Search of Snow* might at first sight be surprising. Neither is the protagonist of this highly symbolic novel a Mexican-American, nor does the narrator explicitly situate his voice in the Chicano community. Moreover, in the first two of three parts not much attention is given to Mexican-American cultural life. In fact, in these first two parts Mexicans are represented in stereotypical outline as menacing to the white Anglo protagonist. However, despite its thematic focus and its farcical style that at least momentarily seem to detach it from much of the more prominent "culturally rooted" Chicano fiction, *In Search of Snow* is most obviously staged as a novel of and about the borderlands. Borrowing Mary Louise Pratt's (1992) term, I read *In Search of Snow* as a novel about the "contact zones" of the cultures of the Southwest and as a fictional account of, what I would like to call, "fossilized contact histories." Pratt defines "contact zones" in the following terms:

> [...] social spaces where disparate cultures meet, clash, and grapple with each other, often in highly asymmetrical relations of domination and subordination—like colonialism, slavery, or their aftermaths as they are lived out across the globe today. (4)

Such encounters and conflicts, as Urrea's novel illustrates, leave traces behind. Contact histories persist through inscriptions that make landscapes, sites and bodies into textual material which as such "remembers." From this perspective I argue that despite the scarce presence of Chicanos/as, *In Search of Snow* does contribute to conceptualizing Chicano border-space by outlining three different spaces of intercultural contact: (1) Cultural conflict zones based on static identities that insist on ethnically marked boundaries, (2) utopian space in the tradition of perceptions of America as wilderness or as a "virgin land," characterized by historical amnesia, and (3) "contact zones" where encounters between historically "rooted" characters are represented as opening a transcultural space where boundaries are acknowledged but at the same time understood as permeable. In the fictional world of *In Search of Snow* this latter space, the "transcultural space," renders possible the dissolving of fixed oppositions. Here transculturation, in Fernando Coronil's words, "breathes life into reified categories, bringing into the open concealed exchanges among peoples and releasing histories buried within fixed identities" (1995: xxx). As the other two outlined notions of intercultural space, the imagined transcultural space in the novel opens a way to draw attention to the American "legacy of conquest" (Limerick 1987: 18), but the transcultural model, in contrast to the other two models, simultaneously depicts identity as not staticly rooted in the past. Translated into Chicano/a discourse, the novel neither invokes *Aztlán* as homeland, nor the borderland as a solely Chicano/a space, but rather attempts to envisage, to give fictional expression to and to textualize contact histories that have affected and are affecting the different cultures that have been interacting in the Southwest.

In my understanding of transculturation I refer to Fernando Ortiz's concept which in the 1940s he proposed as describing the two-way dynamics of colonial situations and intercultural contacts. Silvia Spitta argues that Ortiz's concept of transculturation has to be understood as a "specifically Cuban theory" since it is based on the particular historical situation of an island where "the indigenous populations were completely wiped out in the early years of the Conquest" (1997: 163), and European and African cultures thus interacted on a ground that was emptied of historical "roots." Spitta is certainly right in pointing out that "marginalized cultures in the United States today [...] provide a context very different from that of Cuba" (1997: 163). However, I do think that despite these very important historical and contextual differences the theoretical concept of transculturation offers itself for analysing the contact histories of different ethnic groups as represented in American literature. The concept emphasizes that cultural contact is never enacted solely in unidirectional terms but is to be understood as a two-way dynamic. In other words, markers of history are left in and on everyone involved in contact situations. Thus, I do use the term in Coronil's broader definition as "bringing into the open concealed exchanges among peoples" (1995: xxx).

Set in the 50s, the narrative focuses on the biographies of the protagonist Mike McGurk and his father Turk McGurk who own a Texaco station in the middle of a desolate desert valley near Tucson, Arizona. Narrated in a humorous and satirical tone with laconic, farcical dialogues, the narrative nevertheless is built on very serious historical subtexts that once in a while enter the present of the fictional world. The "hidden existence" of historical subtexts is reflected in the narrative strategies. It is a performative narrative as it includes not just the reader but also the narrator and the protagonist into the deciphering process. Seemingly mere descriptive accounts might turn out to be composed of different layers of meaning and thus demonstrate the "remembering" textuality of history. Most suggestive in this regard is the sketching of Mike's immediate environment, the desert. The desert becomes a textual landscape, full of signifiers that have to be deciphered, signifiers whose meaning has to be brought to the surface. The narrator as well as the characters seem to be involved in this deciphering process that opens up different layers of history.

In the beginning of the narrative a "professor" stops at the Gurks' Texaco station, and tells Mike: "Arizona [...] is an untapped wonderland of fossils" (19). In order to prove his statement, he steps out of his car and picks up an inconspicuous stone that then turns out to be a petrified clam. Mike learns that this clam is a relic from prehistoric times and that his Texaco station is built in a valley that once was a sea. The encounter with the professor explicitly introduces the motives of historical subtexts and layered textuality. After this encounter Mike writes the Latin term for a fossil on the wall of the customers' rest room—which is the place where he as an adolescent discovered all kind of cryptic, but also openly sexist and racist, messages. The reaction to his wall scribbling illustrates how strongly Mike's environment is marked by another history, namely the history of American expansionism, conquest, racism and ethnic conflicts: "ATRYPA RETICULARIS, Mike wrote near the toilet. Two weeks later, it was answered by a timid OH YEAH DAMNED MEXICAN" (29). The reaction reconnects pre-history with the profane present. The Latin term on the rest room wall is perceived by one of the visitors as a Spanish message, and possibly as a sign of reconquering and Mexicanization of the Southwest. The textual reply aggressively rejects the "Mexican" presence on the wall. Analogous to this textual exchange, Mike's search for meaning in the desolate desert valley and his desire to reconstruct his disarranged family history—he knows only fragments about his mother's fate—are constantly intersecting with the history of American expansionism and its reverberations, as well as other collective and individual memories.

In contrast to Mike who is receptive to messages and different histories, the narrator represents Mike's father Turk McGurk, a World War I veteran, as a tough frontier-guy and as eccentricly hostile against any kind of Otherness:

> Though Mike could remember little of his mother, he remembered many of his father's diatribes against every race and ethnic group that didn't have the good fortune to be a McGurk [...]. He saw conspiracy all about him, from the land-grubbing Navajo to the Zionist bankers 'controlling' New York and Hollywood. He hated both unions and scabs, hated the Ku Klux Klan and decried the 'Negro invasion' of white northern cities. He roundly denounced the church in all its manifestations, quoted pointlessly from the Bible, insulted both housewives and 'loose women,' [...] The only apparent solution Turk could see was immediate bombing, followed by [...] hand-to-hand combat. (11)

This war-fare attitude of Mike's father meets counterparts in the aggressiveness of other characters. These aggressive characters are ethnically marked as either white, Mexican or Native American. In the narrative setting the desert valley, in contrast to other places, is represented as a place where different solitary tragic and comic ethnic characters are exposed to, and are themselves re-vitalizing, conflicts that originate in the history of the Southwest. By juxtaposing different visions of intercultural space, the novel proposes ways to deal with the "legacy of conquest." The desert valley is framed as a conflict zone where static conceptions of identities and clear-cut boundaries are upheld by the characters. However, as I want to show in my reading, the narrative dissolves such static concepts of cultural space and identity positions. Most significant for my argument is Urrea's incorporation of international "encounters" that transcend the Mexican-American borderlands and emphasize the novel's thematic focus on questions of intercultural contact and "contact-histories." In the last part of the novel, in addition to the historical subtext of American expansionism, another subtext comes up in the narrative and plagues the memory of the major Chicano character: World War II and the Holocaust.

The McGurks' *Texaco* station turns into the primary memory-site of the novel: The station is built on a prehistoric sea, it is the place of fossilized history and historical inscriptions. History is further staged out symbolically. The station is constantly threatened by the heat of the desert valley. The destructive power of heat is then translated into potential destruction through re-enactments of historical conflicts. The theme of destruction is introduced through the Apache Mr. Sneezy who once, in his youth, was the chief officer of the Apache police of the region. This Apache police force then was under the supervision of Mike's grandfather, Carroll McGurk (9). Although Mr. Sneezy and the McGurks treat each other as long family friends, the narrator retrospectively implies that their relation is overshadowed by the grandfather's involvement in the subjugation of the Apaches: "Carroll McGurk [...] made a good impression on his Apache officers. He was fierce but generally fair and not in the least bigoted toward the Indians—as long as they were 'subjugated'" (32). When Mr. Sneezy unexpectedly shows up at the station, Turk "welcomes" him: "We don't serve no heathen Apaches around these parts" (31). Although this statement here is not meant seriously, it is clear that it is a relic from the time Carroll McGurk was still subjugating the Apaches of the area. The grandfather's activities in the Apache territories thus are introduced as one of the many prehistories of the narrative, a prehistory that remains rather uninvestigated by the characters and the narrator, except of such short remarks as: "Carroll McGurk had once policed the Apache in the company of Tom Horn, the notorious 'regulator'" (9). This prehistory and the conflicts between whites and Native Americans, parodied by Turk and Mr. Sneezy, at other points reverberate more seriously in the present of the fictional world. This is most obvious in the flashback of Mike's childhood experience when Mr. Sneezy introduced his grandson

Ramses Castro as his "Mexican grandson" (33). According to Mr. Sneezy
his grandson's father was Mexican. Ramses, however, insists to be Apache
and adds: "I am a warrior"—not yet clear whether meant as a joke or seri-
ously. The boy Ramses then tells Mike: "I'm an Apache. I'm not Mexican
[...]. Mexicans are the enemy of the Apache, [...] After the white man" (33).
To Mike's surprise, Ramses suggests to play "cowboys and Indians" (34).
Ramses finally traps Mike and beats him up, while commenting his actions:
"Think about it [...]. We are coming back" (34).

       This childhood encounter of the two boys, narrated in the beginning of
the novel, evolves to be of fatal importance in the narrative. It introduces the
character who will eventually kill Turk McGurk, Mike's father. Partly due to
his "military frame of mind" (11), partly to his desire to revive his success as
a professional boxer, Turk later in the narrative time frame challenges
Ramses for a prize fight. Ramses meanwhile has become a professional local
fighting hero. Although Mike and Mr. Sneezy try to convince Turk otherwise, he insists on proving that he still qualifies as a tough guy, a "real
McGurk." The fight then, in a hostile atmosphere is staged as a fight of the
(white) McGurks against the Mexicans and Indians of the town. Ramses
"had with him an entourage of zoot-suiters, Indians, and farmworkers" (66-
68). Mike perceives the Mexicans as threatening:

> They were dangerous, hopped up with new style—greasy ducktail hairdos and
> cavernous draped jackets that dropped past their knees [...]. Mike beat it to the
> other side of the room, into white territory. He maneuvered around behind Turk
> and the boys, where he cast furtive glances at the Mexicans and the Indians. (67-
> 68)

The fight itself, then, doesn't even last one round, as Ramses shows himself
much superior to the old man. With just one blow he destroys Turk: "Ramses
Castro swung his fist up and over. It came down like an ax blow, straight
into the top of Turk's head. Crack" (70). As a result of this blow Turk dies a
week later.

       The fight represents the climax of the hostilities between the different
characters. Hostilities that indirectly are resulting from the history of the
Southwest and that make the desert the location of violence between Native
Americans, Whites and Mexicans. Thus the space that is outlined in these
parts of the narrative, is one characterized by clearcut oppositions stemming
from conflicts that have a history. This space in the novel is allegorized in
the boxing ring, in which individuals are acting in the name of opposed
ethnic groups.

Seemingly as a reaction to the conflicts in the desert valley, Mike day-dreams of escaping, of leaving the valley. He expresses this desire by emphasizing how urgently he wants to see snow—the thing, as is said in the novel, most unlikely to be found in the valley. His dreams of snow are set against the hot and violent desert valley. In Mike's imagination snow gains symbolic meaning for making up a counter world to his immediate environment. When shortly before his death Turk again complains about Mike's "basic weakness" (23), Mike simply responds in his own symbolic language: "I hate heat [...] I want to see snow" (86). And in the prologue which anticipates Mike's cathartic act of setting fire to his father's *Texaco* station after his death, Mike says about snow: "It makes everything nice and white [...] covers it all up" (1). I suggest that Mike in his daydreams imagines a utopian space characterized by harmony and, in American terms, "new beginnings"—but also historical amnesia. On the one hand, Mike's utopia of a void, unlimited, boundless and, from his perspective, non-signifying space that is emptied of history, where snow "covers it all up" (1), sets up a counter-world to the desert valley that despite its vast emptiness still is a historical place plagued by conflict and hostilities. On the other hand, his "search of snow" (the novel's title) to a certain extent epitomizes the ahistorical attitude of the *white* characters in the novel. In contradistinction to the Apache Ramses Castro and the Chicano Bobo García, neither Mike nor his father Turk reflect very much upon their own "historical making" and the role of the legacy of conquest.

Shortly after Turk's death Mike wanders into the desert where he enters an Indian saloon and gets involved in a fight with Ramses Castro. Bobo García rescues him. A day later Ramses and his Apache gang show up at Turk's funeral:

> 'They just don't like me,' Mike said. He was suddenly overcome with the desire to be liked—especially by the Apaches.
> 'Why should they like you? You fucked up their world for them. Killed all their chiefs. Put pinche Phoenix in the middle of the desert to suck up all the water. Those guys been eatin' rocks for ninety years, vato.' [Bobo, the Chicano, said]
> 'I didn't do it!'
> 'Go tell them that.'
> Bobo relented—after all, it was Mike's dad's funeral.
> 'Aw, hell,' he said. 'They don't like Mexicans, either. We went and killed Geronimo's whole family—kids and all.' [...] 'Why should anybody like anybody?'
> 'I don't know,' Mike said. 'I like everybody.'
> 'You're ignorant.' Bobo said. (154)

This conversation shows how little Mike is aware of the wounds left by the history of Spanish colonialism, by the Mexican history of Arizona and by the history of US-expansionism, and how little he realizes to what extent these wounds have affected his own cultural making. I suggest that reading Mike's "search of snow" as the utopia of a space where historical amnesia establishes a new collective harmony, very much corresponds with the cultural logic of such traditional Anglo-American myths as "the virgin land," the New Beginning and American exceptionalism. Hidden in Mike's search of snow are myths that are based on the idea that historical roots are cut and that the new beginning in the Americas replaced the past by the future perspective, where progress reigns over memory.

After his father's death Mike leaves the valley and goes on a journey with Bobo García, who started working as a mechanic for the McGurks the day after the fight. Visiting Bobo's hometown in Arizona, Mike is for the first time exposed to Mexican cultural traditions. Mike experiences a culturally marked place that he feels is not "his own" but—and that is a new experience for him—not hostile against him either. Back in the desert valley—the cultural conflict zone—he, for example, had perceived the section of the fighting arena where the Mexicans gathered as "dangerous." Or, the Indian pub, which he enters in total confusion after Turk's death, is a place where he feels (and is) unwanted: "He was the only white in the building [...] He felt against his chest a tender wave of resentment that tried to push him back out the door" (136). In the saloon Ramses Castro who to Mike's surprise is a guest in the saloon, then addresses Mike:

> 'No offense, McGurk, but me and the People don't want you here [...]. Look at these faces. These here are Navajo and 'Pache faces. No white man comes in here. Why'd you come in here?'
> 'I was lost.'
> Castro snorted. 'Lost! Whole fucking white race is lost' (139)

In contrast to these conflict-ridden encounters with places assigned to either Mexicans or Native Americans in the first two parts of the novel, the third and last part draws another picture of intercultural contact. When approaching the García house which from the outside is decorated with "brightly painted [...] flowerpots" that signify "Mexicanness" for Mike, he is first skeptical whether he is really welcome:

> Mike was terrified. He wanted to go home. He wanted to get out of there before the rest of the Garcías came out—he imagined a whole household of pachuco gardeners, all of them with evil little goatees and switchblades, everybody so [...] Mexican. (189)

However, the García home soon turns into a place where—for the first time in the novel—non-violent intercultural communication is possible, where the characters learn from each other, and in that sense, it becomes a transcultural utopia where historical rootedness can be transcended and at least momentary permeations of boundaries are achieved. After the dinner with the García family, Mike announces: "I want to be a Mexican" (208). Considering the pejorative and racist terminology prevailing in the McGurk household and the desert valley, where Mexicans were called "greasers" or "beaners" the utterance of the wish to want to be Mexican signals that the characters have entered another intercultural space. Although the representation of the Garcías' home tends to suggest a transcultural utopia, it is not framed as a harmonic paradise where historical legacies and power differentials don't matter anymore. The Garcías live in a mining town where unjust working conditions and discrimination are prevalent. For Mike this is not self-evident:

> Yeah, it's nice,' said Bobo. [referring to the Garcías' home]
> But it ain't easy,' Bobo continued.
> How so?'
> Bobo looked at him as if he were an idiot.
> Money, vato. Where do you think they get the money?'
> Money had never occurred to him [Mike]. He thought the García spread was a magic kingdom, utterly separate from the earth.
> 'The ol'man got fucked up royal in them mines,' Bobo said. 'You seen him try to walk?' [...] 'You don't get too much of a break around here. Not when you're a Mexican.' (213)

Thus in contrast to Mike's dream of snowy landscapes as a space of historical amnesia, the García's home is represented as a utopian space were historical wounds are recognized. In this transcultural space the development of cultural "newness," resulting from cultural exchange, can at least be imagined.

At the end of the novel the themes of transculturation and "contact histories" are translated into the fictional world by bringing to the surface an individual trauma that had so far been unacknowledged throughout the novel. A trauma that has not been caused by the historical conflicts of the borderlands. Both, Mike McGurk and Bobo García served in the American army during World War II, Mike in North Africa, Bobo in Europe. This experience tightens their friendship. Although in their conversations they refer to the war in rather superficial coolness, the narrator informs about Bobo's traumatic experiences during the liberation of the concentration camp Buchenwald. His memories of the suffering and the horror he faced there are interpreted by Bobo himself as the impetus for his activities as a

kind of cultural mediator that distinguish him from most of the other characters in the valley. But his experiences in Germany have also alienated him
from his family. The narrator reflects Bobo's thoughts about his family and
their Mexican cultural memory:

> Bobo looked around the bathroom. It was all the same. Everything was in its
> place, his father's straight razor lying half open on a white cloth beside the shav-
> ing mug [...]. Nothing had moved [...]. Not even Buchenwald had moved any-
> thing. Not even the smell of Buchenwald had removed the medicinal odor of
> Mr. García's various herbal cures [...] These people did not comprehend a place
> such as that. When he had tried to tell them, they nodded gently and patted his
> hand. But their eyes remained blank. They barely understood who Hitler was.
> Their imaginations were still riding with Pancho Villa and Emiliano Zapata;
> their dreams were still circling the royal palace of Cuauhtémoc and the ships of
> Cortés. How could they understand ovens?
> He washed his face.
> Mrs. García was clapping her hands together and crying, 'Time to eat!'
> He looked in the mirror and tried on a smile. (206)

This incorporation of World War II and the Holocaust adds an autobiographical note to the novel and to the character Bobo, as Urrea's mother
actually entered Buchenwald right after liberation and suffered from this
experience ever after. In *By the Lake of Sleeping Children* Urrea writes:

> My mother [...] returned from being seriously wounded in World War II, a Red
> Cross front-line doughnut-and-coffee 'girl' who entered Buchenwald with the
> GIs and in some ways never came out. (1996: 3)

I want to suggest that the contextualization of the Mexican-American
borderlands with this trauma of his family which is at the same time the
trauma of modernity and humanity, illustrates the novel's connectedness
with global history and politics, as well as Urrea's skepticism towards
cultural-nationalist standpoints. Urrea's interest in this novel is not primarily
the representation of a specifically Chicano space, but rather he strives to
envisage "contact zones" of different cultures. In the novel it is obvious that
the cultural contact zone of the García home is favored as a place that is
open for intercultural communication and exchange. In the García home
processes of transculturation are "taking place" and are mutually acknowledged as doing so. This certainly connects Urrea's novel with the Chicano
discourses on the borderlands, hybridity and *mestizaje*. In Urrea's account,
the borderland between cultures or the contact zone "breathes life into reified
categories, bringing into the open concealed exchanges among peoples and
releasing histories buried within fixed identities," as Coronil puts the func-

tional dynamics of the concept of transculturation (1995: xxx). Urrea's exploration of the borderlands draws attention to the ways contact histories have shaped and are shaping and affecting ethnic minorities as well as white "Anglo"-culture in the US. Opening up the local knowledge that his receptive characters "learn from fossils," Urrea's staging of history incorporates contact histories that go beyond the Mexican-American borderlands and add a universal dimension to Chicano/a literary discourse.

LANGUAGE AND MALE IDENTITY CONSTRUCTION IN THE CULTURAL BORDERLANDS: RICHARD RODRIGUEZ'S *HUNGER OF MEMORY*

EDUARDO DE GREGORIO

This contribution investigates the role of language in the construction of Chicano writer Richard Rodriguez's male identity in *Hunger of Memory*. The search for a public identity is closely related to the author's acquisition of proficiency in English by means of education, and his subsequent Americanization. Together with this process, male identity is achieved through the implementation of a number of prototypically male discursive features including a pattern of self-imposed silence and reluctance to self-disclose, as well as strong differentiation between male and female conversational topics, and avoidance of female verbosity and gossip. Rodriguez's autobiographical account proves that only when both such linguistic processes and Americanization are completed will his sense of masculinity be assured, the author's masculinity being threatened by a number of hints of gayness throughout the process of identity configuration. Discourse and gender happen thus to be two major parameters of analysis in the construction of identities in the Chicano cultural borderlands.

Richard Rodriguez's autobiographic exploration of his male identity construction is by no means an isolated case in current North-American ethnic literature; in Asian literature, for example, such authors as Frank Chin, Jeffrey Paul Chan or Shawn Hsu Wong embody a whole trend in defining Chinese American manhood (Kim 1982). As it is, the recent interest in masculinity as an object of study is not restricted to Literary Criticism and Cultural Studies (e.g. Berger et al. 1995). Men's Studies is a wide new interdisciplinary approach comprising Psychology (Pleck 1981; Edley and Wetherell 1995; Levant and Pollack 1995), Sociology (Brod 1987; Kimmel 1987; Hearn 1992), Anthropology (Gilmore 1990; Cornwall and Lindisfarne 1994), and Linguistics (Johnson and Meinhof 1997). In an attempt to explore and react against what has been described as the contemporary crisis of masculinity (Horrocks 1994; MacInness 1998) resulting from the attacks of feminists, and gay and lesbian liberation movements (Easthope 1990: 2; Kimmel and Kaufman 1994: 262), Men's Studies call for careful consideration of the masculine as such rather than as an implicit and taken for granted category (Hearn and Collinson 1994: 99).

Drawing on Men's Studies and Linguistics, and leaving aside the primary focus of media interest in *Hunger of Memory*, namely Rodriguez's denunciation of ethnic activism, his corresponding endorsement of conservative cultural and political positions, his attacks on affirmative action and bilingual programs, and his support of traditional American education, institutionalized religion and ethnic assimilation (Paredes 1992: 280), attention will be paid to the role of language in Richard Rodriguez's male identity configuration. In point of fact, not only is the linguistic interest of *Hunger of Memory* clearly stated from the very beginning of the work, as Rodriguez himself claims, "This autobiography, moreover, is a book about language" (1982: 7)[1], but a concern with maleness is also pervasive throughout the autobiography as a whole,

> I turn to consider the boy I once was in order, finally, to describe the man I am now [...] I became a man by becoming a public man [...] Here is the life of a middle-class man; (6-7)

In this respect, language has been admitted to play a fundamental role in the configuration of individuals' personal identity, as suggested by Wetherell:

> To talk at all is to construct an identity. These constructions are shifting rather than stable and draw upon the multiple voices of a culture [...] Discourse analysts and social constructionists suggest that identity is accomplished as people speak. And of course, because the process of speaking has a long history for each individual, which is rooted in childhood, individual human minds become built from the accretion of voices over the years. (1996: 224)

Moreover, given that "we customarily take gender, ethnicity, and class as given parameters and boundaries within which we create our own social identities" (Gumperz and Cook-Gumperz 1982: 1), it seems to be clear that gender and ethnic identity construction may be explored discursively.

Thus, in an attempt to account for Rodriguez's gender configuration from a linguistic perspective, two major processes will be borne in mind. On the one hand, the process of code-switching between English and Spanish will be considered in relation to the establishment of a public/private identity during the author's Americanization. As it can be observed, Rodriguez's

---

[1] Henceforth, when quoting Rodriguez's *Hunger of Memory* (1982), the page only will be indicated.

process of gender identity construction will parallel the (re)definition of his personal ethnic formation in the Chicano linguistic and cultural borderlands[2]. On the other hand, a number of typically male linguistic features will be examined as essential in Rodriguez's gender identity shaping. In both cases, language will be seen as a tool helping configure the male identity of the author, which means considering the fact that "masculinity is socially constructed" (Connell 1995: 71). As a matter of fact, the idea of masculinity presupposes a concept of gender as the socially determined personal and psychological characteristics associated with being male or female, in opposition to sex as the biological differences between males and females (Oakley 1972: 158; Graddol and Swann 1989: 8). In this way, the concept of gender acquires what Butler defines as a "performative value" (1990: 25), that is, gender is not seen as a noun or a set of free-floating attributes, but rather as a doing, since the effect of gender is only performatively produced through "a set of repeated acts within a rigid regulatory frame which congeal over time to produce appearance of substance, of a natural kind of being" (1990: 33). Such a performative concept of gender will be considered below.

The first linguistic process contributing to Richard Rodriguez's male identity construction has to do with the alternative code-switching between Spanish and English, and its relation with the author's search for the con-figuration of a public/private identity. Although a number of linguists have come to the conclusion that, traditionally, male language tends to be associ-ated with the public realm, whereas female ways of speaking tend to be related to the private (Borker 1980: 33; Spender 1980: 80; Coates 1995: 14), Rodriguez seems to be aware that both a public and a private identity happen to be compatible within the male gender,

> As a socially disadvantaged child, I considered Spanish to be a private language. What I needed to learn in school was that I had the right—and the obligation—to speak the public language *of the gringos* [i.e., English]. (19)

However, the personal conflict arising inside Rodriguez is one in which the search for a public identity will involve a struggle to acquire English and abandon Spanish on grounds that the author tends to have assimilated a state of affairs where English is associated with a public identity whereas Spanish is related to a private one,

> Because I wrongly imagined that English was intrinsically a public language

---

[2] Wetherell (1996: 227) suggests that the dividing lines between such variables as gender, race or class are blurred when it comes to exploring the configuration of people's personal identities.

and Spanish an intrinsically private one, I easily noted the difference between classroom language and the language of home. (20)

As a result of this, the progressive acquisition of confidence in English will have a three-dimensional result having effects on the author's identity construction: Firstly, the acquisition of such a public identity will cause an internal cultural conflict inside a Rodriguez who does not quite resign himself to living without a private identity which he tends to associate with the actual use of Spanish, so that his progressive abandonment of such a language produces in him a sense of guilt for forgetting his native society. He depicts this sense of guilt through the names he was called—i.e., *Pocho*—as a Mexican-American who, in becoming an American, forgets his native society. Nonetheless, Richard Rodriguez's gradual proficiency in English will parallel the configuration of his longed-for public identity,

> One day in school I raised my hand to volunteer an answer. I spoke out in a loud voice. And I did not think it remarkable when the entire class understood. That day, I moved very far from the disadvantaged child I had been only days earlier. The belief, the calming assurance I belonged in public, had at last taken hold [...] for I was increasingly confident of my own public identity. (22-25)

Secondly, at some stages Rodriguez experiments a certain sense of guilt of his gradual Americanization feeling that, owing to his learning English, he commits a sin of betrayal against his immediate family, shattering the intimate bond that had once held the family close through their actual speaking of Spanish. However, there seems to be no doubt that Richard Rodriguez's Americanization will be confirmed by his progressive acquisition of confidence in English, "At last, seven years old, I came to believe what had been technically true since my birth: I was an American citizen (22)"; in both processes the influence of Rodriguez's teachers being as remarkable as that of one's parents in first language acquisition, "I came to idolize my grammar school teachers. I began to imitate their accents, using their diction, trusting their very direction" (49). And thirdly, and perhaps most importantly, the author's progressive mastery of English and his subsequent abandonment of Spanish will powerfully contribute to his male identity formation,

> Only when I was able to think of myself as an American, no longer as alien in gringo society, could I seek the right and opportunities necessary for full public individuality. The social and political advantages I enjoyed as a man result from the day that I came to believe that my name, indeed, is *Rich-heard-Road-ree-guess.* (27)

Therefore, it is only when Rodriguez is able to identify English as the language of the private, and not only of the public, that his new identity may be said to have finally arisen. As Rodriguez himself will claim, "this boy became a man" (32). Admittedly, the initial situation where Rodriguez was incapable of breaking the dichotomy inherited from his native Mexican culture where the public tended to be associated with English and the private could only be associated with the actual use of Spanish, seems to have evolved. When full proficiency in English has been acquired and his personal identity is completely consolidated, Rodriguez will be able to identify his use of English with the maintenance of a private identity, which he seemed to have lost, "Making more and more friends outside my house, I began to distinguish intimate voices speaking through English [...] After such movements of intimacy outside the house, I began to trust hearing intimacy conveyed through my family's English [...] *Intimacy is not created by a particular language; it is created by intimates*" (31-32).

Richard Rodriguez's male identity construction materializes through a second process of assimilation of a number of speech features that linguists have described as prototypically masculine. Rodriguez seems to echo what at first sight might seem to be mere stereotypes about gender differences in speech. However, although the author was not certainly aware of the scientific attention to such male-female speech differences, sociolinguists have scientifically proved their existence. Such male features include: Firstly, the acquisition of a pattern of self-imposed silence, which Rodriguez shares with other male members of his family, in special with his father, who is claimed to have never encouraged his children's success (55) or replied to his wife's constant questions about the reasons of the progressive loss of the Mexican style of privacy (57). As it is, young Rodriguez seems to grow a silent man,

> From a very early age, I understood enough, just enough about my classroom experiences to keep what I knew repressed, hidden beneath layers of embarrassment [...] In the midst of preparing dinner, my mother would come up behind me while I was trying to read. Her head just over mine, her breath warmly scented with food. 'What are you reading?' Or, 'Tell me all about your new courses.' I would barely respond, 'Just the usual things, nothing special.' (A half smile, then silence. Her head moving back in the silence. Silence! Instead of the flood of intimate sounds that had once flowed smoothly between us, there was this silence). (45-51)

The assimilation of this pattern of silence by males has been pointed out by a number of linguists like Tannen, for whom one of the most common stereotypes of a real man is the strongly silent type, and the image of the silent father is commonly the model for the lover and husband (1992: 116). In Tannen's view, this pattern of male silence is seen as closely related to a certain reluctance to self-disclose and reveal emotions on the part of men. This is soon learned by Richard Rodriguez,

> More important than any of this was the fact that a man never verbally revealed his emotions. Men did not speak about their unease in moments of crisis or danger [...] At times of illness or death in the family, a man was usually quiet, even silent [...] A married man, if he spoke publicly about love, usually did so with playful, mischievous irony. Younger, unmarried men often were more quiet (The *macho* is a silent suitor). (129)

According to Sattel (1976), male inexpressiveness is bound up with the power and investment men hold as a group in the social division of labor and in existing institutions. Such inexpressiveness is a strategy by which men keep the upper hand. In fact, in a different work, Sattel (1983: 118) emphasizes that much of the recent commentary on men and sex roles in this society has focused on the inability of males to show affection, tenderness, or vulnerability in their dealings with other men and women.

Secondly, the clear delimitation between specifically male and female conversational topics, whose existence is a tendency that has been identified by Eakins and Eakins (1978: 48), Haas (1979: 620-23), Aries and Johnson (1983: 1193) and Bly (1991: 16). They all agree that, while women tend to talk about intimate and family things, men talk about more external activities and seldom about feelings, which is soon assimilated by Rodriguez,

> As a boy, I'd stay in the kitchen (never seeming to attract any notice), listening while my aunts spoke of their pleasure at having light children. (The men, some of whom were dark-skinned from years of working out of doors, would be in another part of the house.) It was the women's spoken concern: the fear of having a dark-skinned son or daughter. (116)

Thirdly, a one-at-a-time turn-taking system in conversation, often as though men's conversations became monologues, in contrast with female conversational patterns, where several women hold the floor at a time taking advantage of each other's interactions, which, again, is a gender difference in topic-development that has been remarked by Coates (1982: 120; 1997: 120), and which Richard Rodriguez echoes in his autobiography as being a typically male feature of speech, "When one heard many voices in a room, it was usually women who were talking.) Men spoke much less rapidly. And often men spoke in monologues (when one voice sounded in a crowded room, it was most often a men's voice one heard)" (128).

Fourthly, avoidance of verbosity and gossip among men on grounds that such features are typical of female speech. As a matter of fact, a number of studies (Ayres 1980; Coates 1986: 103; Tannen 1991: 75) confirm that women talk more than men. On the other hand, being closely intertwined with verbosity, gossip has been linguistically characterized as a female feature of speech (Coates 1986: 115; Johnson and Finlay 1997: 130); and these trends are reflected in *Hunger of Memory,* "But a man was not talkative the way a woman could be. It was permitted a woman to be gossipy and chatty" (128). Once more, it seems that Rodriguez has assimilated a number of gender differences in speech which have been confirmed by linguists, natural though they are presented to be by the author.

Both linguistic processes contribute to Rodriguez's male identity configuration, and, as suggested above, not until English proficiency, public identity acquisition and Americanization, are fulfilled, may the author's masculinity be claimed to be completely consolidated. In actual fact, Rodriguez hints at the threat of a certain gayness as a result of his personal cultural conflict arising during the search of a public identity through an education in English, which is manifested in his "admiration" for the Mexican *braceros,*

> Passing by on the bicycle in summer, I would spy them there, clustered in small groups, talking—frightening and fascinating men [...] I was unwilling to admit the attraction of their lives. I tried to deny it by looking away. But what was denied became strongly desired [...] at such times, I suspected that education was making me effeminate; (114-127)

Together with this admiration for the Mexican *braceros,* such threat of gayness may be guessed by a certain shyness towards women on the part of the author,

> Simply, I judged myself ugly. [...] I felt my dark skin made me unattractive to women [...] I was a teenager shy in the presence of girls. Never dated. Barely could talk to a girl without stammering. In high school I went to several dances, but I never managed to ask a girl to dance. (125-127)

Both such hints of gayness threatening Rodriguez's heterosexual masculinity confirm the performative value of gender discussed above, and confirms the idea that masculinity needs to be proved constantly (Gilmore 1990: 11; Seidler 1996: 64).

Whether Richard Rodriguez's process of identity succeeds in causing English and Spanish to remain completely apart is very much a question of perspective. His English-only option seems to establish an insurmountable barrier between the Mexican and the Anglo, and allows him to start regarding himself as the average American man from an early stage in his life: "Soon I became as Americanized as my classmates—most of whom were two three generations removed from their immigrant ancestors" (79). But if this is the vision of himself he conveys in his narrative, he is not viewed as such by "Americans": he has become a "spokesman" for Chicanos, and frequently speaks on NPR (National Public Radio). This is, in a way, the culmination of a performative linguistic identity, but also the confirmation that Rodriguez cannot switch over entirely into an only English existence. His identity formation, therefore, remains unfinished or on the borderlands.

On balance, the influence of language on Richard Rodriguez's male identity configuration in the Chicano cultural context may be analysed by means of two major linguistic processes. On the one hand, the search for a public identity is closely related to the acquisition of English proficiency through education, and progressive Americanization as a result. On the other hand, male identity is achieved through the implementation of a number of prototypically male linguistic features such as a pattern of self-imposed silence and reluctance to self-disclose and reveal personal feelings, clear differentiation between male and female conversational topics, and avoidance of female verbosity and gossip. However, not until both such linguistic processes, together with Americanization, are completed, will Rodriguez's masculinity be reassured, so that the author's male identity is threatened by a number of hints of gayness throughout the configuration of his manhood involving both the linguistic processes dealt with.

M/OTHER TONGUES IN BORDERLANDS IN CONTEMPORARY LITERATURE IN ENGLISH

M.S. SUÁREZ LAFUENTE

Postmodern concepts such as Otherness, a result of erasing centers of power and, therefore, borders, affect minority languages to the point of bringing mother tongues to the fore. M/other tongues, thus constructed, implement contemporary identities that will now negotiate self-definition through a new agent: the her/story and body of the maternal genealogy. Patriarchal mores and a newly-experienced linguistic power contend within the Borderlands. The outcome is a redefinition of spaces, a new mapping and naming, preceded and followed by the unmapping, unnaming and unlearning of that very place we inhabit. The ensuing literature is unstable and varied, full of fissures and interstices and, therefore, of possibilities. Postmodern, postcolonial literature signals the site of Borderlands.

> Tongue then, an instrument for the (signage) sounds to which we ascribe meaning, the thread that binds a culture together.
> Aritha van Herk

This essay points out some of the possibilities deconstruction offers for the study of language/tongues in contemporary terms. By applying deconstructive critical devices the m/other tongues that influence the development of any language, insofar as they are assimilated into it, come now to the fore, and, by means of the bar (/), point towards their native component (mother tongues) and their importance as (other) "new" languages. Alterity is one of the most active producers of culture today and it starts processes that widen and enrich contemporary literature.

This consideration allows us to work on three hypotheses: first, that the patriarchal construction of language has lost credibility and, therefore, we need alternative means of analysis, such as, for instance, a "mother" tongue, as the most seminal procedure. Patriarchal thought and power have been expanded, through postmodern fissures, into their contraries, "matriarchal" ones, and every possibility that may be articulated in between.

A second hypothesis is that "new" tongues push against the borders of social definition, opening up space for other entities besides the canonical ones, and some tongues even succeed beyond those borders. Although, nowadays, it can safely be said that the "borderland" is yet the site for identity conflicts:

> [T]he border is a persistent metaphor in *el arte de la frontera*, an art that deals with such themes as identity, border crossings, and hybrid imagery.
>
> The border is the locus of resistance, of rupture, of implosion and explosion, and of putting together the fragments and creating a new assemblage. (Anzaldúa, 1998:165)

Anzaldúa's words constitute a superb definition of the doings of postmodernism: after the deconstructive explosion of predefined borders authors re/create as many assemblages as possible with the fragments. No destruction, nor sterile negation are implied in critical deconstructive practices, but a world of possibilities for new voices, for new attitudes, for new experiences.

The third hypothesis derives from the previous one: while a "whole" identity is in the process of being reached, the physical body constitutes the only and most real self we can point to; therefore, authors and critics usually proceed from there.

M/other tongues, either native or new to the territory, have to contend with the colonial or hegemonic language to be able to survive. That process generates borderlands—fusions and contentions that express themselves as experience, history and art in a multiplicity of possibilities depending on the socio-political background, the chronotope and the idiolect of the different contenders. Borderlands constitute, then, a theoretical space originated in any human hegemonic situation.

There is in humanity "a will to immortality" which our mortal condition makes intrinsically impossible, so that our only opportunity to become immortal is through the memory of history. But the door to history has always been closed to "other than white men" (namely women, gay/lesbians and colored people) because it could only be opened with the key that mastered patriarchal language. Given that situation, we wonder what kind of identity could have been acquired by those out of the main social structure. Gloria Anzaldúa's words about the "woman of color" can be extrapolated to cover the circumstances of all those partaking of alterity:

Alienated from her mother culture, 'alien' in the dominant culture, the woman of color does not feel safe within the inner life of her Self. Petrified, she can't respond, her face caught between los intersticios, the spaces between the different worlds she inhabits. (1987:20)

People are trapped within the borders defined by language since minds are modeled by their own linguistic ability. Ability which has always been officially determined, first, in private, by our mother's tongue, then, by the symbolic or male tongue, our social language. This construction of the social world allowed white boys to fit in easily into their public world and let girls and "different" children to stray backwards for a while till they fitted, growing "down," in their predefined slot—the slot of minorities; social minorities being defined by gender, ethnicity, class and religion, to speak only of a few articulations.

Such social construction implies a dangerous psychological fault because its process creates a borderland of differences, and, as Anzaldúa states: "Borders are set up to define the places that are safe and unsafe, to distinguish *us* from *them*" (1987:3). Therefore, in "Borderland" the sense of identity and the right to self-definition are, at best, heatedly argued out, or, at worst, sublimated into a false sameness. "Sameness" meaning the necessary unity to enter the realm of "them"/story. Gayatri Spivak would remind us, at this point, of the fact that subalterns lack a historical discourse and can only express themselves through insurgency and revolution. Childs and Williams produce the useful footnote:

Gramsci used the term subaltern (which means both 'of inferior position or rank' in military terms and 'the particular' in distinction from the universal in logic) to denote a group without class consciousness. Guha, explaining his application of the word, says that for the Subaltern Studies Group the term is used 'as a name for the general attribute of subordination in South Asian society whether this is expressed in terms of class, caste, age, gender and office or in any other way'. (1997: 161)

With the advent of poststructuralism and the postmodern unlocking of cultural reservoirs the deconstruction of the patriarchal structure became socially possible, and the tongue of the mother, the tongue of her/story and the tongue of difference became cultural assets. Tongues "shamed into silence and disuse" (Vevaina 1997: 81) are now put to work to change Tradition and Truth (both with a capital T). Newly acquired voices are intent on preventing the abuse of "innocence," the "I didn't realize," "I didn't mean to;" in the last decades of the twentieth century we cannot avoid knowing that we *know*. No more pretending. Adrienne Rich gives us the clue to this process in her poem "An Atlas of the Difficult World":

> I know you are reading this poem which is not in your language
> guessing at some words while others keep you reading
> and I want to know which words they are. (XIII, lines 489-491, 1990-91)

Difference has to be reached precisely through language by deconstructing, by undoing the linguistic process, widening "los intersticios," the fissures, as the best way to subvert the patriarchal "I." And an elemental subversion is deconstructing the Cartesian cogito; the most appropriate graffiti to this process "pienso, luego estorbo" (I think, therefore I become a nuisance) was read on the wall of a secondary school lavatory in Spain—our children, product of the postmodern condition, understand the step to be taken.

Some writers have already pushed the process into its limits, such critics as Hélène Cixous, Luce Irigaray and Julia Kristeva, Monique Wittig in *The Lesbian Body* and Verena Stefan in *Häutungen*. What they propose is to uncover/discover the mother tongue which lies below the surface structure of male-constructed language, in Irigaray's words, and change language radically in radically changing social, moral and aesthetic points of view. Audre Lorde amplifies the previous theoretical points poetically:

> I
> is the total black, being spoken
> from the earth's inside. ('Coal,' 1976)

Aritha van Herk, in her book of ficto-criticism *A Frozen Tongue*, describes the "Mothertongue"

> as the language one must un-learn, forget, spurn, the language of origin but a language to be lost: neglected, abandoned, forsaken. The illegitimate language, the immigrant language, the native tongue, displaced and shoved aside. Mothertongue: tonguemother. Body, place, land. (19-20)

Most writers stopped within the borderland to work out its possibilities before proceeding onwards to determine the plurality of the "I" of identity, to determine the right each of us has to be subjects of our own self/definition; they stopped to reread and rewrite history, literature and philosophy, to make it possible for alterities to inscribe themselves/ourselves in the world with a multiplicity of "I"'s.

While this process of recovering/uncovering takes place, the body is the most obvious "reality" we possess, the place of/for pleasure, pain, touch, taste [...] life. Especially so in the case of outsiders/others, "migrants" that have their bodies as the only luggage: "we do not *have* bodies, we *are* bodies, and we are ourselves while being in the world" (Trinh Minh-ha 1989: 36). The body is predetermined as the cornerstone of identity, the physical site of the subject in contemporary culture: tattoos and piercing, hair styling, anorexia/bulimia and vigorexia are there to show the world that even if I am denied other chances I am still the master of my own body. The body has been aptly designed as the site of social meanings and a political battle-ground.

We must extrapolate here the female body; which is also motherhood, the mother's body, the threshold to language, our first key to the world:

> the beginning: language, a living body we enter at birth, sustains and contains us. it does not stand in place of anything else, it does not replace the bodies around us. placental, our flat land, our sea, it is both place (where we are situated) and body (that contains us), that body of language we speak, our mother-tongue. it bears us as we are born in it, into cognition. (sic., Daphne Marlatt, qtd. in van Herk 1992: 20)

Our mother's body is our first spatial reference, and in mapping, naming and understanding this space, we come to terms with our own self and grow towards our maturity. This complex process often entails the deconstruction of childhood memories and takes the form of literary auto/biographies, pieced together out of the puzzle bits of life and genealogy (Suárez Lafuente 1993: 192). Hence the rereading of that body, of maternity, which is effected once and again by writers in their pursuit of uncovering the mothertongue. Eavan Boland, in "The Muse Mother" (1982), reads, writes and even tries to decline the maternal body in an attempt to possess the mothertongue:

> If I could only decline her -
> lost noun
> out of context,
> stray figure of speech -
> from this rainy street
> again to her roots,
> she might teach me
> a new language:
> able to speak at last
> my mother tongue.

Susan Swan celebrates the end of the process in *The Biggest Modern Woman of the World*: "Now I am in full voice [...] blowing my own horn."

Maternity, then, constitutes the alternity to his/story, since it gives its subjects the same powerful, rooted feeling history gave to patriarchy. Maternity functions as a chronology that fuses the past with the present and looks to the future. Lola Lemire Tostevin, in the "Afterword" to her book of poetry *Gyno Text* explains that her poems

> are not about the mystification or sacred calling of motherhood defined as duty or end-in-itself but as source of generative creative power and strength. Not about generation as chronology but as signifying space, both corporeal and mental. (in Vevaina 1997: 86)

Australian author Olga Lorenzo's novel, *The Rooms in My Mother's House* (1996) and Canadian Hiromi Goto's *Chorus of Mushrooms* (1994) are two very good examples of what we are arguing here: narratives of a female genealogy, grandmother-mother-daughter, where the grandmother keeps her mother's tongue as her only sign of identity and sanity. "[Dolores] could not find shelter [in] an English that she did not understand. There were so much lacking. She wondered if she would ever feel herself again" (Lorenzo 1996: 260). So, grandmother tries to pass her tongue on to the granddaughter, to assure her survival at least in the girl's memory, while the mother rejects the mothertongue she knows because that excludes her from her new country and prevents her daughter from learning the new language of power. The daughter, posed in-between, exiled from both, exiled at each end, enriches her identity in the conflagration. Although Australian poet Silvana Gardner considers this situation extremely painful, especially for the child:

> One family, yet the grandmother speaks
> a foreign language, mother and father
> yet another and the daughter another again.
> They are not clever for speaking in many tongues!
> Sometimes no one understands what the other says
> least of all the child who blames wars for sifting
> them like sand to countries with no affinities. ('Forbidden Language')

Such characters also enact their frustration and their contentment and find out about each other's feelings and life through the touching and handling of their bodies; kissing, caressing, feeding, washing and combing each other's hair. But such activities are also damaging to themselves and each other, as in the compulsory shaving and plucking of the corporal hair, cutting their nails till they bleed, hitting or kicking one another and even going willingly to surgery. So connected is the body with identity, and both with language:

> Keiko and I, our differences remain. But there are times when one can touch the

other without language to disrupt us. Daughter from my body, but not from my mouth [...] Sometimes we are able to touch the other with gentle thoughts and gentler hands. We still have our hair days, and she still asks me to clean her ears. (Goto 1994: 25-26)

The strategies to subvert definitorial borders are many and varied. Vevaina proposes a few possibilities that derive directly from postmodern practices; for instance erasing the boundaries between literary genres allows the writer to play freely with memory, which takes one directly to the possibilities open by the archaeology of knowledge, such as the unearthing of historical ancestors, and the rewriting, in contemporary terms, of ancient myths and epic characters. Dialects, native rhythms of speech or proverbs are auxiliary agents that evoke an immediate "historical" response in the mind of the readers.

The list does not stop there. The more we read, the more we add to such strategies, memory standing out as the best archive where to look for instances of our mothertongue. Canadian writer Margaret Laurence, in her novel *The Diviners*, renames memory as "memorybank," the place from which we draw whatever item we need at a given point, and, consequently, where we keep, often unconsciously, every bit and piece that might hold us together.

Photographs, with their iconographic power, figure uppermost in the memorybank menu, filling up literary works. To mention some examples, Sunetra Gupta, in *Memories of Rain* (1992), makes photographs the means by which the main character is able to verbalize her situation and make a vital choice. While old photos help Jean Bedford's character in *Love Child* (1986) construct her genealogy. Bedford quotes poet Janis Ian as the introduction to her novel:

> There's never much to read
> Between the lines of what we need
> And what we'll take.
> [...] Between the lines of photographs
> I've seen the past [...]

Mothertongues being language, after all, appear also disseminated in letters and diaries, bushlogs and oral stories. While "official" writers and "public" welldoers were busy progressing in the patriarchal path, describing the main lines of the historical script and making sure everything was well fit in its prescribed slot, people were enriching their mothertongue, quietly dwelling in the borderland of possibilities, dreams and stories. Margaret Atwood aptly describes both activities in "Marsh Languages":

> The dark soft languages are being silenced:
> Mothertongue Mothertongue Mothertongue
> falling one by one back into the moon
> [...]
> Translation was never possible.
> Instead there was always only
> conquest, the influx
> of the language of hard nouns,
> the language of metal,
> the language of either/or,
> the one language that has eaten all the others.

This wealth of everyday experience and cultural development is being transcribed into contemporary literature. Powhiri Rika-Heke calls our attention to that fact in the poem "For my friend": "Hear me / This language is my mother tongue / My mothering tongue." Identities expand through their (m)other/tongues till they burst the borders that constrain them.

John Skinner plays with the parental relationship we are using here to give the argument a twist and introduce a new element, that of the "step-mother tongue," in what he calls New Anglophone Fiction. Skinner draws the symmetry from the meaning stepmothers acquire in folk tales, one of love-hate relationship and essential to the structure of the narrative. Such is the feeling between writers and the English language they use for literary communication, an english "first *adopted* and then *adapted*" (11), the step-mother tongue.

Skinner provides a taxonomic table best to illustrate his theoretical standpoint. The space of the mother tongue is here reserved to Old Literatures in Old Worlds, where "our" land is described by "our" language. This argument would be impeccable in terms of traditionally classic bodies of literature, but it prevents native mother tongues from expressing themselves not only freely but in qualified terms. Only if the notion "Old Literature" is unequivocally made to include Orature as well, can we think of considering it as valid.

Literary post-colonial language can only occupy, according to Skinner, the space of stepmothering. I quote from his table: 1. New Literatures in Old Worlds (our land described by their language): it's applicable to the literatures of Asian, African and South Pacific territories. 2. New Literatures in New Worlds (their land described by their language) covers Afro-American and Caribbean literatures, and 3. Old Literatures in New Worlds (their land described by our language) will correspond to the literatures of Australia, New Zealand, South Africa and Canada. The theory poses interesting possibilities and many conceptual problems, such as the development of language beyond "ownership" or the many ins-and-outs of nationhood and nationality, to state only a few. But it certainly widens the limits of the borderland to cover the globe over.

The result of this postmodern/postcolonial/gender expansion is a multicultural, plural world full of possibilities; a golden pot for literature and readers.

THE BORDERS OF THE SELF: IDENTITY AND COMMUNITY IN LOUISE ERDRICH'S *LOVE MEDICINE* AND PAULE MARSHALL'S *PRAISESONG FOR THE WIDOW*

MARIA DEL MAR GALLEGO

The exploration of the concept of the 'border' is a key issue in Louise Erdrich's *Love Medicine* (1984) and Paule Marshall's *Praisesong for the Widow* (1983), where the authors illustrate the quest for a satisfying sense of identity by means of a redefinition of the crucial notion of self. In these polyphonic narratives the negotiations of 'the borders of self' are intimately connected to a rediscovery of the collective sense of community. The female mixed-blood or diasporic characters depicted by Erdrich and Marshall are deeply engaged in a process of reconciliation with their multicultural heritage and their manifold borders, whereby liminality is assessed as a suitable critical tool to answer their need to shape a sustaining and nurturing sense of identity. Inhabiting a liminal space, these women destabilize Western hegemonic discourse and its gender hierarchy by providing an alternative matriarchal worldview, where women recover their spiritual roles in their communities.

The quest for a satisfying sense of personal identity runs parallel to a rediscovery of the collective sense of community in Louise Erdrich's *Love Medicine* (1984) and Paule Marshall's *Praisesong for the Widow* (1983). In these works both authors explore the productive concept of the "border," especially concerned with a redefinition and reconstruction of the crucial notion of self. The negotiations of "the borders of self" that these two authors undertake in their narratives point out the problematic nature of shaping a sustaining and nurturing sense of identity for mixed-blood or diasporic characters who need to come to terms with their multicultural heritage and their multiethnic allegiances. In so doing, Erdrich as well as Marshall engage in a revisionist project that entails a direct challenge to Western hegemonic discourse and calls into question its gender hierarchy by providing an alternative matriarchal worldview, in which women recover their significant roles in community-building and decision-making.

Before dealing with the texts under discussion, the whole concept of blurred and polifaceted identities should be addressed from the perspective of the border. Locating the self at the crossroads of a multilayered confrontation effectively interrogates the very foundations of Western thought, since it opens up new venues for exposing its inherent contradictions and its manifold gaps. In this sense, it seems appropriate to approach the concept of the border from a theoretical framework that analyzes in depth the profound implications of placing the notion of self in a sort of "in-between space," which serves as main instrument to destabilize the powerful influence of Western dominant discourse and its trend toward categorization and homogenization. Trying to map out a significant theory of the liminal being, I have adopted Arnold Van Gennep and Victor Turner's classical characterization of liminal entities, but I also take into account contemporary renderings of literary liminality.

I- Rites of Passage: Liminality and Community

The anthropological definition of ritual and, more specifically, of "rites of passage" highlights the importance of claiming for an in-between space. The term "rites of passage" was coined in 1900 by Van Gennep, who defined them as "rites which accompany every change of place, state, social position or age" (1960: 11). Three stages are noticeable in any rite of passage: separation, in which the individual is separated from his/her previous life; transition, during which the individual remains in a liminal space preparing him/herself for the integration into a new status; and, finally, incorporation, whereby the individual achieves social acceptance and integration. Using another set of terms, Van Gennep describes these rites as "preliminal, liminal, and postliminal" phases respectively.

The stage that mostly characterizes rites of passage is obviously the so-called "liminal" period. The importance attributed to this period signals its central role for a clear understanding of the whole significance of rites of passage and their socio-cultural implications. The liminal period is charted by the presence of certain distinct liminal features. It becomes associated with the idea of ambiguity, that is, the liminal position is uncertain, as it lies outside any possible social categorization. The liminal persona is not yet classified nor classifiable according to social conventions. He/she has been plucked out of his/her status, as it were. In this ambiguous position the person becomes constantly linked with an entire set of images that deal with the absence of status or the uncertainty of possessing one. As Turner puts it: "liminality is frequently likened to death, to being in the womb, to invisibility, to darkness, to bisexuality, to the wilderness, and to an eclipse of the sun and the moon" (1977: 95). Other features must be added to this description such as the loss of any kind of personal distinguishing attributes such as gender, name, etc. The individual is equated to a tabula rasa, "a blank slate, on which is inscribed the knowledge and wisdom of the group" (Turner 1977: 103). This last quote reminds the reader of the dynamic relationship between liminal entities and society, in which the former is entirely dependent upon the latter.

In fact, liminality is defined by its marginal position with respect to the social system of values. Although it can bring about a certain kind of autonomy, it is nevertheless intrinsically related to the outside world. It can be seen as an "inter-structural" position, that is to say, a position from which society can be both scrutinized and internalized. It also possesses inherent power, which lies at the very heart of the liminal situation due to its transgression of the very norms or rules that regulate social intercourse. From the anthropological standpoint, this power relates to ideas of the sacred and holy because the transitional person literally "wavers between two worlds" (Van Gennep 1960: 18). Even more, this power is seen as positing a threat, due to its potential negation of the arbitrariness and subsequent constructiveness of the social apparatus. However, it is usually directed and controlled by society to perpetuate itself and its value system. This phase is where the actual social creation or social production is prone to take place, since it is the place where the normative expectations and notions of the world are questioned and new expectations are engendered.

The concept of liminality is most productive when applied to the study of literary texts, as Manuel Aguirre, Roberta Quance and Philip Sutton propose in *Margins and Thresholds* (2000). Their definitions of liminality are very useful for our purposes here, since they definitely offer a suitable framework to deal with the two texts under scrutiny. On one hand, they understand the notion of liminal texts as those "generated between two or more discourses, a transition area between two or more universes which thereby shares in two or more poetics" (2000: 9). Erdrich's and Marshall's novels partake of at least two discourses and, therefore, two poetics respectively: in Erdrich's case, these two universes are the Chippewa and Western legacies, whereas for Marshall her Afro-Caribbean roots intertwine with her Westernized education. So the female protagonists portrayed in their novels need to constantly negotiate between those two divergent worlds and allegiances. On the other hand, Aguirre et al. assign another possible meaning to the liminal phenomenon in literary texts which "centered around the notion of the threshold, or whose fundamental theme is the idea of crossover, a transgression or an entry into the Other" (2000: 9). In this second sense, I contend that both novels focus on the key presence of the threshold as an autonomous area by depicting liminal characters who inhabit that threshold, expanding its limits and claiming its central position. Their liminal status allows them to reconsider and reconceptualize themselves and their own community in an attempt to rewrite the "borders of the self," both individually and collectively.

II- *Love Medicine* and *Praisesong for the Widow:*
The Triumph of Liminality

Erdrich and Marshall create polyphonic narratives in which liminality is assessed as an efficient critical tool to unmask Western hegemonic discourse and its imposed univocal definition of self. Employing the "discourse of the threshold," both authors sustain a radical critique of a central Western self by means of depicting characters who figuratively and successfully waver between two worlds and, hence, consistently break away with constraining racial and sexual binary oppositions and rigid categories promoting a more fluid constitution of the female self. I wish to further demonstrate that, in fact, the female characters chosen by Erdrich and Marshall inhabit a liminal space, which becomes thus a suitable scenario, a ritualistic ground, for the enactment of both processes: the personal and the communal quest for identity. Marie Kashpaw and Lulu Lamartine in *Love Medicine* and Avey Johnson in *Praisesong for the Widow* act as living embodiments of liminal selves, mediating the borderlands of their own selves and those of their communities. Being insiders and outsiders simultaneously, they attempt to effect an actual reconciliation of the multiplicity of selves which constantly plague them, in order to reach a satisfactory balance between the need to remember the past and the urge to construct a hopeful future. Although in seemingly different ways in the two cases, the three women are envisioned by their creators as powerful nurturing entities for their communities that defy the established Western patriarchal rule and offer new possibilities for achieving some satisfying sense of self.

For Erdrich, Marie and Lulu personify liminal figures *par excellence* from an ethnic, social and cultural perspective, since from the beginning they seem to step out of the conventional representation of Native American women. Marie acknowledges her mixed origins and considers entering the convent on the grounds that "I don't have that much Indian blood" (Erdrich 1984: 40). Obviously the idea of going to the convent reflects Marie's cultural alienation from her tribal origins, since her main purpose is to turn into a Christian saint rejecting Chippewa traditions and beliefs. Nevertheless, the main motivation behind her desire to enter the convent does not lie in her Christian devotion, but in a sort of competition with another nun, Sister

Leopolda, who happens to be her actual mother though she never finds it out. Her mixed love-hatred feelings with respect to the nun encourage her to embark on a sadistic enterprise at her hands which results in the final abandonment of her religious aspirations and her seemingly reluctant return to the Chippewa community. Lulu also sets herself apart from the rest of the community thanks to what many regard as her "unruly" behavior. Lulu has always been known as a "flirt" (76), and the fact that she has eight boys, all looking completely different from one another, undoubtedly corroborates her unconventional stance. Already from these introductory remarks, Erdrich presents us with autonomous and self-assured women, very unlikely, and perhaps unwilling, to become leaders of their community, which they both seem to reject at first. Throughout the novel they must undergo a process of change and transformation that eventually leads to mutual understanding and finally coming to terms with themselves and their vital role in the community.

The same holds true of Avey, the widow protagonist of Marshall's text, who is radically alienated from her African American/Afro-Caribbean community living in an exclusive upper class neighborhood, and completely estranged from her origins and traditions. As with Erdrich's characters, Avey seems to be an unlikely griot. Nevertheless, she becomes involved in a transformative act, setting out on a journey that will cross oceans and lands. Not only in a strict geographical sense taking her from the United States to the Caribbean Islands, but more fully in a metaphorical way allowing her to meet and reconcile with all her older selves, her forlorn past and her broken dreams. But this reconciliation is not possible without taking into account a sustaining community, which plays a crucial role throughout the narration and also transforms itself by means of Avey's conciliation with herself.

The main factor that is going to affect these three women very deeply in compelling them to establish closer ties with the community is the crucial fact of family and motherhood. Marie and Lulu give birth to many children. As mentioned above, Lulu has eight sons; while Marie not only has many children, she also takes in others all the time allowing for a "surplus of babies" which overflows her house. Mothering is central to the creation and maintenance of the Native American community in both a literal and a symbolic sense. First, having children implies continuity, it repopulates the reservation, re-membering the community and disavowing past policies of extermination of the entire Native American population that went on for a significant number of years and that almost meant the literal death of the community.[1] But from a symbolic point of view, the mother is even more

---

[1] Paula Gunn Allen denounces the policy of what she calls "physical and cultural genocide" (1986: 3) in her groundbreaking work *The Sacred Hoop*, in which

important in Native American tradition because she symbolizes, as Wong
suggests, "not merely one's biological parent; she is all one's relations"
(1991: 177). Indeed, the mother represents the direct link to one's tribe and
therefore to one's tribal identity and heritage. As Wong continues, mothers
and families become the primary source of personal and collective identities
even reaching cosmic dimensions.[2]

On the contrary, Avey's motherhood does not seem to provide any positive ground for self-shaping and self-fashioning, despite the importance
attributed to motherhood in the African diaspora.[3] In these communities
mothering is also conceived as a responsibility for extended women-centered
networks, where it is seen as "a symbol of power" (Hill Collins 1987: 5). So
mothering is also essential for the well-being of the entire community, as it
usually brings along social status and political activism. Coming from an
African perspective on motherhood, the figure of the mother is invested with
the symbolic powers of creativity and continuity. In spite of this positive
vision of motherhood, Avey lives her own as a sort of traumatic nightmare,
or a heavy burden, so this is a clear instance of her estrangement from her
African American/Afro-Caribbean roots. She always connects it to negative
moments of her life, especially to her unsuccessful attempt at abortion when
she gets pregnant for the third time. In her case it is precisely the lack of
familial ties which pushes Avey to recover her lost sense of identity and
identification with her community. When she finally reencounters herself
and her community at the end of the novel, she also reestablishes the lost
links with her children. Then, she becomes a mother once more in a similar
way to Marie and Lulu, that is, a mother for both her own children and all
the future generations to come.

---

she accounts for it as a Western patriarchal response to Native American gynocratic
societies.
    [2] In her article "Adoptive Mothers and Thrown-Away Children in the novels of
Louise Erdrich" (1991), Hertha Wong explains the distinctions between theories of
mothering based on Western constructions of femininity and motherhood and Native
American definitions intrinsically linked to the concepts of tribal identity and
extended family. Therefore the figure of the mother acquires great significance in the
Native American tradition, since it constitutes the main basis for a sense of identity
that goes far beyond mother-child relationships.
    [3] As there are many significant studies devoted to the topic, I can only mention
a few. A groundbreaking work is "The Meaning of Motherhood in Black Culture and
Black Mother/Daughter Relationships" by Patricia Hill Collins (1987), where she
investigates the notion of an Afrocentric ideology of motherhood. Two other publications which analyze the issue in detail are *Claiming the Heritage* (1991) by Missy-
Dehn Kubitschek and *Women of Color* edited by Elisabeth Brown (1996).

III- *Love Medicine:* **Tricksters and Survivors**

Erdrich chooses to stress the liminal position that Marie and Lulu occupy in the novel by means of their identification with trickster figures. As John Slack observes, "many of the stories in *Love Medicine* are related *to* and are a relating *of* the once verbally preserved cycle of Chippewa folk tales of the trickster" (1993: 118; author's emphasis), and then he goes on to recount Marie's and Lulu's stories as two of the "twenty-three possible trickster narratives in *Love Medicine*" (120). What is interesting in Slack's analysis is the condition of survivor that is associated with the trickster figure, which basically fits both Marie's and Lulu's roles in the novel. They are born survivors, since they survive despite all odds. Marie shows this quality in her frightening encounter with Sister Leopolda, who tortures her. Later on, she also survives Nector's rape, transforming it into the beginning of their married life. As far as Lulu is concerned, she also survives different disasters throughout her life such as a fire that leaves her bald, an attempt at eviction and the rage of many women on the reservation who suspect her of ensnaring their husbands.

So Marie and Lulu embody the liminal figure of the trickster in its "dual role of culture-hero and fool" (Catt 1991: 74). On one hand, both characters are honored, especially later in life, for their powers and their important contributions to the community. For instance, at the end of the novel the Chippewas start recognizing Lulu's "knowledge as an old-time traditional" (268). But both of them also play the role of the fool by deliberately violating all taboos, either social or sexual ones. Socially speaking, both characters climb up the social ladder: Marie becomes part of one of the most important families, Kashpaw, by marrying Nector; whereas Lulu obtains all she desires by having children with different men on the reservation. From a sexual point of view, Lulu clearly stands out as the sublimation of sexual greed, "a kind of greed that is typical of the Trickster" (Catt 1991: 78). Although Marie is not so outspoken about sex, the fact that she mothers many children is also a sign of her greedy nature.

Besides, another factor to take into account in their position as border figures concerns their gender identification. Even though Marie and Lulu give prime importance to their role as mothers, their liminal gender status within the community is also signaled in the text by some markers like their continuous gender-crossing, almost exemplifying the prototype of the "berdache" in Native American tradition:

[A] person [...] who was anatomically normal but assumed the dress, occupations and behavior of the other sex to effect a change in their gender status. This

shift was not complete; rather, it was a movement toward a somewhat interme-
diate status that combined social attributes of males and females. (Callender and
Kochems, qted. in Barak 1996: 51)

As Barak has further noticed, berdaches and tricksters share their liminal
status in the community. This liminal position allows for the multiple talents
attributed to them, among which active sex lives, healing abilities and
exceptional skills to combine both traditional male and female activities.
Both Lulu and Marie fit easily into this pattern, since they are basically the
heads of their families, even in the periods when they are actually married,
and perform male and female roles. Thus their behavior questions any neat
separation of genders and promotes a new sexual hierarchy, where again
notions of fluidity, adaptability, and ambiguity are ascribed utmost importance.

The connection between berdaches and tricksters is also very illuminating in their search for a self-defined identity. Both Marie and Lulu seem to
engage in a process of discovery and recovery of their own selves through a
reconstruction of a troubled love relationship, a love triangle, as both are
actually in love with the same man: Nector, Marie's legal husband. This love
posits a serious threat to their friendship, since it seems to represent some
sort of psychological obstacle between them. Tharp accounts for it from a
gender point of view, commenting that "heterosexuality as it has been
influenced by Anglo culture takes over women's community and therefore
divides women and dissipates tribal strength" (1993: 175). In a sense, Tharp
is pointing at the loss of female bonding that takes place when patriarchal
gender is imposed upon Native American women. But the separation between Marie and Lulu can be also understood as a result of the internalization of certain damaging patterns springing from a Western legacy that
eroded the original organization of tribes in matriarchal units. As Allen
remarks, the destruction of the matriarchal tribes justifies an increasingly
tense atmosphere between sexes, bringing about such undesirable consequences as rape, battering, etc., and why not rivalry among women that
never existed before.[4]

Marie and Lulu are *de facto* separated for most of their lives because of
their love for the same man and it is not until Nector dies that the insurmountable impediment is overcome. Then there is some intimation of a
possible return to a traditional sense of matriarchy which has to break away
with centuries of Western domination. In fact, feelings of female bonding

---

[4] Allen considers that this negative aftermath of Western patriarchal imposition
is due, ironically, to the "proximity to the 'civilizing effects' of white Christians"
(1986: 50).

and solidarity emerge right away. These feelings are aptly pictured by Lulu's first description of Marie employing mother-child images: "She swayed down like a dim mountain, huge and blurred, the way a mother must look to her just born child" (236). Here Erdrich is clearly directing the reader's attention to the possibility of new beginnings, metaphorically encoded in the crucial figure of the mother with a child. Obviously, it signifies the vital importance of the mother principle for Native American women like Marie and Lulu who, through recovering their lost links to their real and symbolic mothers, can claim back their rightful position as matriarchs in their community.

Another idea connected to Marie and Lulu's growing friendship is the fact that it also implies a sort of symbolic rebirth, since their "vision" or hidden powers increase in relation to their closeness, achieving what Tharp denominates a "'near divine' power of vision" (1993: 177). The liminal powers of the trickster return with unprecedented strength to them, as Lulu confirms: "[T]he less I saw the more I had developed my senses" (229). If prior to their meeting the two women have been related to trickster abilities as mediators between two worlds, now they finally acquire the power to actually see beyond, in order to heal not only themselves, but also their community from the damaging effects of the Western colonization of the mind. As Tharp further notices, "female friendship enables the women [...] to recreate an empowering matrix that was frequently lost or disrupted through colonization or acculturation" (1993: 179). Envisioning a return to a lost gynocracy, the reconstruction of this "empowering matrix" is regarded by Marie and Lulu as a direct challenge to Western rules and hierarchies. Moreover, I would argue that, through the complementary relation that these two matriarchs establish, Erdrich successfully portrays a twofold mother figure which legitimates her critique of Western dominant ideology. Resisting this imposed code, Marie and Lulu learn together to use their inherent trickster power in order to become political activists in favor of the preservation of the Chippewa land and the Chippewa ways. Hence, they turn into true survivors, since for them to survive is to do so in community, and into useful tricksters that provide "a model for establishing identity in the presence of change" (Catt 1991: 75), ensuring the continuity of the tribe by saving all their children.

IV- *Praisesong for the Widow:* Ritualistic Spiritual Becoming

Here I intend to deal with the transformative process undergone by Avey in the novel, since the crucial notion of liminality is raised by Marshall's conscious redrawing of boundaries, at both a personal and a communal level. A fitting framework for the analysis of Avey's spiritual search is found in the so-called "rites of passage" as explained above. Applying their tripartite structure to Avey's transformation, one can identify the three main stages of any rite of passage: separation from her old self, transition to a new one and then incorporation to the community. These three steps are clearly signaled in the novel by means of temporal, but especially geographical markers, due to the fact that each of the stages roughly corresponds to one of the three main geographical sites in which the story develops: the ship, the island Grenada and Carriacou.[5] I further contend that throughout the story Avey personifies a liminal entity, as she inhabits the threshold between two worlds, Western and African American/Afro-Caribbean, never coming to terms with her liminal status until the very end. So Marshall's use of liminality is twofold: her protagonist needs to undergo a complete rite of passage in order to discover and accept her liminal role in the community.

On board the ship, Avey suffers from a series of nervous disorders that result in her need to abandon it swiftly. Her hasty leaving can be readily associated with a rite of separation, in which Avey realizes the greatness of her loss: she feels she has lost her sense of direction, her self, her past and even her name. On the ship she feels out of place, like a prisoner, or "a sneak thief" (10), who does not fit there, very much in consonance with liminal feelings of not belonging. Her predicament is born out of a lack of harmony with her internal self, as it is made clear in a mirror scene that appears very early in the novel. The fact that there is a mirror scene in each of the phases of Avey's rite of passage emphasizes the significance of her confrontation with the mirror. In this first instance, the pattern for the following scenes is basically set out. When Avey looks at herself in the mirror, she is unable to acknowledge herself. Actually, she contemplates herself as she would do with a stranger:

> And in the way she always did she would quickly note the stranger's clothes. The well-cut suit, coat or ensemble depending on the season. The carefully co-ordinated accessories. The muted colors. Everything in good taste and appropriate to her age. (48)

Thus Avey is portrayed as a woman who is very self-conscious, and even race conscious. But what really marks Avey in this first stage is her constant

---

[5] Although many critics have asserted the importance of the ritualistic structure in the novel (especially Christian 1983; Wilenz 1992: 107; Pettis 1990 and 1995), there has not been any detailed description following Van Gennep and Turner's model.

remembrance of a happier past. This past takes several forms but two figures are really crucial to discern Avey's confusion: her great aunt and her husband. Her great aunt Cuney appears to her in a dream asking her to perform a ritual that was ingrained in her mind as a child: a walk on Tatem Island, which would end with the retelling of the story of Ibo landing. Avey senses that with this story, "the old woman had entrusted her with a mission she couldn't even name yet had felt duty-bound to fulfill" (42). Her dilemma is that she does not comprehend the nature of this mission nor is she ready to fulfill it. She will need to undergo a complete rite of passage to reach that knowledge.

Along with her great aunt, she keeps remembering her past life with her husband. But she actually remembers two husbands, as it were, two different men with two different names: Jay and Jerome. On one hand, she recalls Jay, a man who made life very special in Halsey Street despite their poverty. And then Jerome, the man he became later with a set determination to succeed. But it is Halsey Street the necessary step for Avey to overcome the liminal phase. So she needs to return to her origins, to reclaim them. In this sense, a sentence that Jerome pronounces with reference to Halsey Street becomes very meaningful in the narration: "[Y]ou must want to wind up back where we started" (88). Obviously, Jerome implies his negative vision of their beginnings, especially of the fateful night in which he almost left her, back in the winter of '47. But Avey needs to recover that part of her life to feel whole, so she starts reclaiming Halsey Street as her nurturing origins, where love intermingled with music, dancing, poetry and sex. For her, "those were things which would have counted for little in the world's eye. To an outsider, some of them would even appear ridiculous, childish, *cullud* [...] They had nonetheless been of the utmost importance" (136). Avey realizes the highest significance of those rites for their lives since their loss meant the destruction of their love and their inner selves.

On this journey back to the past, an episode stands out: the annual boat ride up the Hudson River to Bear Mountain. She describes it as follows:

> [S]he would feel what seemed to be hundreds of slender threads streaming out from her navel and from the place where her heart was to enter those around her [...] While the impression lasted she would cease being herself [...] instead, for those moments, she became part of, indeed the center of, a huge wide confraternity. (190-1)

The idea of confraternity is associated to a sense of a nurturing and sustaining community of which Avey felt part back then, which ensured her a link with her past and ancestry. So she needs to return to that feeling of confraternity in order to work out her inner struggle. In one word, she must become a child again. The vision of Avey as a child is a constant trait in her characterization as a liminal figure. Quite appropriately, she is identified with a *tabula rasa*, because "her mind [...] had been emptied of the contents of the past thirty years" (151). So right now she is at the pure transitional or liminal state. A clear illustration can be detected in her name, which sounds "almost like someone else's name" (186). Her naming uncertainty reaches deeper levels, since she finds increasingly difficult to identify with it. Avey's unstable sense of identity is the resulting effect of her liminal status, being unable to find her true self, her true name and her true community. Thus, her personal quest becomes intimately related to the recovery of a sense of confraternity she had felt especially in Tatem, in the annual boat ride, and she will feel again in Carriacou.

The strong sense of correlation between Tatem and the island culture is what triggers off Avey's memories in the first place. Avey has finally come full circle, in the sense that she begins to accept the "hole" that the past thirty years had meant in her life. Once she has reached this step of the process, Avey is definitely ready to face the last stage or incorporation to the community. Two events in the novel signal the preparation for the reintegration: vomiting and washing while crossing over to Carriacou.[6] These acts can be interpreted as part of the process of cleansing the liminal self, in which she finally becomes "the child in the washtub again" (221). Achieving a complete regression to her childhood, she recalls a strong sense of female bonding which facilitates her return to the community. The last part of her rite of passage takes the form of a collective dance in Carriacou, where Avey feels finally free and alive.[7] For her, it is the ultimate step to go back to her great aunt and Tatem, as she describes it: "[S]he had finally after all these decades made it across" (248). But also to that sense of confraternity she used to feel on the annual boat ride. With this return to her source of sustenance, the community, she recovers her lost identity and her name—"Avey, short for Avatara" (251).

What is more important, she finally understands the mission her great aunt had entrusted her with and which has been puzzling her all those years: to continue the tradition that her great aunt had passed down to her by telling her future grandchildren and visitors about the Ibos and their pride in their community, as the only possible source and fountain for wholeness in life. In

---

[6] Some critics have brilliantly argued that Avey's journey to Carriacou can be defined as the "Middle Passage back" following Washington's term (1981: 324), by means of which Avey experiences "the horrors of Middle Passage" (Lindberg-Seyersted 1994: 44) in order to be able to reintegrate into her community.

[7] For a fuller account of the significance of this communal dance, see Denniston 1983; Collier 1984; and Gikandi 1996.

the closing pages of the novel Avey has rediscovered her rightful place in her community. As a mother figure, she is going to nurture future generations and preserve traditions in order to ensure the continuation of the community. Having completed a rite of passage to return to her community, Avey is finally able to come to terms with her liminal status. Recovering her place in the community assures her a liminal role in it as a mediator between two worlds—Afro-Caribbean and Western—and between the borders of her self and those of her community. By going back to the island, Avey demonstrates her willingness to perform the mission of spiritual mother following her aunt's steps. Hence, she acknowledges liminality "in a more, or less permanent way" (Aguirre 74, n. 13) as Erdrich's characters. Accepting their role as empowered liminal beings, the three characters are thus able to continue inhabiting the productive liminal territory of the border, and to offer an alternative worldview to the dominant order.

V- Conclusion

Both Marshall's and Erdrich's novels postulate that to feel restored to a "proper axis" means to acknowledge differences as enriching the personal and communal processes of coming to terms with the notion of a multiple self that can encompass diversity and still suggest unity. Moreover, their exploration of the issue of liminality highlights similar concerns in their redefinition of the notion of female identity as inhabiting a threshold zone which relates two worlds, two universes at the same time: Afro-Caribbean/Western in Marshall, and Chippewa/Western in Erdrich. Nevertheless, they present different perspectives about approaching liminality: Marshall prefers to portray Avey as a pure liminal entity undergoing an entire rite of passage, whereas Erdrich endows her female protagonists with trickster abilities. Despite their apparent differences, both novelists reach a similar conclusion: the only way to work out a satisfying sense of self for their female protagonists is to fulfill their mission as mother figures for their communities. Hence, to feel reconnected to the community and to be restored to their role of matriarchs proves crucial for the three protagonists' reconciliation with themselves and their manifold borders. So for these spiritual mother figures transcending the boundaries of their own selves to nurture others becomes a plausible way to inhabit liminality. Their liminal status enables them to overthrow Western hegemonic discourse and to make sense of the multiethnic reality these women face by means of a female-based alternative conception of motherhood.

A TWO-HEADED FREAK AND A BAD WIFE SEARCH FOR HOME: BORDER CROSSING IN *NISEI DAUGHTER* AND *THE MIXQUIAHUALA LETTERS*

JANET COOPER

Monica Sone's *Nisei Daughter* and Ana Castillo's *The Mixquiahuala Letters* both focus on a protagonist who has no home. Sone's Kazuko does not belong anywhere because, as she insists, 'I didn't see how I could be a Yankee and Japanese at the same time.' The source of Castillo's protagonist Teresa's two-headedness is also a clash of cultures; it hinges on the sexism of her Chicano culture rather than a racist national political agenda. Both authors employ border crossing to dramatize their characters' attempts to mitigate their feelings of cultural homelessness. In their search for home and identity, Kazuko engages in three different physical border crossings, while Teresa crosses the Mexican-American border three times. However, neither protagonist finds a home through border crossing. Both authors ultimately employ the device of border crossing to imply that more than a physical crossing of borders is necessary to fully negotiate a comfortable space that each protagonist can call home.

One significant aspect that Monica Sone's *Nisei Daughter* and Ana Castillo's *The Mixquiahuala Letters* share is a protagonist who has no home. Sone's protagonist Kazuko is without a home because of her concurrent socialization in American and Japanese cultures. She memorably describes this dilemma by insisting, "I didn't see how I could be a Yankee and Japanese at the same time. It was like being born with two heads. It sounded freakish and a lot of trouble" (Sone 1979: 19). This simile aptly captures Kazuko's belief that she cannot be both Japanese and American, and that her "Japanese face" distinguishes her from other Americans. Kazuko's homelessness intensifies on December 7, 1941 when Japan attacks Pearl Harbor and the United States declares war on Japan, and people of Japanese ancestry living on the west coast of the United States are forcibly relocated to internment camps by the authority of Executive Order 9066. Although Kazuko identifies herself as an

American, institutional and social prejudice make it impossible for her to enact this identity. She is thus left somewhere between these identities in a state of figurative homelessness. The source of Castillo's protagonist Teresa's homelessness is also a clash of cultures. However, Castillo places more emphasis on Teresa's resistance to the sexism of her Chicano culture than on a racist national political agenda as the cause of Teresa's lack of a home. Feeling suffocated by the cultural dictates of her Mexican immigrant family that she be a subservient and self-effacing wife and that "bad wives [are] bad people," Teresa desires another community that is less restrictive in its behavioral expectations and more nurturing of her spirit.

Sone and Castillo each employ border crossing as a means of dramatizing their characters' attempts to mitigate their feelings of cultural homelessness. Chicana lesbian feminist poet Gloria Anzaldúa examines border crossing as a metaphor for the reconciliation of internal identity conflict in her historical and sociological study *Borderlands/La Frontera*. Citing the competing influences of Indian, Spanish, and Anglo cultures on the identity construction of Mexican Americans, Anzaldúa offers the concept of *mestiza consciousness* as an ideal site in which a synthesis of competing cultures is achieved through the creation of a new culture, "a new story to explain the world and our participation in it, a new value system [...] that questions the definitions of light and dark and gives them new meanings" (1987: 81). Constructors of such a consciousness are thus both without a geographical homeland and the architects of a cultural homeland that enables them to metaphorically carry their "homes" on their backs like turtles (1987: 21).

Anzaldúa's work implies the potential of the ethnic American author to deploy external migration as a metaphor for an internal negotiation of multiple influences. However, the border crossings that Sone and Castillo deploy in their novels do not represent internal negotiations that aim to construct new cultural spaces. Instead of examining their beliefs, attitudes, and assumptions as they migrate across national and pseudo-national borders, as Anzaldúa suggests, both protagonists believe that they will find their identities ready-made by a change of location. While Kazuko crosses three different national or intranational borders in her journeys from Seattle to Japan, from Seattle to an internment camp, and from the camp to a Midwestern university, Teresa crosses the Mexican-American border three times. Both protagonists seem to believe that location determines identity and that they will change who they are by changing their surroundings. Consequently, Kazuko's and Teresa's border crossings do not result in the synthesis of the competing values of two or more cultures into a coherent whole as Anzaldúa proposes, but in the rejection of aspects of their identities that they deem unacceptable. For example, Kazuko rejects her Japanese ancestry after a trip to Japan, while Teresa declares that she is Mexican once she has set foot on the Mexican side of the Mexican-American border. Because their acts of border crossing are a denial rather than an interrogation of the ambivalence that leads them to states of cultural homelessness, neither protagonist negotiates a viable identity through border crossing. Kazuko's crossings serve only to highlight her abandonment of Japanese culture and her Japanese American community. Teresa, on the other hand, knows that her trips have failed to yield the identity she seeks, although she does not know why. Sone's and Castillo's employments of border crossing ultimately validate Anzaldúa's concept of *mestiza consciousness* by implying that more than a physical crossing of borders is necessary in order to find a home. Kazuko and Teresa must instead negotiate a synthesis of the competing cultures that threaten their coherent sense of self. Significantly, Castillo and Sone communicate an important message by revealing what prevents this complex negotiation of identity for both characters. While Castillo implies that socialization within Chicano communities prevents Chicanas from constructing coherent ethnic and gender identities outside of strictly imposed gender roles, Sone shows that the Japanese internment and the widely disseminated anti-Japanese sentiment that produced it made the construction of a truly Japanese American identity impossible.

Monica Sone's 1953 *Nisei Daughter* was the second narrative written by a Japanese American published by a mainstream American press after World War II. Although Sone has implied that her work is a piece of autobiography, critics such as Traise Yamamoto classify the work as an internment narrative.[1] Yamamoto defines internment narratives thematically and identifies the central tension in these narratives as the dueling impulses to bear witness and to fit into mainstream American culture (1999: 105). While many internment narratives do reveal this struggle, more critical work on the parameters of the internment narrative as a distinctive genre needs to be done. For the purposes of this examination, I define an internment narrative as a combination of autobiography and history. Although autobiography is sometimes construed as a form of history because it catalogues the life of an individual, it is usually not predominantly based on primary sources such as legislation, quantitative data, and the compilation of various personal reports like what James Olney calls "standard histories" are (1980: 15). Thus, autobiography is not conferred with the same authority as standard histories.[2] The nature of the

---

[1] Yamamoto makes this classification in her 1999 study of Japanese American women's fiction, *Masking Selves, Making Subjects*. Sone implied that her work was autobiography in a 1976 letter declining participation in an Asian American literature conference in Seattle, explaining that she did not see herself as a writer because *Nisei Daughter* was non-fiction (Sumida 1992: 207).

[2] Olney makes this argument in his 1980 study *Autobiography: Essays Theoretical and Critical*. Later in this work, he insists that the self constructed in an

combination of autobiography and history in the internment narrative is similar to a continuum and is reliant on the narrativist's goal and historical, social, and political context. For example, Sandra Taylor's 1993 *Jewel of the Desert* resembles a standard history by her reporting of quantitative data, reciting of the dates and language of discriminatory laws, and restating of the opinions of others on their camp experiences. By contrast, Jeanne Houston's 1973 *Farewell to Manzanar* is much more like an autobiography by its focus on her personal reaction to the internment. Sone's text is positioned between these two examples on the continuum of history and autobiography. However, all three narratives attempt to educate readers and prevent future injustices towards other groups. Thus, their primary audience is not Japanese Americans, who would be aware of this history, but middle and upper socioeconomically classed whites.

One of Sone's models for her work was the first internment narrative, Mine Okubo's 1946 *Citizen 13660*. In a later interview, Okubo asserted that it was very difficult to get her book published because shortly after World War II, "anything Japanese was still poison" (Gesensway and Roseman 1987: 74). By 1953 anti-Japanese sentiment was not as virulent as it had been during World War II, and Sone could more freely express her feelings on the internment. However, her work is not as openly critical of the American government as the deluge of internment narratives that came later, such as Estelle Ishigo's *Lone Heart Mountain* (1972), Jeanne (Wakatsuki) Houston's *Farewell to Manzanar* (1973), and Yoshiko Uchida's *Desert Exile* (1982). Thus, social and political context influence the tone, form, and content of the internment narrative.

One of the themes of Sone's narrative is Monica's ambivalence towards her dual Japanese and American ancestry, a subject that Okubo described as poisonous just years before Sone published her work. In order to explore this issue, Sone employs the metaphor of border crossing, thus masking a theme that her audience may have found either unimportant or offensive under the guise of a historical or autobiographical account. Kazuko's first act of border crossing occurs at an early age, shortly after she makes "the shocking discovery that I had Japanese blood. I was a Japanese" (Sone 1979: 3). These words reveal Kazuko's belief that identity is biologically determined. Her parents then take her to Japan to meet her relatives in the chapter aptly titled

---

autobiography is a fiction, so autobiography is a form of fiction (22). Although autobiographers are strategically selective regarding the portions of their lives that they represent and their works encourage a more empathic reaction in readers than standard histories, which may result in the reader constructing a self that is not strictly factual, it is significant that the reader assumes autobiographies to be true life stories.

"We Meet Real Japanese." As the title suggests, the content of the chapter does much to prove that Kazuko and her family are not "real" Japanese, but visitors in a strange land. Kazuko's actions reinforce this implication. She performs an alarming breach of etiquette when she attempts to walk on the sacred Shinkyo Bridge, an honor reserved for Emperors (94). She is also unfeminine enough to engage in physical altercations, with both her female cousin Yoshiye and the village boys who taunt her and her brother by calling them "American-jin" or American, thereby refusing to acknowledge their Japanese identity (97-8). These examples prove that Kazuko is a tourist in Japan. Because her experience in Japan is so frustrating, Kazuko is over-joyed when she sees the Seattle coastline on her return: "Suddenly as if a heavy weight had been lifted from my chest, I realized we were home again [...] We had explored the exotic island of the Japanese [...] but I had felt I was an alien among them" (107-8). This trip shows Kazuko that she is not a "real" Japanese. It establishes her home as America by revealing that she does not share the values and beliefs of her native Japanese relatives.

Kazuko comfortably inhabits her negatively defined American identity until the United States declares war on Japan on December 7, 1941. How-ever, long before Japan attacked Pearl Harbor, Japanese immigrants and their children experienced difficulty in being accepted as Americans. Although Japanese Americans were allowed to begin immigrating to the United States in 1868, first generation Japanese immigrants or Issei were not granted citizenship until 1952 (Weglyn 1976: 66). In the early twentieth century, several American state governments passed discriminatory legislation which was upheld and reinforced by key Supreme Court decisions, starting with the 1913 California Alien Land Act, which declared that "aliens ineligible for citizenship" could not own land.[3] In 1922, the United States Supreme Court upheld the 1870 revision to the 14th Amendment of the Constitution, which declared that only "white persons and persons of African descent" could be citizens. This decision determined that Japanese immigrants were ineligible for naturalization solely because of their race (Chan 1991: 95; Kitano and Daniels 1988: 13). Finally, the Immigration Act of 1924 blocked immigra-tion by aliens ineligible for citizenship (Daniels et al 1991: xv).

These discriminatory legal measures were complemented by strong anti-Japanese sentiments on the West Coast. By 1925, Japanese immigrants, although a mere one per cent of the California population, controlled fifty percent of commercial truck crops and were serious economic competition to white farmers (Weglyn 1976: 37). The responses to this competition were successful lobbying for anti-Japanese legislation and a deluge of "yellow

---

[3] In 1921, the Supreme Court upheld the constitutionality of the Alien Land Act in Terrace vs. Thompson.

peril" propaganda. For example, James Phelan was elected as a Senator of California in 1920 on a platform of keeping California white to confront the Yellow Menace (Nakano 1990: 31). Asians were characterized as dirty, immoral, unassimilable, and threatening to American values by politicians such as Phelan, newspaper articles such as those written by Hearst columnist Henry McLemore, and civics groups such as the Native Sons of the Golden West (Chan 1991: 127). As a result of such racism and propaganda, many Caucasians feared and opposed Japanese economic and cultural influence. Japanese immigrants and Japanese Americans were refused jobs and residences outside of their own ethnic enclaves, which created parallel communities such as Los Angeles' Little Tokyo. The separation of Japanese immigrants and their American children from mainstream American society reinforced beliefs that Japanese Americans were alien and could not fit in as Americans (Kitano and Daniels 1988: 74).

The attack on Pearl Harbor drove anti-Japanese sentiment in America to a feverish pitch. As a result, there was no public protest of President Roosevelt's Executive Order 9066, which was signed on February 19, 1942. This order approved the removal of "any persons whose presence was deemed prejudicial to the national defense" (qtd. in Nakano 1990: 131). Although it could have been enforced against Italian Americans and German Americans as well, only American citizens of Japanese ancestry were forced into internment camps under the authority of Executive Order 9066. As a result, 110,000 persons of Japanese ancestry—including over 70,000 Nisei or children of Japanese immigrants who were American citizens—were involuntarily relocated from the West Coast and confined into ten euphemistically-named "relocation centers" (Daniels et al 1991: xvi-xxi).

Kazuko's second act of border crossing thus highlights internal borders within the United States and is against her will. She literally moves from considering herself an American to having the identity of an enemy alien imposed on her. This identity contradicts the information the reader has learned throughout the text about the apple pie eating, self-proclaimed "roustabout Yankee" protagonist. Once she crosses the boundaries of the Minidoka internment camp in southeast Idaho, she is stripped of her civil rights as an American citizen. She and her fellow internees are imprisoned in a desert camp behind barbed wire guarded by armed soldiers. Internees were also stripped of individual distinctions such as property, social position and occupation. This ultimate personal outrage and devaluation is dramatized by the number that the government assigns Kazuko's family: "from then on, we were known as Family #10710" (166). Crossing the camp border is therefore both an imposition of identity and an erasure of it.

Kazuko's initial reaction to her internment is anger. She summarizes, "the wire fence was real. I no longer had the right to walk out of it. It was because I had Japanese ancestry. It was also because some people had little faith in the ideas and ideals of democracy. They said that after all these were but words and could not possibly insure loyalty. New laws and camps were surer devices" (178). She struggles against the identity imposed by the camp administration that is so unlike the self she has carefully constructed. However, Kazuko cannot maintain this anger and bitterness. She soon experiences a spiritual awakening in which she declares that, "the evacuation had been the biggest blow, but there was little to be gained in bitterness and cynicism because we felt that people had failed us. The time had come when it was more important to examine our own souls, to keep our faith in God and help to build that way of life which we so desired" (186). One way to interpret this passage is that rather than allow her spirit to be imprisoned, Kazuko struggles to create internal peace. But Sau-ling Wong argues that by making Kazuko's search for identity internal through spirituality rather than external by overtly protesting the injustice of the internment, Sone conveniently avoids a rigorous analysis of Kazuko's anger and ambivalence. As a result, Sone diminishes the impact of the internment—and thus the culpability of the United States government and people—on the psyches of Japanese immigrants and Japanese Americans (1993: 111). The most problematic ramification of Sone's spiritual conversion is that Japanese Americans can be content and fully functional adults regardless of discrimination if they call upon a higher power. When viewed in this light, Sone seems to be more concerned with not offending readers of the white Christian majority than with exploring the ramifications of the internment on Japanese American identity or the negotiation of identity in the context of enforced mobility and imposed identity. Rather than interrogate the effect this act of border crossing has on her national and ethnic identity, Kazuko chooses to ignore her painful ambivalence.

Kazuko leaves Camp Minidoka to embark on her third act of border crossing in the chapter "Eastward, Nisei." Although this chapter title signifies on the slogan of Manifest Destiny, the careful reader will find no subversion of the American master narrative that insists that Anglo-Saxon Americans possess a divine right to exploit non-whites such as Native Americans in the name of progress.[4] While the slogan of Manifest Destiny

---

[4] Dominant or master narratives depend on the dialectic between the dominant and subordinate group; they aim to inform the identity of the dominant group and justify and perpetuate the inferior status of those outside of it (Young 1990: 65). Unfortunately, they may also cause members of minority groups to internalize their own inferiority. One example of such a narrative is the Protestant Ethic, which establishes and reinforces the belief in the superiority of the traits of hard work and

designated the American West as a site of opportunity that the Caucasian Christian was entitled to, Sone suggests that success is only possible for publicly inoffensive Nisei east of the border created by Executive Order 9066. Thus, Kazuko's play on the master narrative of Manifest Destiny reinforces rather than challenges this narrative. In preparation for her move, Kazuko asserts that she has shed her past, which is symbolized by her well-intentioned white host family renaming her Monica. This name implies a separation between Kazuko and her Japanese American heritage by both its European derivation and the fact that it is her white host family, who meta-phorically replaces her parents, who bestows it upon her.

Less covert instances also confirm her distance from her Japanese American heritage. For example, before she leaves Minidoka, she is in-structed by a pamphlet issued to all internees who leave the camps by camp administration to avoid interactions with groups of Japanese Americans and to "behave as inconspicuously as possible so as not to offend the sensitive public eye." Rather than bristle at these racist instructions and exult in her newfound freedom, the newly named Monica resolves to "make myself scarce and invisible" (219). She wants to blend into mainstream America in order to re-inhabit the American identity she constructed before World War II. Thus, she does not protest racist treatment such as shop clerks compli-menting her on her English or being mistaken for the Chinese dancer Ming Toy. Her expectations for fair treatment are so slight that the implication in these instances that people of Asian decent are not Americans and are indistinguishable from one another does not upset her. Instead, she is "over-whelmed to find that we [the Nisei leaving the camps] were made welcome everywhere" (221). She thus works to blend in so that she may inhabit an American identity.

Her ability to fit in comes at the cost of her Japanese identity, which, ac-cording to Shirley Geok-lin Lim, is most overtly signified by her abandon-ment of her mother (1990: 298). After she visits her parents in Minidoka and boards the bus to return to the Midwest, Kazuko reveals her distance from her parents by insisting that they "look like wistful immigrants" from the bus window (237). By geography, occupation, culture, and language, Kazuko is literally and figuratively miles away from her parents by the end of the text. While she can move east to start a new life, they are contained in the intern-ment camps where the identity of numbered aliens is imposed on them. Kazuko's actions after her border crossing to an American society beyond the barbed wire of the camps exhibit her abandonment of Japanese culture and ties with other Japanese Americans in favor of an American identity.

---

perseverance in the dominant group while simultaneously fostering stereotypes of non-white ethnics as lazy and dirty, thus explaining their lack of material success.

Her third act of border crossing thus reveals her rejection of her Japanese American identity in favor of a non-ethnic American identity. Ironically, the internment and the instances of social and institutional racism that surrounded it revealed that people of Japanese descent were not allowed to inhabit such an identity. Indeed, as continued stereotyping of Japanese Americans as the model minority shows, phenotypic distinctions prevent people of Asian descent from blending into the famed melting pot of the American mainstream. Kazuko's border crossings are thus circular. Kazuko's trip to Japan in her childhood reveals her rejection of her Japanese heritage. Her internment forces her to confront the fact that the Americans who possess political and economic power refuse to grant her an American identity. However, she does not dwell on this reality; instead, she again rejects her Japanese heritage and Japanese American family and friends in order to embrace an unproblematized, unexamined American identity. Rather than deploy border crossing as a metaphor to reveal Kazuko's construction of a mestiza-like consciousness, Sone deploys the metaphor of border crossing in combination with dramatic irony to reveal Kazuko's struggle. Kazuko does not see any impediment to her embrace of an American identity, nor does she hold ill-will towards the government who interned her or the American people who stood by without protesting such an injustice. However, Sone's readers may not be as forgiving as Kazuko about the racist injustice of her internment. While Kazuko does not overtly rail against the discrimination she has experienced, instances of it are shown clearly enough for the average reader to both recognize and bristle against. Thus, through dramatic irony Sone could be protesting the injustice of the internment. Similarly, such readers may thus recognize the impediments of constructing an identity that is both Japanese and American. During the time Sone wrote her internment narrative, a construction of an identity that was both Japanese and American in values, culture, and consciousness was not possible. This is perhaps the largest injustice of the internment: the enforced eclipse of Japanese American identity.[5]

While Sone conveys her message through her subtle revision of the autobiography, in which she informs her reader of the history of the internment in a non-threatening manner, Castillo dismantles the genre of the epistolary novel. By doing so, Castillo implies that traditional forms are not an adequate means by which to reveal the specific experiences and ambivalence of the construction of an Ethnic American woman's identity. Castillo's work flies in the face of the conventions of the epistolary novel established in the

---

[5] More recent texts such as Cynthia Kadohata's *The Floating World* imply that it is no easier to construct an identity that is both Japanese and American a generation removed from the internment.

British tradition with Samuel Richardson's 1740 *Pamela* and in the American tradition with Hannah Webster Foster's 1797 *The Coquette*. Castillo's letters lack dates and traditional or consistent addresses and signatures. She often fluctuates between writing the letters in third and first person. Some of her letters are written in prose, while others are poems, and still others contain both forms. Finally, her protagonist Teresa does not end the novel as do traditional heroines in the epistolary tradition (e.g., either married or dead), but still seeking, exploring, and refusing prescribed modes of behavior (i.e., still a bad wife).

Castillo also signifies on the structure and style of Argentinean writer Julio Cortázar's 1963 epistolary novel *Rayuela* (translated into English as *Hopscotch*). Cortázar revised the epistolary novel genre by providing a table of instructions at the beginning of his text that provides a non-chronological sequence in which to read the second half of his work. Castillo moves beyond Cortázar by providing the reader with three different sequences in which to read the text: one for the conformist, one for the cynic, and one for the quixotic. As Erlinda Gonzales-Berry points out, the reader must examine himself or herself before deciding which option to take, or before simply reading the letters in the order they appear in the text (1993: 302). The various options may imply that Castillo is aiming her work toward a large and diverse readership. However, the subject matter and challenging stylistics of the novel, which may make it difficult for some readers who are unfamiliar with Chicano culture to comprehend, implies a smaller audience of non-white ethnic and white women. Her frequent critiques of male privilege also imply a reader who is sympathetic to a feminist consciousness.

Castillo uses border crossing to problematize Teresa's construction of a Mexican American female identity without the fear of offending her audience that so constricted Sone. Teresa openly confronts aspects of Mexican American and American culture that she finds distasteful. For example, Teresa reports with exasperation that a woman in her family is not allowed to go "gallivant[ing] around without her man" (Castillo 1992: 18). As her three trips to Mexico without a male escort demonstrate, Teresa refuses to be bound by this expectation. Teresa also protests against the expectation that a woman will marry, have children, and be limited to the home. However, she is no more effective than Kazuko in constructing a mestiza consciousness in which she can be both committed to a man and independent. Instead, Teresa travels to Mexico three times in the hopes of finding a ready-made identity. She is spurred to engage in her first act of border crossing by a desire to escape:

> It was apparent I was no longer prepared to face a mundane life of need and resentment, accept monogamous commitments and honor patriarchal traditions,

and wanted to be rid of the husband's guiding hand, holidays with families and in-laws, led by a contradicting God, society, road and street signs, and, most of all, my poverty. (28-9)

Teresa is weary of the social rules and restrictions that are dictated by her gender, class, and ethnicity. She believes that her trip to Mexico will free her from these restrictions by embracing a Mexican identity.

However, as Debra Castillo reveals in "Borderliners: Federico Campbell and Ana Castillo," much of what attracts Teresa to Mexico during this first trip, such as its ruins, scenic vistas and pre-Conquest villages, are exotic tourist attractions. Teresa's tourist orientation to Mexico is further highlighted by the fact that Mexico is Teresa's homeland only while she is in the United States (1994: 149). Like Kazuko, once Teresa leaves the United States, she realizes that she is more American than she previously thought. In Mexico she rejects patriarchal Mexican customs and beliefs that do not reflect her own, such as the need for a respectable woman to have a chaperone when spending time with a man to whom she is not related. Furthermore, in Mexico Teresa is rejected by the men and women she comes in contact with. The men, who consider her and her friend Alicia Malinches as sexually available but socially undesirable women because they travel alone, subject her to "ridicule, abuse, [and] disrespect" (65). Teresa and Alicia are repeatedly asked to leave the homes of hostesses who are offended by the hours they keep and their casual interactions with men. After one hostess asks them to leave, Teresa reflects, "I belonged no more in that family's home than anywhere else we had stayed during our trip [...] we had practiced the role of unwanted foreigners and continued it with disappointment when we realized we weren't among friends" (99).

It is significant that Teresa alludes to her foreign-ness as a role, implying that it is contrived rather than real. However, she treats many Mexican customs that pertain to women with disdain and is clearly rejected by Mexican men and women for her failure to respect these practices. Although she recognizes the virgin/whore dichotomy that the Mexicans she interacts with believe in because of analogous beliefs in Chicano culture, she does not seem to understand where these roles for women originate in Mexican history or where they derive their continued power in Mexican communities.[6] It therefore seems that Teresa is not contriving foreign-ness, but that

---

[6] The virgin figure was inspired by the Virgin appearing to the Indian Juan Diego in Tepeyac, Mexico in 1531. For an excellent analysis of the origin and trajectory of the belief in the Virgin of Guadalupe in Mexico, see Eric Wolf's 1958 "The Virgin of Guadalupe: A Mexican National Symbol," in *Journal of American Folklore* 71: 34-9. The whore or Malinche figure can be traced to Cortés' conquest of Mexico in 1521. Malinche was a Nahuatl Indian girl who was sold to Cortés, acted as his

Mexican culture is indeed not her own. Teresa's tourist orientation towards Mexico implies that her rejection of Mexican culture relies more on an attraction for the exotic, romanticized past of her ancestors than on an understanding of Mexican culture. Thus, Teresa's attempt to find herself through border crossing in this example is hindered by superficiality.

Teresa's second trip to Mexico is compelled by her divorce and the guilt and pain she experiences from her mother's reaction that "bad wives [are] bad people." While her first journey to Mexico was an escape from her failing marriage, her second trip is spurred by feelings of incompleteness. She believes that her trip to Mexico will provide the missing aspects of her identity. She muses, "there was a definite call to find a place to satisfy my yearning spirit [...] I searched for my home [...] I chose Mexico" (52). This statement is problematic because it implies Teresa's belief that she can choose her home. This contradicts the belief advanced by Michael Omi and Howard Winant in *Racial Formation in the United States* that one's home is determined by both descent and culture, which includes religion, language, customs, nationality, and political identification (1994: 15). Although Mexico was the home of Teresa's mother before she immigrated to the United States, Teresa was born in the United States, and many of her beliefs and behaviors are antithetical to those of many Mexicans. Teresa explains that her sense of identification with Mexico comes from her "Indian-marked face, fluent use of the language, [and] undeniable Spanish name" (25). This assertion equates identity with genetics, or descent, and language. Such an assertion is problematic, however; it ignores the aspect of identity that Werner Sollors describes as consent, or the cultural codes one chooses to organize his or her life around (1986: 6). For example, Teresa is bilingual. If language indicates consent, then both Mexico and America, or some mestiza-like site negotiated between the two, should be her home. In any case, Teresa cannot simply reject the influence of the United States as she attempts to negotiate her identity, because there is at least as much that ties her to the United States as there is that ties her to Mexico.

Unfortunately, this act of border crossing is no more successful than her first. Teresa allows herself to be deceived by a fairy tale dream of marriage to a rich Mexican entrepreneur who unceremoniously dumps her. She and Alicia are again rejected by hostesses and threatened by sexual violence from Mexican men. The two return to the United States, defeated and de-

---

interpreter, and ultimately bore him a son. She has thus been construed as both complicitous in the conquest and the origin of the mixture of Aztec and Spanish blood. For a more thorough investigation of Malinche's legacy, see Tey Diana Rebolledo and Eliana S. Rivero's 1993 essay, "Myths and Archetypes," in their anthology *Infinite Divisions* (Tucson: University of Arizona Press), pages 189-95.

pleted in spirit and weary in body. The metaphor Castillo deploys in which location confers identity repeatedly highlights Teresa's failure to find a viable identity through border crossing. It also implies why this quest is not a success, and inversely, where the successful negotiation of identity lies. Teresa's quest is unsuccessful because she naively desires to belong in a land where she does not believe in or even understand the basic values that govern behavior and relationships. For example, when she is cheated on by a lover who had insisted that he and Teresa hide their affair from his family, Teresa rages: "I'd had enough of the country where relationships were never clear and straightforward but a tangle of contradictions and hypocrisies" (60). This anger clearly marks her as an outsider to this culture; she does not understand the basic assumptions that inform the behavior of the man or his family, but rages at the superficial ramifications of these actions. For her to truly belong in Mexico she needs to understand rather than simply reject the beliefs, values, and behaviors of the culture. Teresa's string of failed relationships with men in Mexico provide an excellent starting point for the construction of her identity. If she could understand why these relationships fail, she would have a better understanding of Mexican and Mexican American culture. This knowledge would grant her the means to negotiate these cultures and her own space within them.

The third trip Teresa takes to Mexico, about which she vows, "I want to take on my ghosts, Alicia, confront them face to face," therefore seems like a fruitful beginning for her negotiation of identity (130). This potential, however, is again foiled by superficiality. She does not confront the physical ghost by talking with Sergio or exploring her memory of the failed relationship with this rich Mexican entrepreneur, but engages in a harmless drive by of his home. Additionally, she does not overtly explore the ghosts within herself, especially her ambivalent feelings towards men. For example, although her early marriage made her hate the "deathtrap" of a woman's role as wife, she was easily seduced by the physical, financial, and emotional security that a marriage to Sergio promised (118, 67). Teresa's letter does not explore her feelings toward Sergio or why she was so easily fooled, leaving the reader to doubt how successful she is in confronting her ghosts. By the end of the text, while Teresa still feels compelled to return to Mexico and is sure that it holds part of her identity, she understands neither why nor how she can use Mexico to construct a more complete identity. Castillo's use of the metaphor of border crossing does not reveal Teresa's successful negotiation of a border space in which she can be both a strong woman and have a fulfilling relationship with a man. The most successful aspect of this strategy is that it implies that more than mere physical movement is necessary for identity construction.

Indeed, both authors may make a more radical assertion by their representation of ethnic women protagonists who cannot construct a site in which they can be recognizably ethnic and American and independent yet loving women. For example, Sone ends her text by Monica's proclamation that "I don't resent my Japanese blood anymore [...] It's really nice to be born into two cultures, like getting a real bargain in life, two for the price of one [...] I used to feel like a two-headed monstrosity, but now I find that two heads are better than one" (236). However, the evidence that amasses by the end of the text contradicts her. Suffering acutely from the prejudice aimed toward those of Japanese ancestry after World War II, Kazuko assimilates to mainstream American culture and resolves to make herself as inconspicuous as possible to avoid further ill-treatment. The fact that Kazuko does not effectively negotiate a space in which she can combine her Japanese and American heritage by the end of her text is very much determined by her historical, social, and political context. Her context makes the construction of a Japanese American identity impossible. Sone's self-contradicting ending reinforces this fact, and implies that before such identities can be constructed, the histories of the internment must be told.

Sone's point is made subtly in order to avoid offending her middle-class, white, and Christian reader, many of whom still held animosity toward Japanese Americans. Castillo is less afraid of insulting her audience. She demonstrates this when her protagonist Teresa criticizes Mexican and Mexican American cultural practices such as the need for proper young women to travel with an escort. She also criticizes the Mexican and Mexican American belief that the ultimate goal of a woman is to become a wife and a mother. Castillo similarly criticizes African American and mainstream American values and cultural practices. Finally, she turns a mirror on Chicanas when she reveals Teresa's complicity in her own victimization by her internalization of the need to seek validation through sexual relationships with men. Like Sone, Castillo does not represent a protagonist who successfully constructs a mestiza consciousness in order to inform a strong Mexican American female identity. Castillo may mean to imply that a fully actualized identity, like a novel, is a fiction, and that all people are in the act of becoming. She also points to the strategy that will facilitate this becoming by the epistolary form of her work: the act of negotiating experience through writing. Another possible explanation for Teresa's ineffectiveness in achieving a viable identity is a more revolutionary call for change. Perhaps Castillo believes that the current socialization of Chicanas renders them unable to neutralize stereotypic expectations enough to dispel them. Although the ability to recognize and deconstruct prescribed behaviors is an important first step, Teresa still does not have the power to completely avoid them and to construct an identity free from their compulsions. In other words, bad wives cannot become viable, happy, and healthy people because of their internalization of the belief that they are bad wives.

Kazuko and Teresa unsuccessfully struggle with dual cultural heritages and imposed gender roles in an attempt to discover how two heads or multiple influences can be better than one. However, because their efforts focus on physical migrations or a desire to escape rather than internal negotiations, their efforts are ultimately unsuccessful. What Sone and Castillo do succeed at is representing the difficulties of constructing an identity that is both ethnic and American due to historical context and competing institutions of socialization. In addition, both authors point to possible future avenues of the successful negotiation of Ethnic American gendered identity: the reconstruction of history and the exploration of identity through writing. Both options provide sites in which the negotiation of competing influences through a *mestiza*-like consciousness can take place.

INSIDERS/OUTSIDERS: FINDING ONE'S SELF IN THE CULTURAL BORDERLANDS

CHRISSI HARRIS

This paper looks at the significance of living in what can be considered to be the cultural borderlands of Britain's London and of New Zealand, both areas of a long reaching history of colonialism that is perpetuated by degrees in the present day. The chosen works, by Andrea Levy, Hanif Kureishi and Alan Duff, highlight the variety of experiences that are produced by belonging to a cultural minority and the resulting uncertainty of cultural identity that ensues. The border is a figurative and permeable condition upon which the discovery of one's identity through concerted choices is reliant, for belonging to a marginalized community forces a movement across boundaries which can either include or exclude. The three works provide examples of the kind of circumstances which are at play in bringing about how one comes to be an insider, an outsider, or someone who is simply, and confusingly, caught in between.

In the introduction to George Lamming's autobiographical work *In the Castle of My Skin,* he writes about a fractured consciousness:

> [...] the totalitarian demands of White supremacy, in a British colony, the psychological injury inflicted by the sacred rule that all forms of social status would be determined by the degrees of skin complexion; the ambiguities among Blacks themselves about the credibility of their own spiritual history. (1991 [1983]: xxxvii).

Lamming refers here to a life in the Caribbean under British colonial rule. The social and political forces that have since been responsible for migrations, exiles and displacements have engendered new and revised definitions of people's identity which are based on a more fluid transition of cultures that merge and create changed identities. Borders of national identity are no longer as distinctive or clear cut, and border culture, where, in Anzaldúa's words, "people of different races occupy the same territory" (1987: Preface), signifies an all-encompassing concept of place, placement and displacement: it necessarily initiates an oppositional positioning of location with dislocation, memberment and dis-memberment; the inevitable creation of invisible boundaries within a given space and within a given society. The focus on race alone becomes secondary to a focus on identities which grow out of issues of class, gender and ethnicity when it comes to determining the real significance of border cultures. Anzaldúa's thesis refers to the particular circumstance of the Chicanos on the geographical border between North America and Mexico, but is, in its fundamental premise, applicable to the border encounters to be found world-wide, even when no visible geographical border is extant.

Wherever there is a co-existence of members of different ethnic origins, the literature which it produces permits an exploration of the many facets of existing in such borderlands; so we find these different aspects (class, gender, ethnicity) treated in works originating from areas as diverse as the Asian and West Indian communities in Britain, right across to literature from New Zealand which considers the Maori experience. In the works I examine, my intention is to highlight the way the writers' own experience, as authors who are either of mixed race descent or born into a different culture from that of their parents, informs the work and describes the effects that their heritage has upon them. We encounter three possible conditions the border experience can give rise to, which I classify as creating insiders, outsiders, or as those who are caught somewhere in-between. My selection provides an example of each of these three determining conditions: from Britain, Andrea Levy's novel *The Fruit of the Lemon* and Hanif Kureishi's *The Black Album* present the parallel yet contrasting nature of the West Indian and Asian experience in London; from New Zealand, Alan Duff's *Once Were Warriors* is an example of the long-term devastating effects of colonialism on the colonized, and the resulting struggle on the part of a marginalized people to reclaim their pride and dignity by discovering their spiritual history. The characters in all three works are developed by using a high degree of psychological penetration by the authors, whose particular circumstances and background manifestly permeate and suffuse the fiction.

The inclusion/exclusion experience is, in itself, nothing new. It has predominated in much of the well-known literature by Caribbean writers, Sam Selvon's *The Lonely Londoners* (1956), V.S. Naipaul's *A House for Mr Biswas* (1961) and George Lamming's *In the Castle of My Skin* (1970) for example, were all written while residing in Britain at a time when many West Indians were welcomed to the country only to find discrimination awaiting and conflict arising in cultural practices. What is perhaps alarming is that thirty and even forty years later the struggle for acceptance appears to continue. Outwardly, Britain no longer retains the "hostility" that Caryl

Phillips refers to in an interview with Frank Birbalsingh about the British attitude to black people and to West Indians in particular[1], but the unrest still permeates and penetrates the lives of those who make up its society. As Phillips points out, the present generation of West Indians, and the same can be applied to Asians, will have to go through the same problems "because of intractable British attitudes" (1986: 184). The novels portray people whose interiors are made to flounder in a sea of uncertainty, still trying to establish who they are and where they should stand. They have become post-modern subjects of one of the past's great fables; positioned by a colonialism that, in spite of being lodged and filed away as part of the grand narrative, is even today perpetuated and manipulated in oddly disconcerting ways.

Andrea Levy's latest novel *Fruit of the Lemon* is a fictional work that is loosely based on facts of her own family compiled together with details from families of others. Levy was born in England to Jamaican parents, and the novel sets about exploring the history of colonialism and Jamaica's links to a colonial past that extend to Cuba and Panama, New York and Scotland and link back into modern day Britain, building up a family tree that relates in part to her own personal background. Making the connections between Britain and Jamaica reveals how the two places are both going through a colonial process. The principal character is Faith Jackson, named after a goat her mother once kept and loved in Jamaica, and whose name bequeaths upon her an innocent belief and trust in all her endeavors. She is a bright young British Jamaican fashion and textiles graduate who is setting out on a career in television. She has grown up in Britain, has suffered the childhood taunts of being called a "darkie" and she typifies those children of immigrants who have grown up with "different cultural priorities and expectations from those of their parents," which Frank Birbalsingh in the introduction to his collection of literary contemplations on the frontier condition observes as representing a common problem (1996: x). True to her name, she is confident that her color will not hinder her progressive rise through the ranks of the BBC from the costume department to dresser and eventually through all the areas of television production. So it shocks her to find that obstacles, in the way of attitudes, are variously placed before her, and she is positively perplexed by the notion that promotion itself can be an act of racism, hopelessly failing to understand that Britain's policy for racial equality is little more than a contorted position. Suddenly she finds her desire for independence from her overbearing but loving family shattered, when her parents announce their

---

[1] See Caryl Phillips in an Interview with Frank Birbalsingh, 15 Oct. 1986, "Caryl Phillips: The legacy of Othello, Part (1)" (Birbalsingh 1996: 183-190).

intention to retire back to Jamaica[2] now that she is assumed to be making her own way in the world. Faith's situation here is an inversion of the alienation of culture and severing of ties normally encountered in post-colonial writing. Whereas writers such as those previously referred to (Selvon, Naipaul, Lamming) leave the Caribbean for the imperialist motherland of Britain or, more recently, like Jamaica Kincaid to the US, Levy posits the dialectic equivalent consternation of the island culture being that which robs the character of her own familiar culture. Further inverted parallels can be found to Kincaid's work in the sense of the mother-daughter relationship, i.e. the Caribbean-England relationship. Here the maternal matrix is a displaced center; the mother has essentially provided concocted origins, only to suddenly one day pronounce that Faith is to be abandoned in this duplicitous and faithless environment while the mother recovers her own. That this news provokes in Faith a total withdrawal from all activity moves the parents to suggest that Faith pay a holiday visit to Jamaica, to visit her auntie, finally begging her to go on the grounds that "everyone should know where they come from" (1999:162).

Having spent her whole life in Britain up to this point, her arrival in Kingston presents her with a feeling of total "culture shock." Faith is the non-immigration border subject whose roots have lost their hold but have still retained an element of attachment and are waiting to be nourished and revived. When she arrives in Jamaica and finds herself in the airport lounge "packed with black faces" everywhere she turns (168), she feels "out of place—everything was a little familiar but not quite. Like a dream" (169). The significance of this as an alarming, disorienting experience is made the more powerful for coming shortly after an episode where Faith has witnessed a racist attack on a bookshop by so-called members of the National Front in Islington, London. That the woman who ran the shop is described merely as "a black woman" (150), of undefined race, is indicative of Faith's obsession and assimilation with being visibly different in the only society she has known since birth, having grown up accustomed to being referred to as a "coon" or a nig-nog" (85) by the kind of people who hold the same consideration for "women drivers" (86). The aftermath of the experience finds her retreating to her bed, enclosing herself in the dark, but not so dark that she couldn't see herself reflected in the mirror. What she sees is "a black

---

[2] A common situation in reality for immigrants in Britain who reach a point in their lives where they want to go back to the land of their roots, according to Caryl Phillips in an interview with Frank Birbalsingh recorded in Toronto on 15 October 1986 (Birbalsingh 1996: 183-190). Phillips remarks that the romantic vision of discovering the Caribbean as somebody who has grown up in North America or Britain usually ends in disappointment.

girl lying in a bed," and the measures she takes to disclaim this image—
covering over one mirror with a towel and the other with a tee-shirt—delude
her into thinking she can solve her deep-rooted anxiety of not wanting "to be
black any more." "Voilá! I was no longer black" (160) she jubilantly ex-
claims.

Faith's meeting with her family in Jamaica is initially one of an over-
obsessively close observation to details of their physical appearance. When
she meets Gloria, her cousin Vincent's very dark blue-black-skinned wife,
she cannot avoid being reminded of the Black and White Minstrels. Her
recollection of this as a feature of her British upbringing: "white people
made up to look black—caricatured with thick dark make-up and woolly
hair—that I used to watch on Saturday night television, singing and dancing
and entertaining the British. I was ashamed of the thought and lowered my
eyes away from her" (206), initiates a personal awareness of the attitudes
that she has unconsciously adopted through her country of birth. Her earlier
efforts to suppress and even eliminate that same image which echoes her
own reflection in the mirror complicates her acceptance of recognizing it as
her own; her shame comes from her realization that she has attempted to
disclaim it all together. The inner conflict is evidence of the intricate source
of competing demands derived from and informed by the London city
dweller and her ancestral history. This of course takes us back to Fanon's
theory of psychic trauma which results, as Loomba reminds us, when realization dawns that the subject "can never attain the whiteness he has been
taught to desire, or shed the blackness he has learnt to devalue" (1998:176).
Through conversations with her aunt Coral, Faith's journey into her family
background leads her into the discovery that she is not the only one who has
harbored uncomfortable thoughts on the significance of one's color, indeed
she finds in Jamaica that pigmentocracy[3] was rife throughout the Jamaica of
her ancestors; to be of the right color was of prime importance to one's
standing in society. Faith's paternal grandparents themselves were purport-
edly descendants of a combination of Scottish and French/Arawak/Indian
who enjoyed mixing with the "high society [...] light skin and white people"
(284). Consequently, her father's acquaintance with Mildred, her "too dark"
mother, necessitated an investigation into whether she was "a quadroon, an
octoroon, a half-breed or just black" (288), and the revealing evidence that
she had "too much African in her blood" resulted in a marriage without
consent and a flight to England from disowning parents. The pinnacle of the
color pyramid was, of course, to be white—the whiter one was the more
middle class one was assumed to be, regardless of financial standing, except

---

[3] The term "pigmentocracy" is one used by Andrea Levy in an interview with
Harriet Gilbert on "Meridian Books," BBC World Service, March 18th 1999.

however, when one was discovered to be ascended from a slave background, like Faith's mother's cousin Nelson who was turned down from the best private Catholic Church school in Jamaica "even though he had the money and the complexion" (267) for being unfortunately considered to be of the wrong class. Faith learns bit by bit about all the members of her extended family, and is gradually able to fulfill her quest to find pride in her blackness through an understanding of her heritage. Not only does she establish the historical connections between the Caribbean and British societies, but Levy also reveals the contemporary reverberations that a British born Jamaican can experience and feel, so allowing a construction of the bridge that helps cross the great divide. The sense of pride discovered in knowing her background gives Faith more confidence to return to Britain's racial atmosphere with a dignity and self respect, no longer embarrassed but exalted to think that her mum and dad had come to England on a banana boat. The novel both commences and ends with this reference which acts as a metaphor for the history of the West-Indian slaves and the (mis)conceptions that the term "banana boat" conjure up. Faith's school history lessons served as little more than a stimulus for self-rejection and it is only when she experiences first-hand who her forebears are that she can take on and accept her identity.

Levy reveals the importance attached to the different degrees of whiteness produced by interracial relations in colonized Jamaica, for they provided the means to climb the social ladder and reach a degree of superiority. In the post-colonial period, Homi Bhabha suggests that these hybrid and differential identities have become performative, negotiating spaces that are continually "opening out, remaking the boundaries, exposing the limits of any claim to a singular or autonomous sign of difference—be it class, gender or race." (Bhabha 1994: 219). Difference, he goes on to say, "is neither One nor the Other, but something else besides, in-between," itself a potential threat to the neat dialectic classification; what emerges from the melting pot pushes the boundaries over the abyss into confusion and defies denominational authority, resulting in a marginalization that is no longer clearly demarcated.

The British Asian writer Hanif Kureishi, son of a Pakistani father and British mother, creates characters which illuminate the social and psychological effects of growing up in a hybrid society. As Stuart Hall posits, Kureishi's films *My Beautiful Launderette* and *Sammy and Rosie Get Laid*, which deal with the upwardly mobile Pakistani immigrant, demonstrate that "the question of the black subject cannot be represented without reference to the dimensions of class, gender, sexuality and ethnicity" (1995:226). Kureishi has therefore consistently explored the burden of marginalization in his writings, notably in his first novel *The Buddha of Suburbia* (1990) which above all examined the racial tensions in suburban Britain. In his second

work of fiction which is examined here, *The Black Album* (1995), the principal character is Shahid Hasan, a young British Asian who has grown up in
the provinces and moved to London. He confesses that he feels paranoid
about who he is: "I began to be scared of going into certain places. I didn't
know what they were thinking. I was convinced they were full of sneering
and disgust and hatred. And if they were pleasant, I imagined they were
hypocrites. I became paranoid. I couldn't go out. I knew I was confused [...]
I didn't know what to do" (1995: 10). In Shahid, Hanif Kureishi has created
a character who is described by the book's jacket as one who finds himself
caught between liberalism and fundamentalism. The character becomes
Bhabha's universalized hybrid, that is to say he is a subject that contains all
of the diverse modalities that Ella Shohat suggests need discriminating
between: "forced assimilation, internalized self-rejection, political co-
optation, social conformism, cultural mimicry and creative transcendence"
(1993:110). Right from the start of the novel, the reader is drawn into the
psyche of the character who, as a Pakistani subjected to having been "kicked
around and chased a lot" (1995:10), has developed a fearsome desire to
become a racist in order to become like his fellow citizens, hating "all
foreign bastards" so that he can "swagger around pissing on others for being
inferior"(11), while at the same time recognizing that in such thoughts lies
the potential for turning into a monster. Such complex psychological emotions are not uncommon in places like London where society is formed of a
plethora of cultures, all jostling with each other and attempting to preserve
individual cultural identity yet at the same time integrate sufficiently to be
able to mingle unnoticed and indistinguishable from the masses and the
majority in order to avoid being singled out for attack. It is the perfect site of
the borderland, where multiple identities "collide and/or renegotiate" the
space they cohabit (Boyce Davies, 1994: 66). Collision or renegotiations
depend on the individual's degree of adaptation, together with strength of
character for maintaining a personal identity. Those who stand firm may
clash, while those who bend risk losing sight of their inner self. To align
with the majority and fit into the mould of society does not always bring
about peace of mind either, as Shahid discovers to his consternation. His
contempt for all other blacks becomes a contorted Manichean position which
results from the general air of malaise in his society as regards role and
identity.

Although the novel is picaresque and with a plot that borders on farce—
the protection of and devotion for an aubergine which is believed to bear an
inscription of holy words from God in its interior flesh and which has
therefore been declared a holy symbol worthy of pilgrimage is symptomatic
of the extremes to which Riaz, the angry Muslim fundamentalist leader of
the "militant Muhammadans" (1995:190), feels he needs to go in order to

generate faith and loyalty in his people—it is littered with acute observations and emotions of the Asian English experience. Kureishi is quoted as saying in 1993: "I write about riots and street life and so on because I feel that writing is a way of forming a discussion about the sort of society we live in."[4] This need for discussion is still present two years later, and in *The Black Album* London is faithfully depicted as a multi-cultural melting pot, where an elderly white couple are quite capable of selling refreshments from their front garden to the crowds of believers queuing to see the sacred miracle; their hand-painted sign advertises the word "hallal" on it, which is interpreted by Shahid as supposing the guarantee of "some kind of immunity" (173). When David Dabydeen optimistically says "there are no identities which cannot be transferred or modified" (1996:180), identities can be read here as "borders" which are equally permeable and shifting. Dabydeen faithfully upholds the premise that the negative aspects of colonial fragmentation are slowly but surely transforming into a more positively regarded multiplicity, but the deeply ingrained wounds do not heal easily, and multiplicity has taken on board the psychological effects of uncertainty that go with the desire and the will to integrate fully and disregard difference against the odds, creating in the act a trope of anarchy and confusion. As Dabydeen goes on to say, "[a]ll this revelling and confusion can, at one level, mean an enormous loss of the self or self-confidence" (180). Shahid is emotionally trapped between being in love with a white liberal college lecturer and having a sense of obligation to his fellow Muslims fighting for their cause, not entirely convinced that either situation is really helping him to find the answers to his deep uncertainties. He had been taught little about religion by his parents, a fact which frequently gives him cause for anxiety and a sense of failure: for example when he finds himself in the midst of his Muslim friends he is aware of a spirituality "taking place" in their faces (1995: 96), yet he struggles to fight off the desire and yearning he gets for the darkness of a pub and a pint—mundane perhaps but further proof of the constant dilemma within him. A visit to the mosque brings him closer to understanding a little about belief being an act of joining, but this same visit also makes him reflect on how the world was "breaking up into political and religious tribes," how London was partitioned into divided races: those invisible borders between blacks, Pakistanis, Bengalis or whites, with little mixing and plenty of implicit hostility (133-4), which he concludes can only lead to different kinds of civil war and which gives him a more pressing anxiety over which group he really belonged to.

The character's British upbringing and ethnic siting by virtue of his color and his ancestry are definitely out of joint. Stuart Hall offers a definition of

---

[4] "Passnotes—Hanif Kureishi," *The Guardian*, November 3, 1993, N° 276

ethnicity as that which "acknowledges the place of history, language and culture in the construction of subjectivity and identity" (1989: 226). In a society such as the one depicted by Kureishi, of London in the nineties, ethnicity cannot be clearly demarcated and, for obvious reasons, Hall suggests that the term, once grounded in difference, must be dis-articulated from this position in the discourse of "multiculturalism" or, as Loomba refers to it, of the "cut and mix" processes that have produced the new black ethnicities in contemporary Britain (1998:176). The effects of this reinforce Dabydeen's explanation for loss of self-confidence, while Shahid's divided loyalties and the dubiety of his own beliefs, at a stage of his life where he is testing all the waters to find the most buoyant, bring him at times to a state of self-hate. Neither mimicry, assimilation, nor rebellion bring relief to his fluctuating condition; he is neither an insider nor an outsider, but lost somewhere in-between, condemned to an identity of chaotic disarray. The novel concludes on this note, with Shahid pondering on the fact that "there was no fixed self; surely our several selves melted and mutated daily? There had to be innumerable ways of being in the world" (1995: 274), so taking the decision to "spread himself out." An apposite description of his experience can be found in Antonio Benítez-Rojo's discerning appraisal of postmodernity:

> Within postmodernity there cannot be any single truth, but instead there are many practical and momentary ones, truths without beginning or ends, local truths, displaced truths, provisional and peremptory truths of a pragmatic nature that barely make up a fugitive archipelago of regular rhythms in the midst of entropy's turbulence and noise. (1996: 151)

The novel depicts the difficult appropriation of the shifting meaning of ethnicity in post-modern Britain. Hall's representation of a more diverse conception of ethnicity as one that comes from the margins, or periphery, and which is not contained by its position (1989: 227) is displayed clearly here as one that is still in the making. Shahid, this postmodern subject, is forced to try out all possible identities, following his curiosity, and Kureishi thereby reinforces the temporality of being that a multicultural post-modern existence is bringing about, the partial-existence of being permanently trapped in this land of many borders.

While self-hate can develop from a lack of conviction or assurance, such as that endured by Shahid, it can also result from a loss of self-pride, and is a condition easily suffered by minority groups wherever they have been stripped of their heritage under colonial rule. In New Zealand, the Maori people have to a great extent become regarded as second-class citizens, a status which has generated an irreconcilable malcontent as though the centripetal force of circumstances has trapped them into a never-ending vicious circle from where there is little hope of escape. The Maori, Beth Heke, in Alan Duff's novel *Once Were Warriors* is introduced to the reader as she spies on her people, with her thoughts of them as "the going-nowhere nobodies who populate this state-owned, half of us state-fed, slum," although she feels like a traitor for her own deprecatory thoughts of them as their "own worst enemies" (1990: 14). The novel's Maori community all live in a mile-long government housing development where, when it rained, the gutters and drains would block up with rubbish, with their "own discarded filth" (1990: 14). The homes are described as "two storey, side-by-side misery boxes" (7) and are sited right in front of the big house owned by the white, Pakeha, Mr Trambert, secure in its surround of "rolling green pasture-land" (1990: 7). They are thus contained behind both physical and political borders. The big house becomes a reference for the colonial power and dominance, and for accentuating the marginality and existence on the border, not unlike Lamming's big house on the hill on the small Caribbean island of Barbados amidst the trees where the landlords live in *In The Castle of My Skin* (1991: 25). The physical separation in both accounts is clearly established, while the boundary of landscape and geography functions as a metaphor for the divisions and collisions of class, race and, by extrapolation, opportunity. In *Once Were Warriors* home itself is problematized—not a safe or comfortable space for the mother whose husband Jake "the Muss" Heke equates the glorified Maori warrior culture of the past with his own muscular strength and macho brutality in the only way he knows how—with violence—and who sees the kids on the Pine Block estate with no future other than to be the violent adults of the future themselves. Jake's attitude is intensely colored by his own personal heritage of slavery, which he tries unconsciously to redress by a tendency to seek power over others through aggression and physical might. We cannot help but be reminded of the reverberations here of the colonizing powers who once exerted their own pressures on the existing communities of the land. The Maori revolts of the 19th century in response to losing their land to the colonizers resulted in concessions being made, but concessions do not equal land-owning rights, and the Maoris have ever since borne resentment. Once again, rather like Kureishi's character Shahid, the reactions to a feeling of displacement and dislocation within society are made manifest in violent emotions.

The turning point for Beth's desolate perspective on life comes with tragedy, the tragedy of her teenage daughter Grace's suicide; itself a powerful statement of frustration and impotence of a young girl who feels trapped within a community of no-hopers. Grace chooses to hang herself from the branches of the Trambert's tree from where she would watch the Pakeha family having dinner; to her "like they were a film, a TV show; the eatings and goings-on of the other species" (1990: 116). It is interesting to note once again the concurrence here with Lamming's novel: the estate in Barbados, where the villagers would steal through the woods to watch secretly how "tea was served in the big house" (Lamming 1991: 25); and where the ones who eventually hold responsible positions adopt the image of the "low-down nigger people" as the enemy and the ones who let you down (26-27), as though they automatically and instinctively accept that the whites' social mores were, after all, superior. That is matched in Duff's novel by the successful Maori welfare officer who reprimands the Maoris for not attending to their lawful responsibilities (Duff 1990: 30-31). Even the style of writing has a certain parallel—the narrative modes that intertwine and overlap—which Duff employs by juxtaposing a highly perceptive and eloquent omniscient narrator with the vernacular, psycho-realist train-of-thought narration coming right from within the character's experience, as shown by the following extract from *Once Were Warriors* taken from just before Grace hangs herself, while she is watching the Tramberts enjoy their dinner party:

> Their accents, their demeanours, their soberness, their every communication so so different.
> [...] A girl thinking: What if you people came over to our world, joined our party? What'd happen? Imagining the novelty of havin not just Pakehas in their midst but posh ones at that; [...] Eyin em up, the men, for trouble to pick. The women for what they—Oh can't even think about it. Then sure as eggs (fried eggs) someone'd walk up to one ofem and ask: The fuck're you lookin at, cunt? Then, Tramberts and friends, they'll punch the shit out of you [...] For they know it is the only taste of victory they get from life. (1990: 118)

Again, rather like Lamming's essential message in *In the Castle of My Skin* that the West Indians go back to before the colonizers changed their lives, Duff emphasizes that the Maoris have a history, yet lack a history by including two chapters entitled: "Those who have history." The first presses home the fact that white history, albeit shorter than the indigenous history in New Zealand, had become infinitely more powerful. In a scene where Grace's little brother Boogie has to appear before the judge for truancy, Grace is overawed by the atmosphere in the courthouse; the huge paintings of all the past magistrates and especially the magistrate, "(God)" (33), who has the power to decide her brother's fate (he is made a ward of court), represent for her the ones with "History. (He's got history, Grace and Boogie Heke, and you ain't)" (35). The second marks the beginning of the turning point for Beth. Grace's funeral is entirely taken over by the Maori elders, and the three day ritual, held in a language "a mother did not understand" (120) introduces her to the people and customs of her rightful heritage. She discovers, for example, that the traditional carved totem constitutes a "bookless society's equivalent of several volumes"[5] (121), and she is gradually helped to understand the importance of remembering their Maori past in order to have a future, finally learning of the great Maori ancestors, the poets, the warriors and the culture that was their own. Once again, David Dabydeen's observations are relevant here when he says: "You cannot be cultural unless you have a sense of boundaries. [...] the absence of boundaries can be very dangerous. It can mean [...] that you have no roots or attachment or commitment" (1990: 181). A sense of commitment and an understanding of those boundaries is what grows from Beth's discovery of her real culture, and it becomes the driving force to set about improving the conditions for her neighborhood and her people by involving them too in this learning process. She comes to realize that there is much more to be gained from wholeheartedly embracing what it means to be a Maori than of despairing their ways and giving them up for lost amidst the overbearing colonial panorama. I would venture to claim that Duff's attempt in this novel to expose the effects and consequences of colonial rule in New Zealand is resoundingly similar to what Lamming intended to reveal about the Caribbean in *In The Castle of My Skin* quoted at the beginning of this article.

Alan Duff is, like Kureishi, the son of a mixed-race marriage—his scientist father a Pakeha New Zealander and his mother a Maori—and his life experience is not unlike that described in *Once Were Warriors*: his parents split up when he was ten and he was raised by Maori relatives in Rotorua, who struggled to contain his wild nature which resulted in expulsion not only from school, but later also from Social Welfare homes and even from Borstal. This background has enabled him to succeed in getting inside the Maori psyche and displaying their predicament with a force that highlights the importance of being aware of the significance of cultural borders. His overriding message is one that heavily and openly rejects the attitude of "you owe us" as being the most profitable way forward. The novel is an example of what it means to be on the "outside," and shows that assimilation is not the only way; that to ignore the need for choosing on which side of the "border" you wish to be is to be either at odds with one's inner self or to deny that self a wholeness of being. Unlike Kureishi's premise that the boundaries are fluid and permeable, or Levy's perspective that although on the "inside" there is still an intangible part somehow missing, Duff's premise

---

[5] The Maori communities are renowned for their lack of books and their disadvantaged children often attend the poorest of the nation's primary schools. Alan Duff is credited with founding a 'flourishing' campaign: "Books in homes" in 1995 which now reaches "56,000 children in low-income schools, with each child getting five books a year [...] ownership being the key to the scheme's success" (McLoughlin 1999: 55).

is that differences do matter and are to be embraced wholeheartedly and built on.

There is one common factor in these three works that is their depiction of post-colonial societies where the metaphor of Prospero and Caliban is made manifest in its several guises. As Linda Hutcheon explains: "a sense of duality was the mark of the colonial"; doubleness and difference occur within colonialism by its "paradoxical move to enforce cultural sameness" (1995: 134). In other words, the post-colonial subject's legacy is to be torn between the two worlds, two cultures, both jostling for dominance, demanding the subject to straddle the border and suffer the dilemma of choosing. The three novels, coming from both hemispheres of the globe, display the fact that cultural boundaries exist and are manifest in a wide variety of contexts and geographical locations, and produce a contingent range of pressures and responses for multicultural societies to negotiate, both at the individual and the collective level.

BIBLIOGRAPHY

Aguirre, M., R. Quance, P. Sutton 2000. *Margins and Thresholds. An Enquiry into the Concept of Liminality in Text Studies. Studies in Liminality and Literature 1.* Madrid: The Gateway Press.

Allen, Paula Gunn 1996. "The Sacred Hoop: A Contemporary Perspective." In Glotfelty & Fromm, eds., 241-263.

Allen, Paula Gunn 1986. *The Sacred Hoop.* Boston: Beacon Press.

Altman, I. 1975. *The Environment and Social Behavior: Privacy, Personal Space, Territory, and Crowding.* Monterey, California: Brooks/Cole Publishing Co.

Altman, Irwin and Martin M. Chemers 1984. *Culture and Environment.* Cambridge: Cambridge University Press.

Anaya, Rudolfo A. 1972. *Bless Me, Última.* Berkeley: Tonatiuh-Quinto Sol International.

_____ 1976. *Heart of Aztlán.* Albuquerque: University of New Mexico Press.

_____ 1977. "The Writer's Landscape: Epiphany in Landscape." *Latin American Literary Review* 5.10: 98-102.

_____ 1984. "The Silence of the Llano: Notes from the Author." *MELUS* 2.4: 47-57.

_____ 1988. *Heart of Aztlán.* Albuquerque: University of New Mexico Press.

_____ 1988. *Tortuga.* Albuquerque: University of New Mexico Press.

_____ 1992. *Alburquerque.* New York: Warner Books.

_____ 1995. *Zia Summer.* New York: Time Warner.

_____ 1996. *Río Grande Fall.* New York: Time Warner.

_____ 1999. *Shaman Winter.* New York: Time Warner.

Anzaldúa, Gloria 1987. *Borderlands/La Frontera.* San Francisco: Aunt Lute.

_____ 1999. "Chicana Artists: Exploring Nepantla, el Lugar de la Frontera." In Antonia Darder and Rodolfo D. Torres, eds. *The Latino Studies Reader: Culture, Economy and Society.* London: Blackwell.

Aparicio, Frances R. 1994. "On Subversive Signifiers: US Latina/o writers tropicalize English." *American Literature* 66: 795-801.

Aries, Elizabeth and Fern Johnson 1983. "Close friendship in adulthood.

Conversational content between same-sex friends." *Sex Roles* 9.12: 183-196.

Arteaga, Alfred 1991. *Cantos*. San José: Chusma House Publications.

_____ 1997. *Chicano Poetics*. Cambridge: Cambridge University Press.

Ashcroft, B. G. Griffiths, & H. Tiffin, eds. 1995. *The Post-Colonial Studies Reader*. Routledge, London.

Ayres, Joe 1980. "Relationship Stages and Sex as Factors in Topic Dwell Time." *Western Journal of Speech Communication* 44: 253-60.

Baker, Houston 1984. *Blues, Ideology, and Afro-American Literature*. Chicago: The University of Chicago Press.

Bakhtin, M. M. 1981. *The Dialogic Imagination*. Caryl Emerson & Michael Holquist, trans. Austin & London: University of Texas Press.

_____ 1984. *Rabelais and His World*. Bloomington: Indiana University Press.

Barak, Julie 1996. "Blurs, Blens, Berdaches: Gender Mixing in the Novels of Louise Erdrich." *Sail* 8.3: 49-62.

Bhabha, Homi 1990. "The Third Space." In J. Rutheford, ed. *Identity, Community, Culture and Difference*. London: Lawrence and Wishart.

_____ 1988. "Cultural Diversity and Cultural Difference." In B. Ashcroft, G. Griffiths, and H. Tiffin, eds. 1995: *The Post-Colonial Studies Reader*. London: Routledge. 206-209.

_____ 1994. *The Location of Culture*. London: Routledge.

Benítez Rojo, Antonio 1996. 2nd ed. *The Repeating Island: The Caribbean and the Postmodern Perspective*. Durham: Duke University Press.

Berger, Maurice *e. a.*, eds. 1995. *Constructing Masculinities*. New York: Routledge.

Birbalsingh, Frank, ed. 1996. "Introduction." *Frontiers of Caribbean Literatures in English*. London: Macmillan. ix-xxiii.

Bly, Robert 1991. *Iron John: A Book About Men*. London: Element Books.

Borker, Ruth 1980. "Anthropology: Social and Cultural Perspectives." In Sally McConnel-Ginet *e. a.*, eds. *Women and Language in Literature and Society*. New York: Praeger. 26-44.

Boyce Davies, Carole 1994. *Black Women, Writing and Identity, Migrations of the Subject*. London: Routledge.

Breau, Elisabeth 1993. "Identifying Satire: *Our Nig*." *Callaloo* 16. 2: 455-66.

Brod, Harry 1987. *The Making of Masculinities*. London: Allen & Unwin.

Brown, Elisabeth, ed. 1996. *Women of Color. Mother-Daughter Relationships in Twentieth Century Literature*. Austin: University of Texas Press.

Butler, Judith 1990. *Gender Trouble: Feminism and the Subversion of Identity*. New York: Routledge.

Carby, Hazel V. 1987. *Reconstructing Womanhood: The Emergence of the Afro-American Woman Novelist.* New York and Oxford: Oxford University Press.

Carchidi, Victoria 1995. "'Orbiting': Bharati Mukherjee's Kaleidoscope Vision." *MELUS* 20.1: 91-101.

Castillo, Ana 1992. *The Mixquiahuala Letters.* New York: Doubleday.

Castillo, Debra 1994. "Borderliners: Federico Campbell and Ana Castillo." In Margaret Higonnet and Joan Templeton, eds. *Reconfigured Spheres.* Amherst: University of Massachusetts Press. 147-70.

———— 1999. "Border Theory and the Canon." In D. L. Madsen, ed. *Post-Colonial Literatures: Expanding the Canon.* London: Pluto Press. 180-205.

Castronovo, Russ 1997. "Compromised Narratives along the Border: The Mason-Dixon Line, Resistance, and Hegemony." In David E. Johnson & Scott Michaelson, eds. 195-220.

Catt, Catherine 1991. "Ancient Myth in Modern America: The Trickster in the Fiction of Louise Erdrich." *Platte-Valley Review* 19.1: 71-81.

Chambers, Iain 1994. *Migrancy, Culture, Identity.* London and New York: Routledge.

Chan, Sucheng 1991. *Asian Americans.* Boston: Twayne.

Christian, Barbara 1983. "Ritualistic Process and the Structure of Paule Marshall's *Praisesong for the Widow*." *Callaloo* 6.2: 74-84.

Coates, Jennifer 1982. "Gossip Revisited: Language in All-Female Groups." In Jennifer Coates and Deborah Cameron, eds. *Women in Their Speech Communities.* Harlow: Longman. 94-121.

———— 1986. *Women, Men and Language.* Harlow: Longman.

———— 1995. "Language, Gender and Career." In Sarah Mills, ed. *Language & Gender.* London: Longman. 13-30.

———— 1997. "One-at-a-time: the Organization of Men's Talk." In Sally Johnson and Ulrike Meinhof, eds. *Language and Masculinity.* Oxford: Blackwell. 107-129.

Childs, Peter and Patrick Williams 1997. *An Introduction to Post-Colonial Theory.* London: Prentice Hall/Harvester Wheatsheaf.

Collier, Eugenia 1984. "The Closing of the Circle: Movement from Division to Wholeness in Paule Marshall's Fiction." In Mari Evans, ed. *Black Women Writers (1950-80).* New York: Doubleday. 295-315.

Connell, Robert 1995. *Masculinities.* Cambridge: Polity Press.

Cornwall, Andrea and Nancy Lindisfarne, eds. 1994. *Dislocating Masculinity. Comparative Ethnographies.* London: Routledge.

Coronil, Fernando 1995. "Introduction." In Fernando Ortiz. *Cuban Counterpoint: Tobacco and Sugar.* Durham and London: Duke University Press. ix-lvii.

Cortazár, Julio 1987 (1966). *Rayuela*. Transl. Gregory Rabassa. New York: Pantheon Books 1987.

Dabydeen, David 1996. "Coolie Odysse." Interview with Frank Birbalsingh, 18 April, 1990. In F. Birbalsingh, ed. *Frontiers of Caribbean Literatures in English*. London: Macmillan. 167-182.

Daniels, Roger, Sandra C. Taylor and Harry H. L. Kitano, eds. 1991. *Japanese Americans: From Relocation to Redress*. 2nd ed. Seattle: University of Washington Press.

Denniston, Dorothy 1983. "Recognition and Discovery." *The Fiction of Paule Marshall*. Knoxville: University of Tennessee Press. 126-45.

Dew, Thomas 1963. "Review of the Debate in the Virginia Legislature." In Eric McKirtrick, ed. *Slavery Defended: The Views of the Old South*. Englewood: Prentice Hall.

D'haen, Theo 1997. "Magic Realism and Postmodernism: Decentering Privileged Centers." In L. Parkinson Zamora and W. Faris, eds. 191-208.

Doriani, Beth Macklay 1991. "Black Womanhood in Nineteenth-Century America: Subversion and Self-Construction in Two Women's Autobiographies." *American Quarterly* 43.2: 199-222.

Dougherty, William H. 1995. "Crossing." *The Language Quarterly* 21.4: 5-7.

Duff, Alan 1990. *Once Were Warriors*. Tandem: New Zealand.

Eakins, Barbara and Gene Eakins 1978. *Sex Differences in Human Communication*. Boston: Houghton Mifflin.

Easthope, Anthony 1990 (1986). *What a Man's Gotta Do. The Masculine Myth in Popular Culture*. Boston: Unwin Hyman.

Eckard, Paula Gallant 1994. "The Interplay of Music, Language, and Narrative in Toni Morrison's *Jazz*." *CLA Journal* 37.1: 11-19.

_____ 1995. "The Prismatic Past in *Oral History* and *Mama Day*." *MELUS* 20.3: 121-135.

Edley, Nigel and Margaret Wetherell 1995. *Men in Perspective. Practice, Power and Identity*. London: Prentice Hall/Harvester Wheatsheaf.

Elder, Arlene A. 1996. "Criticizing from the Borderlands." *Modern Language Studies* 26: 6-11.

Ellison, Ralph W. 1987. *Going to the Territory*. New York: Vintage Books.

Erdrich, Louise 1984. *Love Medicine*. New York: Bantam.

Ernest, John 1994. "Economies of Identity: Harriet E. Wilson's *Our Nig*." *PMLA* 109.3: 424-38.

Evernden, Neil 1996. "Beyond Ecology: Self, Place, and the Pathetic Fallacy." In Glotfelty & Fromm, eds. 92-104.

Felman, Shoshana & M.D. Dori Laub 1991. *Testimony: Crises of Witnessing in Literature, Psychoanalysis, and History*. New York: Routledge.

Finkle, Michael 2000. "America, or Death." *NYTM*, June 18, 2000.

Flores, Juan and George Yudice 1994. "Living Borders/Buscando America: Languages of Latino Self-Formation." In Juan Flores, ed. *Essays on Puerto Rican Identity*. Houston: Arte Público Press.

Flys, Carmen 1998. *Place and Spatial Metaphors in the Quest for Cultural and Artistic Epiphany: James Baldwin and Rudolfo Anaya*. Unpubl. Diss. University of Alcalá.

_____ 2000. "Writing Against the Grain: Rudolfo Anaya's Murder Mysteries." In P. Gallardo and E. Llurda, eds. 519-524.

Fox-Genovese, Elizabeth 1990. "My Statue, My Self: Autobiographical Writings of Afro-American Women." In Henry L. Gates, ed. *Reading Black, Reading Feminist: A Critical Anthology*. New York: Meridian Book. 176-203.

Fuentes, Carlos 1995. *La frontera de Cristal*. Madrid: Alfaguara.

Galeano, Eduardo 1988. "In Defense of the Word." *The Graywolf Annual five: Multicultural literacy*. Saint Paul: Graywolf Press.

Gallardo, P. And E. Llurda, eds. 2000. *Proceedings of the 22nd International Conference of AEDEAN*. Lleida: Universitat de Lleida.

Gates, Henry L. 1987. "Parallel Discursive Universes: Fictions of the Self in Harriet E. Wilson's *Our Nig*." In *Figures in Black*. New York and Oxford: Oxford University Press. 125-63.

_____ 1983. "Introduction" to Harriet E. Wilson, *Our Nig; or Sketches from the Life of a Free Black*, New York: Vintage Books. ix-lix.

_____ 1993. Review of *Jazz*. In Henry Louis Gates, Jr., and K. A. Apiah, eds. *Toni Morrison: Critical Perspectives Past and Present*. New York: Amistad. 52-53

Geok-lim Lin, Shirley 1990. "Japanese American Women's Life Stories: Maternality in Monica Sone's *Nisei Daughter* and Joy Kogawa's *Obasan*." *Feminist Studies* 16.2: 289-312.

Gesensway, Deborah and Mindy Roseman 1987. *Beyond Words: Images from America's Concentration Camps*. Ithaca: Cornell University Press.

Gikandi, Simon 1996. "The Circle of Meaning: Paule Marshall, Modernism and the Masks of History." In Ade Ojo, ed. *Of Dreams Deferred, Dead or Alive*. Westport, Conn: Greenwood Press. 143-55.

Gilmore, David 1990. *Manhood in the Making. Cultural Concepts of Masculinity*. New Haven: Yale University Press

Giroux, Henry A. 1992. *Border Crossings: Cultural Workers and the Politics of Education*. London: Routledge.

Glotfelty, Cheryl & Harold Fromm, eds. 1996. *The Ecocriticism Reader. Landmarks in Literary Ecology*. Athens, Ga.: University of Georgia Press.

Goetz, Jill 1996. "Viramontes is awarded the John Dos Passos literature prize for 1995." *The Cornell Chronicle. Cornell University News Service* (on-line). August 8.

Gómez-Peña, G. 1988. "Documented/Undocumented," *The Graywolf Annual Five: Multi-Cultural Literacy*. Saint Paul: Graywolf Press.

_____ 1993. *Warrior for Gringostroika*. Saint Paul: Graywolf Press.

Gonzalez-Berry, Erlinda 1993. "Malinche Past: Selections from *Paletitas de Guayaba*." In Rebolledo and Rivero, eds. 207-12.

González-T, César A, ed. 1990. *Rudolfo A. Anaya: Focus on Criticism*. La Jolla: Lalo Press.

Goto, Hiromi 1994. *Chorus of Mushrooms*. Penguin Books Canada.

Graddol, David and Joan Swann 1989. *Gender Voices*. Oxford: Blackwell.

Gray, Paul 1998. "Paradise Found." *Time* 151.2: 62-68.

Grewal, Gurleen 1998. *Circles of Sorrow, Lines of Struggle*. Baton Rouge: Louisiana State University Press.

Gumperz, John and Jenny Cook-Gumperz 1982. "Introduction: Language and the Communication of Social Identity." In John Gumperz, ed. *Language and Social Identity*. Cambridge: Cambridge University Press. 1-21.

Haas, A. 1979. "Male and Female Spoken Language Differences: Stereotypes and Evidence." *Psychological Bulletin* 86. 3: 616-26.

Hall, Stuart 1995 (1989). "'New Ethnicities' Black Film, British Cinema." ICA Documents 7, London: Institute of Contemporary Arts, in B. Ashcroft, G. Griffiths, & H. Tiffin, eds. 223-227.

Harris, Trudier 1991. *Fiction and Folklore: The Novels of Toni Morrison*. Knoxville: The University of Tennessee Press.

Harris, Wilson 1983. *The Womb of Space. The Cross-Cultural Imagination*. Westport: Greenwood Press.

Hearn, Jeff 1992. *Men in the Public Eye*. London: Routledge.

Hearn, Jeff and David Collinson 1994. "Theorizing Unities and Differences between Men and between Masculinities." In Harry Brod and Michael Kaufman, eds. *Theorizing Masculinities*. London: Sage. 97-118.

Hicks, D. Emily 1991. *Border Writing: The Multidimensional Text*. Minneapolis and Oxford: University of Minnesota Press.

Hill Collins, Patricia 1987. "The Meaning of Motherhood in Black Culture and Black Mother/Daughter Relationships." *Sage* 4.2: 3-9.

Horrocks, Roger 1994. *Masculinity in Crisis*. London: The Macmillan Press, Ltd.

House, Elizabeth 1990. "Toni Morrison's Ghost: The Beloved Who Is Not Beloved." *Studies in American Fiction* 18: 17-26.

Houston, Jeane Wakatsuki and James Houston 1973. *Farewell to Manzanar*. Boston: Houghton Mifflin.

Hutcheon, Linda 1995. "Circling the Downspout of Empire." In B. Ashcroft, G. Griffiths, & H. Tiffin, eds., 130-135.

Jay, Paul 1997. "Critical Theory, American Literature, and Border Studies."

Contingency Blues: The Search for Foundations in American Criticism. University of Wisconsin Press.

Jehlen, Myra 1993. "Why Did the Europeans Cross the Ocean?" In Amy Kaplan and Donald E. Pease, eds. *Cultures of US Imperialism.* Durham and London: Duke University Press. 41-58.

Johnson, Sally and Frank Finlay 1997. "Do Men Gossip? An Analysis of Football Talk on Television." In Sally Johnson and Ulrike Meinhof, eds.130-143.

Johnson, Sally and Ulrike Meinhof, eds. 1997. *Language and Masculinity.* Oxford: Blackwell.

Joyce, James 1992. *A Portrait of the Artist as a Young Man.* Harmondsworth: Penguin Books.

Kim, Elaine 1982. *Asian American Literature. An Introduction to the Writings in their Social Context.* Philadelphia: Temple University Press.

Kimmel, Michael 1987. *Changing Men: New Directions in Research on Men and Masculinity.* Newbury Park: Sage.

Kimmel, Michael and Michael Kaufman 1994. "Weekend Warriors. The New Men's Movement." In Harry Brod and Michael Kaufman, eds. *Theorizing Masculinities.* London: Sage. 259-288.

Kitano, Harry H. L. and Roger Daniels 1988. *Asian Americans: Emerging Minorities.* Englewood Cliffs: Prentice Hall.

Krupat, Arnold 1996. *The Turn to the Native: Studies in Criticism and Culture.* Lincoln: University of Nebraska Press.

Kubitschek, Missy Dehn 1991. *Claiming the Heritage.* Jackson: University Press of Mississippi.

Kureishi, Hanif 1995. *The Black Album.* London: Faber & Faber.

Johnson, David E. and Scott Michaelson 1997. "Border Secrets: An Introduction." In David E. Johnson & Scott Michaelson, eds. *Border Theory: The Limits of Cultural Politics.* Minneapolis: University of Minnesota Press.

Lamming, George 1991 (1983). "Introduction." *In the Castle of My Skin.* Ann Arbor, Michigan.

Larsen, Neil 1991. "Preface." In E. Hicks, *Border Writing: The Multidimensional Text.* Minneapolis and Oxford: University of Minnesota Press.

Lauter, Paul, ed. 1998 (3rd edition). *The Heath Anthology of American Literature.* Boston: Houghton Mifflin.

Layton, Bentley 1986. "The Riddle of The Thunder (NHC VI,2): The Function of Paradox in a Gnostic Text from Nag Hammadi." In Charles W. and Robert Hodgson, Jr., eds. *Nag Hammadi, Gnosticism and Early Christianity.* Hedrick, Peabody, Massachusetts: Hendrickson Publishers. 37-54.

Lee, A. Robert 1998. *Designs of Blackness: Mappings in the Literature and*

Culture of Afro-America. London and Virginia: Pluto Press.

Levant, Ronald and William Pollack, eds. 1995. *A New Psychology of Men*. New York: Harper Collins Publishers, Basic Books.

Levy, Andrea, 1999. *Fruit of the Lemon*. London: Review.

Lewis, Barbara Williams 1997. "The Function of Jazz in Toni Morrison's Jazz." In David L. Middleton, ed. *Toni Morrison's Fiction: Contemporary Criticism*. 271-281.

Limerick, Patricia Nelson 1987. *The Legacy of Conquest: The Unbroken Past of the American West*. New York and London: Norton.

Lindberg-Seyersted, Brita 1994. *Black and Female*. Oslo: Scandinavian University Press.

Lmrabet, Alí 2000. "Así crucé el Estrecho." *El País*, October 1, 2000.

Loomba, Ania 1998. *Colonialism/Postcolonialism*. London: Routledge. 1998.

Lorenzo, Olga 1996. *The Rooms in My Mother's House*. Penguin Australia.

MacInness, John 1998. *The End of Masculinity. The Confusion of Sexual Genesis and Sexual Difference in Modern Society*. Buckingham: Open University Press.

McHale, Brian 1987. *Postmodernist Fiction*. New York and London: Methuen.

Marlatt, Daphne 1984. *Touch to My Tongue*. Edmonton, Alberta: Longspoon Press.

Marshall, Paule 1983. *Praisesong for the Widow*. New York: Dutton.

Martínez, Rubén 2000. "The Next Chapter: America's Next Great Revolution in Race Relations Is Already Under Way." *NYTM*, July 16.

McCarthy, Cormac 1992. *All the Pretty Horses*. New York: Vintage Books.

_____ 1994. *The Crossing*. New York: Vintage Books.

_____ 1998. *Cities of the Plain*. New York: Alfred A. Knopf.

McKenna, Teresa 1997. *Migrant Song*. Austin: University of Texas Press.

McLoughlin, David, 1999. "The Runner University Press." *North and South*, Jan 1999: 54-56

Meaney, Gerardine 1993. *(Un)Like Subjects: Women, Theory, Fiction*. London: Routledge.

Minh-ha, Trinh 1989. *Woman, Native, Other: Writing Postcoloniality and Feminism*. Bloomington: Indiana University Press.

Mitchell, Angelyn 1992. "Her Side of His Story: A Feminist Analysis of Two Nineteenth-Century Antebellum Novels: William Wells Brown's *Clotel* and Harriet E. Wilson's *Our Nig*." *American Literary Realism* 24.3: 7-21.

Morrison, Toni 1998. *Paradise*. New York & Toronto: Alfred A. Knopf.

_____ 1995. "Nobel Lecture" (December 7, 1993). *The Georgia Review* 49.1: 318-323.

_____ 1992. *Jazz*. London: Chatto & Windus.

_____ 1987. *Beloved*. New York: Alfred A. Knopf.

_____ 1984. *Tar Baby*. London: Triad/Panther Books.

_____ 1980. *Song of Solomon*. London: Triad/Panther Books.

_____ 1970. *The Bluest Eye*. New York: Alfred A. Knopf.

Munton, Alan 1997. "Misreading Morrison, Mishearing Jazz: A Response to Toni Morrison's Jazz Critics." *Journal of American Studies* 31.2: 235-251.

The Nag Hammadi Library in English 1977. Trans. by members of the Coptic Gnostic Library Project of the Institute for Antiquity and Christianity. James M. Robinson, Director. San Francisco: Harper & Row, Publishers.

Nakano, Mei 1990. *Japanese American Women: Three Generations 1890-1990*. Berkeley: Mina Press Publishing.

Oakley, Ann 1972. *Sex, Gender and Society*. Melbourne: Temple Smith.

Okubo, Mine 1946. *Citizen 13660*. New York: Columbia University Press.

Olney, James, ed. 1980. *Autobiography: Essays Theoretical and Critical*. Princeton: University of Princeton Press. 3-27.

Omi, Michael and Howard Winant 1994. *Racial Formation in the United States*. 2nd ed. New York and London: Routledge.

Ortiz, Fernando 1995. *Cuban Counterpoint: Tobacco and Sugar*. Durham and London: Duke University Press.

Paredes, Raymund 1992. "Autobiography and Ethnic Politics: Richard Rodriguez's *Hunger of Memory*." In James Payne, ed. *Multicultural Autobiography*. Knoxville: The University of Tennessee Press. 280-296.

Parkinson Zamora, Lois and Wendy Faris, eds. 1997. *Magical Realism. Theory, History, Community*. Durham: Duke University Press.

Pettis, Joyce 1990. "Self-Definition and Redefinition in Paule Marshall's *Praisesong for the Widow*." In Harry Shaw, ed. *Perspectives of Black Popular Culture*. Bowling Green: Bowling Green State University Popular Press, 93-100.

_____ 1995. "The Journey Completed: Spiritual Regeneration in *Praisesong for the Widow*." *Toward Wholeness In Paule Marshall's Fiction*. Charlottesville: University Press of Virginia. 106-135.

Phillips, Caryl 1996. "Caryl Phillips: The legacy of Othello, Part (1)." Interview with Frank Birbalsingh, 15 Oct. 1986. In Frank Birbalsingh, ed. 183-190.

Piedra, José 1993. "The Black Stud's Spanish Birth." *Callaloo* 16: 820-848.

Pleck, Joseph 1981. *The Myth of Masculinity*. Cambridge, Mass.: M. I. T. Press.

Pratt, Mary Louise 1992. *Imperial Eyes: Travel Writing and Transcul-*

turaltion. London: Routledge.

Rebolledo, Tey Diana and Eliana S. Rivero, eds. 1993. *Infinite Divisions: An Anthology of Chicana Literature*. Tucson: University of Arizona Press.

Rice, Herbert William 1996. *Toni Morrison and the American Tradition: A Rhetorical Reading*. New York: Peter Lang.

Rodriguez, Richard 1982. *Hunger of Memory. The Education of Richard Rodriguez*. New York: Bentan Books.

Rowe, John Carlos 1990. "Structure." In Frank Lentricchia and Thomas McLaughlin, ed. *Critical Terms for Literary Study*. Chicago: University of Chicago Press. 23-38.

Rutherford, Jonathan 1988. "Who's That Man?" In Jonathan Rutherford and Rowena Chapman, eds. *Male Order: Unwrapping Masculinity*. London: Wishart. 21-67.

Said, Edward 1979. *Orientalism*. New York: Random House, Vintage.

Sattel, Jack 1976."The Inexpressive Male: Tragedy or Sexual Politics?" *Social Problems* 22: 469-77.

_____ 1983. "Men, Inexpressiveness and Power." In Barrie Thorne et al., eds. *Language, Gender and Society*. Cambridge, Mass: Newbury House. 119-124.

Seidler, Victor 1996. "Masculinity and Violence." In Larry May et al., eds. *Rethinking Masculinity: Philosophical Explanations in Light of Feminism*. New York: Rowman & Littlefield. 63-75.

Shohat, Ella 1993. "Notes on the Postcolonial." *Social Text* 31/32: 99-113.

Showalter, Elaine 1997. *Hystories*. New York: Columbia University Press.

Skinner, John 1998. *The Stepmother Tongue*. London: Macmillan Press.

Slack, John 1993. "The Comic Savior: The Dominance of the Trickster in Louise Erdrich's *Love Medicine*." *North Dakota Quarterly* 61.3: 118-29.

Sollors, Werner 1986. *Beyond Ethnicity: Consent and Descent in American Culture*. New York and Oxford: Oxford University Press.

Sone, Monica 1979 (1953). *Nisei Daughter*. Seattle: University of Washington Press.

Spender, Dale 1980. *Man Made Language*. London: Routledge & Kegan Paul.

Spitta, Silvia 1997. "Transculturation, the Caribbean, and the Cuban-American Imaginary." In Frances R. Aparicio and Susana Chávez-Silverman, eds. *Tropicalizations: Transcultural Representations of Latinidad*. Hanover and London: Dartmouth College. 160-183.

Steele, Fritz 1981. *The Sense of Place*. Boston, Mass.: CBI Publications.

Steinberg, Stephen 1989. *The Ethnic Myth: Race, Ethnicity and Class in America*. Boston: Beacon Press.

Suárez Lafuente, M.S. 1993. "Echoes of Mother." In C. C. Barfoot and Theo

D'haen, eds. *Shades of Empire in Colonial and Post-Colonial Literatures*. Amsterdam: Rodopi. 190-198.

Sumida, Stephen H. 1992. "Protests and Accommodation, Self-Satire and Self-Effacement in Monica Sone's *Nisei Daughter*." James Robert Payne, ed. *Multicultural Autobiography: American Lives*. Knoxville: University of Tennessee Press. 207-43.

Tate, Claudia 1998. *Psychoanalysis and Black Novels: Desire and the Protocols of Race*. New York and Oxford: Oxford University Press.

Tate, Claudia 1990. "Allegories of Black Female Desire; or Rereading Nineteenth-Century Sentimental Novels of Black Female Authority." In Cheryl A. Wall, ed. *Changing our Own Words: Essays on Criticism, Theory, and Writing by Black Women*. London: Routledge. 98-126.

Tally, Justine 1999a. *Paradise Reconsidered: Toni Morrison's (Hi)stories and Truths*. Hamburg: Lit Verlag.

———— 1999b. "'A Specter I Have to Behold and Be Held By': the Southern Legacy in Toni Morrison's *Jazz*." In Waldemar Zacharasiewicz, ed. *Remembering the Individual/Regional/National Past*. Tuebingen, Germany: Stauffenberg Publishers. 215-128.

Tannen, Deborah 1991. *You Just Don't Understand. Women and Men in Conversation*. London: Virago.

———— 1992 (1986). *That's Not What I Meant! How Conversational Style Makes Or Breaks Your Relations With Others*. London: Virago.

Taylor, Sandra C. 1993. *Jewel of the Desert: Japanese American Internment at Topaz*. Berkeley: University of California Press.

Tharp, Julie 1993. "Women's Community and Survival in the Novels of Louise Erdrich." In Janet Ward and Joanna Mink, eds. *Communication and Women's Friendship*. Bowling Green, Ohio: Popular. 165-80.

Thyagarajan, K. & A.K. Ghatak 1981: *Lasers: Theory and Applications*. New York: Plenum Press.

Tuan, Yi-Fu 1977. *Space and Place: The Perspective of Experience*. Minneapolis: University of Minnesota.

Turner, Victor 1977 (1969). *The Ritual Process*. Ithaca, New York: Cornell University Press.

Urrea, Luis Alberto 1993. *Across the Wire: Life and Hard Times on the Mexican Border*. New York and London: Anchor Books.

———— 1994. *In Search of Snow*. New York: Harper.

———— 1996. *By the Lake of Sleeping Children: The Secret Life of the Mexican Border*. New York, London: Anchor Books.

Van Gennep, Arnold 1960 (1908). *The Rites of Passage*. Trans. Monika V. Vizedom and Gabrielle L. Caffee. Chicago: The University of Chicago Press.

Van Herk, Aritha, 1992. *A Frozen Tongue*. Coventry: Dangaroo Press.

Vevaina, Coomi S. 1997. "Wom(b)enspeak: Modes of 'detoxifying' the Mastertongue in Canadian Women's Writing." *Revista Española de Estudios Canadienses* 3.2: 77-97.

Viramontes, Helena María 1984. "The Cariboo Cafe." *The Moths and Other Stories* (1985). Houston: Arte Público Press. Reprinted in P. Lauter, ed. 1998. 3083-3093.

Washington, Mary Helen 1981 (1959). "Afterword." *Brown Girl, Brownstones*. Old Westbury, NY: Feminist Press. 311-24.

Weil, Simone 1952. *The Need for Roots*. Trans. A. F. Wills. New York: Putman's Sons.

Wetherell, Margaret 1996. "Group conflict and the social psychology of racism." In Margaret Wetherell, ed. *Identities, Groups and Social Issues*. London: Sage. 175-238.

Wilenz, Gay 1992. *Binding Cultures*. Bloomington: Indiana University Press.

Wilson, Harriet E. 1983 (1859). *Our Nig; or Sketches from the Life of a Free Black, In A Two-Story White House, North. Showing that Slavery's Shadows Fall Even There. by "Our Nig."* New York: Vintage Books.

Weglyn, Michi Nishiura 1976. *Years of Infamy*. New York: William Morrow.

Wilson, Rowdon 1997. "The Metamorphoses of Fictional Space: Magical Realism." In L. Parkinson Zamora and W. Faris, eds. 209-234.

Wolf, Eric 1958. "The Virgin of Guadalupe: A Mexican National Symbol." *Journal of American Folklore* 71: 34-9.

Wong, Hertha 1991. "Adoptive Mothers and Thrown-Away Children in the Novels of Louise Erdrich." In Brenda Dally and Maureen Reddy, eds. *Narrating Mothers: Theorising Maternal Subjectivies*. Knoxville: University of Tennessee Press. 174-192.

Wong, Sau-ling Cynthia 1993. *Reading Asian American Literature*. Princeton: Princeton University Press.

Yamamoto, Traise 1999. *Masking Selves, Making Subjects*. Berkeley: University of California Press.

Young, Robert 1990. *White Mythologies: Writing History and the West*. London: Routledge.

Zimmerman, Marc 1991. *U.S. Latino Literature: An Essay and Annotated Bibliography* (web version at *http://www.uic.edu/~marczim/latlit*). Chicago: March/Abrazo Press.

CONTRIBUTORS

Dr. Jesús Benito is professor of American Literature and Literary Theory at the University of Castilla-La Mancha. He has published extensively in the field of Ethnic American Literature, as well as on other 19th century and contemporary American writers. He is the author of *La estética del recuerdo: la narrativa del James Baldwin y Toni Morrison* (1994), and has co-edited *Narratives of Resistance* (1999) as well as several bilingual editions of works by Frederick Douglass, W. E. B. DuBois, Olaudah Equiano, among others.

Dr. Janet Cooper earned a Ph.D. in American Literature with a concentration in African American and Ethnic American Literature from the Pennsylvania State University in 2000.

Dr. María del Mar Gallego Durán teaches American and Ethnic Literatures at the University of Huelva. She has published several articles dealing with contemporary women writers and gender issues. She is currently co-editing a volume on the Vietnam era and completing a book that analyzes the production of "passing" novels during the Harlem Renaissance.

Dr. Carmen Flys-Junquera is an Associate Professor of American Literature at the University of Alcalá. She is currently also the Secretary to the Institute of North American Studies of the same University. Dr. Flys, an American residing permanently in Spain, has co-edited the books *El Poder Hispano* (1994*), El Nuevo Horizonte: España/Estados Unidos* (2001), and is finalizing the co-edition of an anthology, *Family Reflections: Representing the Contemporary American Family in the Arts*. Most of her published articles deal with contemporary American ethnic literature, particularly Latino and African American, and the sense of place found in these works.

Eduardo de Gregorio Godeo teaches English as a foreign language at the University of Castilla-La Mancha in Spain. At the moment he is working on his Ph.D. thesis, where he investigates the role of discourse in the construction of gender identities in contemporary British media. His research interests include Language and Gender, Critical Discourse Analysis, and Men's Studies.

Chrissi Harris is Associate Lecturer of English at the University of Castilla-La Mancha, Cuenca. Her work on Caribbean and Indian women writers has appeared in Spanish journals, and she has contributed to other books dealing with literature of resistance and ethnicity. She is currently working on her postgraduate study on Caribbean women poets and exploring the changing position of Black British writers.

Markus Heide teaches American cultural history at *Amerika-Institut* of Ludwig-Maximilians-Universität München. Currently he is completing his Ph.D. thesis on *Transgression/Translation: Strategies of literary encounter in Chicano/a Fiction*. He has published essays on Chicano/a literature, performance art, and postcolonial literary and cultural theory.

Dr. Aitor Ibarrola-Armendariz is a Lecturer in American Literature at the University of Deusto, Bilbao. He specializes in late 19th-century American literature, minority and immigrant fiction and academic writing. His publications include articles on the works of authors such as Stephen Crane, Kate Chopin, Charles Chesnutt, Richard Rodriguez, Sherman Alexie or Pietro di Donato. Right now he is working on a new edition of Mark *Twain's Adventures of Huckleberry Finn* and a course book on academic writing.

Dr. Francisco A. Lomelí is Full Professor in Chicano Studies and Spanish and Portuguese from the University of California at Santa Barbara. He has published extensively in both Chicano Literature/Studies and Latin American Literature/Studies. His numerous books document the emerging field of Chicano Studies historically, culturally and thematically, while his studies in Latin American Literature/Studies tend to concentrate on literary expression. Some of his known works include *Aztlán: Essays on the Chicano Homeland* (co-editor Rudy Anaya, 1989*)*, *Chicano Literature: A Reference Guide* (co-editor Julio Martinez, 1985), *La novelística de Carlos Drougett* (1983*)*, *Dictionary of Literary; Chicano Authors* (vols. 1-3, co-editor Carl Shirley, 1989, 1993, 2000), *Handbook of Hispanic Cultures in The US: Literature and Art* (1993), *US Latino Literatures and Cultures: Transnational Perspectives* (co-editor Karin Ikas, 2000). Currently, he is completing a manuscript on a New Mexican writer from the 18th century titled *Miguel de Quintana: New Mexican Poet in a State of Disenchantment* (co-written with Clark Colahan).

Dr. Ana María Manzanas is professor of American Literature at the University of Salamanca. She has contributed articles and chapters of books to

Spanish and American journals and volumes. She has a joint volume on Toni Morrison and James Baldwin (1994), and has co-edited and translated into Spanish selections of the works of Olaudah Equiano (1994), W.E.B. DuBois (1995), Martin Luther King (1997), and Frederick Douglass (2000). She has also co-edited the anthology *Narratives of Resistance: Literature and Ethnicity in the United States and the Caribbean* (1999).

Dr. Begoña Simal teaches at the University of Coruña. She has published a book, *Identidad étnica y género en la narrativa de escritoras chinoamericanas* (2000). Her articles have appeared in Spanish and American journals such as *MELUS Journal, Amerasia Journal* and *Critical Mass*. She has also contributed chapters to several books on American literature edited both in Spain and in the US.

Dr. Isabel Soto currently teaches in the English Department at Madrid's Universidad Nacional de Educación a Distancia. Her interests lie in African American writing and discourse that explores thresholds, boundaries, limina. She is founding member of The Gateway Press (Madrid: 2000) and General Editor of the series Studies in Liminality and Literature.

Dr. M.S. Suárez Lafuente is Professor of English Philology at the University of Oviedo, northern Spain, where she teaches contemporary English Literature and Literatures in English. She is interested in literary theory and women's studies and has published extensively within her field of research. She is currently President of the Spanish Association of University Women's Studies (AUDEM) and partner of the European Research Group ATHENA.

Dr. Justine Tally is Professor of American Literature at the University of La Laguna, Tenerife, Spain, where she specializes in African American Literature and Culture. Her latest publications include *Paradise Reconsidered: Toni Morrison's (Hi)stories and Truths* (Hamburg: Lit Verlag, 1999, and Rutgers, NJ: Transaction Press, 1999) and *The Story of Jazz: Toni Morrison's Dialogic Imagination* (Hamburg: Lit Verlag, 2001, and Rutgers, NJ: Transaction Press, 2001). She is a member of the Board for the Collegium for African American Literature and serves as its treasurer.